Gaining Control

Oliver Wight Manufacturing Series

Gaining Control

Capacity Management and Scheduling

Second Edition

James G. Correll
Norris W. Edson

John Wiley & Sons, Inc.

New York · Chichester · Weinheim · Brisbane · Singapore · Toronto

This book is printed on acid-free paper. ∞

Published by John Wiley & Sons, Inc.
Published simultaneously in Canada.

This publication is designed to provide accurate and authoritative information in regard to the subject matter covered. It is sold with the understanding that the publisher is not engaged in rendering legal, accounting, or other professional services. If legal advice or other expert assistance is required, the services of a competent professional person should be sought.

Library of Congress Cataloging-in-Publication Data

Correll, James G.
   Gaining control : capacity management and scheduling / James G. Correll, Norris W. Edson. — 2nd ed.
      p.   cm. — (Oliver Wight manufacturing series)
   Includes index.
   ISBN 0-471-29167-6 (cloth : alk. paper)
   1. Production scheduling.   2. Manufacturing resource planning.
3. Just-in-time systems.   4. Industrial capacity—Management.
I. Edson, Norris W.   II. Title.   III. Series.
TS157.5.C67   1998
658.5′3—dc21   98-28269
                                                                    CIP

Printed in the United States of America

10 9 8 7 6 5 4 3 2 1

Contents

CHAPTER NINE
Continuous Improvement

CHAPTER TEN
Moving Ahead

Acknowledgments

Making a revision to a previously published book is not all that much easier than producing the original. It takes the cooperative effort of a lot of people. We would like to extend our heartfelt thanks to the many people who played a part in bringing both the original and this revision to fruition.

First and foremost, we thank our wives, Donna Correll and Margaret Edson. The hours that we spent pounding away on the word processor or conferring on the phone instead of spending time with them were countless. Our love and thanks go to them for all their patience and support.

Next, we would like to reiterate our thanks to those who made the first edition of this book possible: our writer, Ron Schultz; our editor and publisher, Dana Scannell, and his production assistant, Rachel Snyder; and Donna Correll for her work in developing the graphics. Thanks again to Terry Tuttle of Nutrilite Products, Inc., Ron Hawkins of Kop-Flex Company, Sue Mazzio of the Boeing Company, and Mike Laker of Douglas Aircraft Company for their help in reviewing the original manuscript.

For encouraging us to update the book, we want to thank the publisher of this revised edition, John Wiley and Sons. We appreciate the patience and persistence of Julia Seto, Jeanne Glasser, and Debra Alpern of the John Wiley editorial staff. After all, this is a book about meeting schedules, isn't it?

We would also like to give special recognition to all of our associates who read drafts, listened to our ideas, and critiqued our work on both editions, especially Walt Goddard, Darryl Landvater, Pete Skurla, Steve Souza, Bill Sandras, and John Dougherty. The input from these people was sometimes tough to take, but it was what we needed.

Finally, we would like to acknowledge all of the people we have worked with over the years who have operated in the informal environment, especially those who have pulled themselves out of the chaos to get control of their businesses. This is really their story, and they seldom receive recognition for what they accomplish or gratitude for getting the product out the door in spite of all the obstacles. To them, we say thanks a million for your unknowing contributions to the book.

James G. Correll
Gresham, Oregon

Norris W. Edson
Lake Wildwood, California

October, 1998

Introduction

Throughout our professional careers, while working in industry, teaching seminars, and consulting with companies, we have been troubled by the apparent inability of manufacturing departments to get control of their operations. It's like the story that one company president related not long ago. He said that as president of a very large enterprise, people believed that he had a great deal of control over what the company did. But, he said, he felt a lot like the little boy in the circus parade riding the big elephant. The little boy had a little stick, and when he would tap the elephant on the back, the elephant would speed up. When he tapped him on the forehead, he would slow down; tap him on the right ear and he'd turn right. Everyone was amazed that the little boy had so much control over the elephant. They forgot, said the president, that the elephant could go anywhere he pleased. The little boy was merely making suggestions. That was how the president felt. He was not in control of the company; he was merely making suggestions.

Have you ever felt that way? And worse yet, has the elephant been doing what it wants to do and not anything you want it to? There are two things you can do: get a bigger stick or educate the elephant. This book is aimed at educating elephants.

One of the big hurdles we face constantly in industry is understanding terminology. We have tried to be consistent with our terminology, and have for the most part adopted the terminology of the American Production and Inventory Control Society (APICS). We are fully aware that you may use different terminology in your plant. Furthermore, in the eight years since the original publication of this book, not only have new methods and techniques been introduced, but the terminology has changed also. The technology explosion has led to a terminology/process explosion.

The most obvious of these terminology changes are the use of ERP (Enterprise Resource Planning) in place of MRP II (Manufacturing Resource Planning) and Lean Manufacturing in place of Just-in-Time. Although there are differences of opinion, there is wide-spread acceptance that the new terms (ERP and Lean) are logical extensions of the earlier processes, and that the change in terminology conveys an expansion of scope more than a change in concepts and processes. Throughout this book, we continue to use the terms MRP and MRP II rather than ERP. We are fully aware of and embrace the advances in technology that form the foundation of the migration to ERP. However, we have chosen to stay with the MRP II terminology to emphasize the people issues rather than the software.

Of a different nature is the introduction of new terminology that in many cases does indeed reflect new concepts and processes. Finite Capacity Scheduling (FCS), Capacity-Constrained Scheduling (CCS), Manufacturing Execution Systems (MES), Theory of Constraints (TOC), Drum-Buffer-Rope (DBR), Process Flow Scheduling (PFS), Quick Response Manufacturing (QRM), and Advanced Planning and Scheduling (APS) are those that we have come across in recent years.

It is not our intention to either ignore or give full treatment to these matters. To do so would expand the book unrealistically. There are ample publications on these and other techniques, and we encourage you to research them. Our belief is that you need to do the fundamentals well first before you attempt the more exotic. As the legendary Vince Lombardi said, winning football is about blocking and tackling—doing the fundamentals well. This is a book about fundamentals.

In this book, you will meet Brian Miller, a manager in a manufacturing company that is certainly out of control. Brian and the other people in the book are fictitious characters, composites of the people we have met and worked with over the years. While they are not real people, they may seem very familiar. You may think you recognize them as your coworkers or neighbors, or perhaps even yourself.

The story takes place in the Hayes Tractor Company, a midsize manufacturing company located in the town of Somewhere, USA. The situations encountered in the story represent a collage of our experiences, and any inference to an actual company is purely coincidental.

Hayes Tractor has Material Requirements Planning (MRP) implemented. But that alone doesn't do the job. They have to "close the loop" with formal scheduling of operations on the factory floor and balancing available capacities with what is required to meet the schedules. As the story progresses, Brian and his associates find out how to gain control of their manufacturing operation by implementing and using the tools and techniques available through Manufacturing Resource Planning (MRP II) and Lean Manufacturing.

Their focus is on those tools that help schedule production work and plan resources, as well as control both the utilization of capacities and the execution of schedules. Although the primary story line takes place in the Hayes Tractor Company, a metal fabrication and assembly shop, the concepts and principles explained in this book are applicable to any environment. As you will see, Brian and his associates learn from many other companies. Examples are used from a variety of industries, including electronic assembly, food processing, aerospace and defense, repetitive manufacturing, and others who have used the tools successfully. It is by putting together these collective experiences from a wide variety of manufacturing environments that Hayes is able to solve its problems.

Throughout this book we have used the term "he," "him," or "his" instead of "he or she," "him or her," or "his or hers." This is for ease of reading and is not intended as a gender bias. If you like, anywhere you read "he" can be read as "she," "him" can be read as "her," and "his" can be read as "hers."

Our objective in writing this book is to help you understand what you have to do to get the real benefit from MRP II and Lean Manufacturing. The answer is in gaining control of the factory floor, often referred to as "closing the loop," and this book shows you how.

We wanted the book to be fun and interesting to read. We hope we have accomplished that through the use of the Hayes story to reveal true-to-life examples of how bad it is sometimes, but also how the problems can be solved with understanding and perseverance. We wish you the best of success in applying these tools to your company.

Cast of Characters

(Names are in alphabetical order by first name.)

HAYES TRACTOR COMPANY

Alex Handly	Engineering Manager
Brian Miller	Machine Shop Manager
Carl Mueller	Material Planner
Carol Barrow	Quality Control Manager
Cecil Nickerson	Machinist
Dan Milkosky	Fabrication Manager
Elliot Hathaway	Manufacturing Engineering Manager
Hank Jones	Second Shift Welding Supervisor
Harold Bloom	Purchasing Manager
Ivan Solokov	Maintenance Manager
Jim Romero	Grinding Supervisor
Joan Van Schot	Production Control Manager
José García	Machine Shop Supervisor
Larry Placarde	Second Shift Machine Shop Supervisor
Laura Sanderford	IT Systems Analyst
Lenny Youngman	VP, Sales and Marketing
Lloyd Adams	Design Engineering Manager
Mac Helm	Personnel Manager, ex-Machine Shop Manager
Mickey Issacson	Assembly Manager

Pete Smith	General Manager
Ralph Barnard	Production Manager
Roy O'Brien	Materials Manager
Sharon Levy	Controller
Tony Alonso	Machine Shop Expeditor/Capacity Planner

OUTSIDE CONTACTS

Buster Jones	Manufacturing Manager, McNally Machine Tool
Frank Snider	Teacher, local junior college
Hal Beckman	Materials Manager, Good Health Vitamins
Harvey Piscoli	Production Manager, ERON Technology
Joe Crowe	Production Manager, Supreme Enterprises
John Hall	General Supervisor, Precision Air Components
Marty Bloch	Plant Superintendent, Beartone Manufacturing
Rob Ericson	Production Manager, Mercury Electronics
Sue Corey-Smith	Production Manager, Missile Systems Company
Tom Huang	Master Scheduler, Supreme Enterprises

Gaining
Control

Chapter One

Out of Control

Brian Miller rebuilt the 1960 Chevy convertible for his wife as he had planned. He knew what parts he needed and had them there when it was time to install them. He figured out the proper sequence in which to reconstruct his pride and joy. He even scheduled his weeknights and weekends to ensure that he would complete the car to coincide with his wife's 30th birthday. Because things never seemed to work out exactly as planned, he constantly rescheduled his time to get things done. He met his target date a day early. On her birthday night, he ceremoniously opened the door of the Chevy for his wife. She seated herself, turned the key, and took Brian for a ride in her new car.

His planning and execution had resulted in an on-time completed project. Why then, he thought from his office at the Hayes Tractor plant, couldn't he get his three production shifts running smoothly? He was the manager of the machine shop. He had a computerized planning and scheduling system that was supposed to provide schedules with which he could run the machine shop. Why was it that he couldn't meet with the same success he'd had rebuilding the Chevy?

Brian had been at the West Coast plant for only two months, having transferred from the company's Midwest division. He was the new guy on the block, and he was learning how to survive in this good-ol'-boy environment. As he looked out over the shop, he was not a happy man. The plant was in real trouble. Product was never delivered on time, lead times were unpredictable, and productivity was atrocious. The schedule that was generated by the computer was useless and might as well have been thrown in the trash as soon as it arrived. Things were simply out of control.

It had been six months since Pete Smith had been promoted from the Midwest plant to succeed the retiring general manager. Pete had slowly begun to prune the ranks of the old-guard managers, replacing them with a group of more forward-thinking people.

Brian was one of these. The former machine shop manager, who had been with the company for 45 years, had been moved to the Human Relations Department. The fact that Brian had come from Quality Control to the machine shop didn't make the people in the shop too happy: They thought the new manager should have been elevated from within their own ranks. Ralph Barnard, the Production Manager, had thought so, too.

On Brian's first day on the job, he was called into Ralph's office. Pete had known Brian at the Midwest plant and had arranged for his transfer, feeling that Brian's management style and quality perspective were needed at Hayes. Ralph, on the other hand, didn't know Brian at all. Ralph, in his early sixties, with a constant sour smile as if his stomach were continually in revolt, closed the door and sank down heavily into the high-backed chair behind his desk.

Ralph's desk was covered with production reports, shipping schedules, product drawings, engineering changes, and memos about missed schedules. What caught Brian's attention, however, was a statue of a steel-gloved hand with a lightning bolt stuck through it. The inscription read: "Cause it to happen!" This exemplified Ralph's attitude.

"All right, it's as simple as this," Ralph said, leaning back in his chair. "You've been brought in here as the Machine Shop Manager. But here's the deal, Miller: you've got three months to get productivity up and shortages down. Nobody expects you to meet the schedules that come out of Production Control. That would be virtually impossible since they're so screwed up. What I want you to concentrate on is the hot list from Mickey in Assembly. That will tell you the real priorities, and that's what I want you to work on. If you don't, I'll find someone who will!"

Brian slowly lifted himself from his chair. He straightened his tie and thought to himself, "What have I gotten myself into?" He said,

"Well, Ralph, I appreciate your vote of confidence. And I guarantee you I'll work hard to get the job done. I know I can do it."

"I hope so, kid." Ralph couldn't suppress his smile.

Needless to say, when Brian left the office, he was concerned about his lukewarm welcome; but he was also even more determined to make a difference at Hayes. He had little idea of what he was up against.

He knew his first move was to try and establish a working relationship with his people. Brian had his foremen take him around and introduce him to everyone. He wanted to let these people know that at least he was a friendly sort and not one to stay holed up in his office.

The second part of Brian's plan was to enroll quietly in a machine shop class at the local community college. Since his knowledge about machining parts was limited, he figured it would be in his best interest to get some hands-on experience.

The teacher, Frank Snider, soon noticed that Brian's hands weren't the hardened hands of a machinist. After the third class session, he asked, "Where do you work, Brian?"

"Hayes."

"Oh, really? What's your position over there?"

"I'm the Machine Shop Manager," Brian said.

Frank just about fell over in surprise. He had retired from Hayes's machine shop and now was teaching this class to stay busy. "I'll give you all the help I can," was Frank's generous reply. Fortunately Brian liked working with the equipment and proved himself to be a quick learner.

Several weeks later, Frank returned to Hayes to pick up some scrapped parts that Hayes had agreed to give the college for its students' use. Brian was on the shop floor expediting a past-due part when he found Frank chatting with a group of Brian's machinists, some of Frank's old buddies. Frank made a point of telling them all about his new star pupil. Brian was embarrassed. But, contrary to his fear that the news would lower his workers' estimation of him, it earned Brian a good deal of respect.

Brian, however, had bigger problems to face at his new job than just earning the respect of his workers. First, there were the daily 8:30 A.M. part-shortage meetings.

The company had installed a computerized Material Requirements Planning system (MRP) that generated information that told the material planners when to release orders. The computer also provided Brian with schedules and machine-load reports for each of the work centers. The only problem was they were completely worthless. They didn't reflect the work that *really* needed to be done, and a large percentage of the scheduled orders were already past due. Consequently, everyone was using hot lists to communicate the real priorities.

The Production Control people constantly told Brian that there wasn't anything wrong with the computer system. The problem was with the people, who simply were not following the schedules. Brian knew that they were including him in their comments, but he had no idea what he was doing wrong.

Brian also knew there were problems with management. Top management didn't seem to understand the limitations of the manufacturing process at all: They just wished things would happen and then expected Brian and the other managers to get them done on time. The Sales Department, for example, continually promised new orders with less-than-normal lead times and expected them to be shipped on time. To say the least, the job ahead of Brian was not going to be easy or pleasant.

Brian arrived at the factory each morning around 6:30. He wasn't expected to be in the office until 8:00, but expectation and reality had already been proven to be two different things. First, he would find his third-shift supervisor to see what went on the night before. Then, he would track down the expeditor. "Tony," he would yell, through the constant noise that permeated the plant, "where's the hot sheet? Get me an update, will you?"

The next half hour or so would be spent going through the parts on the hot list, checking their status with Tony, and, at the same time, trying to assess what progress had been made and where he needed to concentrate his effort to "cause it to happen." Brian would walk into the plant and check with his own eyes to make sure that the parts on the hot list were running on the machines. Built in the 1920s, the Hayes facility was an old shop, with a smattering of new, state-of-the-art equipment mixed in with mostly older machines. Even though everything had been painted and repainted over the years, there was no escaping the age of the plant and its equipment.

At 8:30 each morning, several of the managers gathered for the part-shortage meeting: Dan, the Fabrication Manager; Mickey, the Assembly Manager; Joan the Production Control Manager; Roy, the Materials Manager; and Harold, the Purchasing Manager, were usually present. Dan and Mickey were the ones who made Brian's life difficult, but they probably felt the same way about Brian.

Dan was in his mid-forties and had been a buddy of Ralph's for years. They were regular golfing partners and football couch potatoes; and they'd been known to enjoy a beer or two together as well. Mickey was in his thirties—the same age, in fact, as Brian. Ralph's relationship with Mickey was also special. Although Ralph had a son of his own, he looked upon Mickey as a son, too. The only problem in this little group was that Dan and Mickey didn't like each other. Neither had an advantage over the other with the boss. Their only common ground was that they could both gang up on Brian.

On this particular day, the shortage meeting got under way right on time. It was one of the few things at Hayes that was on schedule. As they did every morning, they started at the top of the list of shortages, which was typically over 300 parts. The status of each and every part was reviewed. Brian was prepared. He'd done his homework and knew where most parts on the shortage list were and when they should be delivered to Mickey or Dan. Invariably, Mickey's response was, "That's not good enough! I need that part at least two days earlier." Of course, everyone in the room knew that Mickey always wanted everything before he really needed it. If a part from Dan's Fabrication Department was late, Dan always pointed a finger at Mickey and said "The parts are in the Paint Shop," which was under Mickey's jurisdiction. It was how Dan always got off the hook. This time Mickey had decided to push back.

Reading down the list, Ralph came to a cover which was supposed to be coming out of Fabrication on its way to Assembly. Dan, without blinking, said, "It's in Paint." Mickey was ready for this, and jumped right on Dan.

"That's a bunch of bull!" Mickey shouted. "I just came from there. That cover's not in Paint—it's sitting in your hand-grind area."

This infuriated Dan. "You're wrong as usual, Mickey! We've completed enough on that order to cover the shortage, and they're in Paint!" Ralph interceded and cooled the two men down. Brian shook his head in dismay. This was the daily atmosphere in which he now found himself.

After the meeting, Brian, trying to learn more about the Hayes environment, went looking for Dan, who had taken off immediately. Brian asked him if the covers he had so adamantly insisted were in Paint were really there. Dan smiled, and said, "The parts are always there when Mickey goes back to look. And they'll be there this time, too. I'll see to that." Brian was beginning to realize intimidation was the only way to survive in this environment. You tried to intimidate the boss, you tried to intimidate your peers, and you absolutely had to intimidate the people that worked for you.

It was surprising that anything got built in this factory. It did, but only through sheer brute force and the dedication of guys like Mickey in Assembly. Mickey battled against confusion and chaos and stayed in constant communication with his people and the expeditors. He knew what must ship and when. He also knew what was missing to make those shipments and he made sure he let everyone else know.

For Brian, that meant approximately 150 different parts in his shop were all past due or due that week. Each part had a specific day during the week when it was needed, and it took constant watching to make sure that Mickey got the parts that he needed when he needed them. Brian was continually checking to make sure the right parts were running on the machines.

Every day, however, Mickey would come in with a list of additional parts that weren't on the original shortage list. "You know that motor mount we thought we had. Well, we had some screw-up and we need more." Those extra shortages—and the extra work they caused—really annoyed Brian.

Once the part-shortage meeting had been completed, everyone had a new set of priorities. Brian rounded up his foremen, Tony, and the rest of the expeditors, and let them know about the additions. "Guess what, guys, more hot parts." No one seemed the least bit surprised. "What I live for," said one of the expeditors reviewing the list. Tony added these new items onto the original hot sheets and passed them around to the foremen. Afterward, Brian was once again out on the floor making sure they were running the right parts.

With 170 employees in his machine shop to manage, Brian's life was rarely dull. There were grievances to arbitrate, promotions to consider, attendance problems, fixture breakdowns, and industrial engineers plotting new equipment layouts. "The new Libiher hobb won't fit in the same position as the old hobb and the foundation for it requires a pit larger than we expected," said an engineer, looking over the drawing. "This means we'll have to move the horizontal broach." Next there were the personnel meetings to review all the problems about hiring new people.

Finally, it was time for lunch. Brian closed the door to his office. He didn't want to see anybody. He just wanted to eat his sandwich in peace. The phone rang. It was his wife. "Yes, dear, just another day in paradise."

After lunch, it was more of the same. More meetings, more problems, more expedited parts. The frustration level continued to rise. "All I want," Brian thought to himself, "is some decent, reliable information. At least, then, I might be able to come up with some sort of game plan." At 35 years old, Brian hadn't reached the point where he was ready to accept that things couldn't and wouldn't get better. He knew that lots of things were wrong at Hayes. He had graduated from college as an industrial engineer, and that supposedly had trained him to find better ways. Although he wasn't exactly sure just how it was supposed to be, he knew it was not supposed to be like this.

One day while waiting in the expeditor's office, which was located in the middle of the shop, Brian picked up the computer-printed schedule. It listed everything that was supposed to be made in each work center for the next week, sorted by due date. He took it to Tony and asked, "Why don't we start using these instead of hot lists?"

Tony sighed disgustedly and told him that the first 12 items on the schedule for the lathes were parts nobody seemed to need. Then he pointed out that the 23rd item on the schedule was the hottest job in the whole factory, according to the shortage meeting that morning. Brian was confused. He stared down at the computer printout. It was the right concept, but the information on it seemed useless. Not knowing where the information came from or how it was developed, he was at a loss.

Brian realized that the key to getting work done on time was having the right number of people at the right time. To accomplish that, he needed visibility of what was required. All he had was a machine-load report that the computer generated every week. It showed the total amount of work in standard hours that were scheduled to be completed week by week for each work center. The trouble was that it always contained a lot of work that was already past due. A month out in the future, however, there was hardly any workload at all. Brian knew there was going to be work next month, but the report gave him no idea how much. This was why he couldn't believe the report. He didn't know whether to hire additional people to take care of the past due or to lay people off because there was no work scheduled for the future. Brian decided to check it out with Mac, the former machine shop manager, now Manager of Human Relations. He must have had some way to predict when and where people and equipment were needed.

Brian walked into Mac's office. Mac was behind his desk, as gruff and grumpy as if he had never left the shop floor. He didn't really like his new position, but he wasn't about to leave Hayes after 45 years. Brian put the machine-load report on the desk before Mac. "I'm having a terrible time trying to plan the number of people I need. Is it possible to really plan with this machine-load report?"

Mac let out an abrupt laugh. "You look at that thing and you tell me." Being his replacement, Brian knew Mac had resented him, and no amount of charm was about to melt that girded exterior.

"Well, it seems obvious to me that it's useless. So what did you use to plan with?"

"Well," Mac drawled, enjoying the fact that Brian was having such problems, "when you get a little more experience, you'll get the 'gut feel', and you'll know."

Brian stared at Mac blankly. He had precious little time to turn things around. Mac had had 45 years, and Brian could see by the chaos on the shop floor that after all those years, Mac hadn't done very well at balancing capacity. Brian felt a very deep emptiness.

He walked into his office like a condemned man. He picked up the phone and called Tony. Brian had confidence in Tony. He knew that a good expeditor was the key to survival, and Tony knew a lot about the shop at Hayes.

Tony entered the office tentatively. The tone of Brian's voice on the phone had suggested that Brian wasn't very happy. Tony pulled a chair out and sat down. "So, what's the story?" he asked. It was how Tony approached every encounter.

"Tony, what do I do about planning capacity in this place? I can't tell if we're coming or going."

"Is that all this is about?" Tony asked, having already assumed that Brian would want to reschedule the whole shop. "Man, that's a piece of cake."

"A piece of cake?"

"Sure. I'll show you." Tony led Brian onto the shop floor amidst the constant roar and clatter. "A piece of cake," Brian thought. "Okay, maybe I will survive this place." He was starting to feel better.

Tony walked him over to the Warner-Swasey 2ACs. A box was attached to a column nearby and it was jammed full of work orders to be completed. "You see that?" Tony asked, raising his voice over the noise, as one of machines peeled a string of metal chips from a part. "You can just look at the work-order box and know we're in big trouble on these machines. We have to have more capacity, so we're going to have to work overtime." The two walked down the aisle to a drill press that had one work order. "See that?" Tony pointed to the only order in the box. "We don't have any capacity problems here."

"That's great, Tony. That's just great," Brian said as the sinking feeling returned. "But, it's all after the fact. It's too late to do anything about it. I mean, if I need to hire people, I need to do it a lot sooner than when the work goes past due."

Tony smiled. "When I said it was a piece of cake, I meant that I'd show you how we did it. I never said it worked, but that's the way we've always done it. The problem now is that we're just too big to operate like this anymore."

"That's not all," Brian said, "late shipments aren't going to be tolerated anymore. Our jobs are on the line here."

Later, leaning back in his chair, staring vacantly at the Timken Bearing Company calendar on the wall, Brian counted his days left. He stared down at the schedule and the machine-load reports on his desk. He had the tools that were supposed to be giving him the information he needed, but they weren't providing accurate information. "The computer can't be the answer," he thought. "Look what it produces—junk. If only I knew what I had to do to solve the problem. No matter how difficult the solution might be, at least I could apply myself and do it." But Brian didn't even know what the problem was. And the frustration continued to build.

Then he thought about his wife's Chevy sitting in the garage at home. He remembered when he had finally finished it, turned the ignition key, and couldn't get it started. Why wouldn't it start? He had had to go back and, without a clue, track down the problem. But once he found the problem, even though it meant additional hours of work, he knew what he had to do. He never minded the hard work. The frustration at Hayes was maddening because he couldn't find the problem.

The frustration didn't just stay at the factory. Every night Brian brought it home. He was tired, angry, and sick of all the endless problems without solutions. He'd snap at his wife when she showed her hurt and anger because her husband was never home. All of his waking hours were consumed by a job that seemed without reward, a job that seemed to be tearing them apart. Brian tried to explain how much everything was out of control, but he didn't have the words. All he had was this continual, unnerving agitation. It was often all he could do to keep himself under control. He wanted her to understand, but the problem was that he himself didn't understand. Something had to give. Maybe they should go back to the Midwest. Things had been better there.

Sitting in his office, Brian tried to sort through the problems he was encountering. He even thought back to a management problem-solving class he'd taken in college, and suddenly a vision of Harvey Piscoli's face appeared in his mind. Harvey! Why hadn't he thought of him earlier? Brian was on the phone in a second. Harvey was one of Brian's best buddies in college and he was now the production manager at ERON Technology, located a few blocks from Brian's old Midwest plant. Brian had never been sure what Harvey's company built, but it had something to do with scientific-research instrumentation.

"Piscoli!" Brian said, with Harvey on the other end. "I have to tell you, buddy, I think I've gotten myself in over my head by taking this transfer to the West Coast. And I'm afraid to admit it, but I think I need some help." It lifted Brian's spirits just to hear Harvey's laugh. Brian then explained his desperate and deteriorating situation. "I tell you, Harvey, I come to work each day wondering how I'm going to meet my schedules and productivity goals. I don't even know what the real schedule is. Everyone seems to have his own. I spend most of my time chasing after parts shortages."

Brian continued; "My schedule calls for 800 hours of output one week, 700 the next, and 900 the week after that. And my machine-load report always has a bunch of past-due work but nothing beyond the next six or eight weeks. It's gotten so bad, Harvey," Brian said, "I don't have time to think about who is going to be on vacation next week or what tooling I need or which machines need maintenance."

"Brian, I have been in that situation before. What are you guys using for a scheduling system?" Harvey asked.

"We've got an MRP system, but it certainly doesn't seem to be much help," said Brian. "I spend half my day trying to keep up with the changes."

"Sounds like you guys have to close the loop," Harvey said.

"Harvey, they've got me jumping *through* the loop. In fact, it feels like that loop is getting tightened around my neck." Both Brian and Harvey laughed.

"Tell me, Brian, are you getting valid schedules for each work center every day?"

"We have a weekly schedule for the shop, but nobody uses it. The schedules I get now are unreliable; either the dates change constantly, or they're way past due."

"What about Capacity Requirements Planning? Are you guys doing that?" Harvey asked.

"I get that machine-load report every week," Brian said. "It's supposed to tell me how much capacity I need, but I haven't found it very useful either because it only shows me released work, not what is planned for the future."

"I'll tell you, partner," Harvey said, "Capacity Requirements Planning has made an amazing difference for us. We're even able to anticipate capacity problems and take the action necessary to avoid them. The visibility we're getting today has made this job one even you could probably do, Miller."

"Talk to me, Harvey. All I wish is that I had some idea of what was really going to happen tomorrow."

"Not to gloat, buddy, but we're able to tell what's happening months in advance. And if we don't think we can meet the schedule, we get together with the planners and expeditors before the problem gets to the crisis stage, and we work it out."

"Your system's supporting all that for you? How do you stay on top of it all? I tell you, Harvey, my boss is constantly monitoring the efficiency, utilization, and output of my departments. If we miss any of the goals he sets for us, . . . well, you can guess what it's like. Then, if I try to talk to him about how far behind we are, he tells me, 'Put a little pressure on your people. They'll get the work out. They always have.'"

"Well, don't get too down on yourself, Brian. It sounds similar to this place a few years ago." Harvey went on to explain that ERON now had an overall operating plan and the schedules that supported that plan. The impact on his job was significant. His responsibility now was to meet the Master Production Schedule. That meant making sure he had the equipment, tooling, and manpower necessary to address the demand. "But, the most important part, Brian, is that we have all the information we need to run the factory and meet our schedules. Now, management expects me to meet the schedule, but they've also given me the authority to make sure that we do."

All Brian could do was shake his head in disbelief. "Obviously, we're not getting the most out of our MRP system. And, I have to tell you, Harvey, it'll be tough to get people at Hayes to change the way they do things. They've been doing them this way since creation. I also know they've been doing it wrong that long, too. So, where do we even start?"

Harvey tried to reassure his friend. "You have to have accurate data to start with. When we first got going, our data was about as reliable as a stopped watch: It was only accurate twice a day. If I were you, I would make sure that the data feeding into MRP is accurate. Then, I would take a look at the routings."

"Piscoli, I knew you were the man I had to talk to. Now, all I have to do is figure out what you're talking *about* and go do it, right? Thanks, buddy."

Brian realized he still had a lot to learn and there would be a great deal of work involved. But, it was like he had always said: "Hard work isn't the problem." When you know what you have to do, you do it. It's the not knowing that makes everyone crazy. Then, you're just working against yourself, and that's the hardest work you can do.

Chapter Two

Constructing Routings and Work Centers

A few days later, Brian was called up to Ralph's office. He wasn't sure what to expect. He did know things hadn't improved much since he had started, and he was never quite sure when the ax might fall. As he entered the office, Dan, Mickey, and Joan, the Production Control Manager, were already seated. "Have a seat, Miller," Ralph said, motioning to the remaining empty chair. "I realize that things are pretty hard for you guys with this scheduling system of ours, although I'm not accepting any excuses because of it. And Brian has been telling me that he doesn't have any way to predict what his capacity requirements are going to be. There's no question but that we have to find a better way to run this place. That's why I want the four of you to attend a seminar on capacity management next week. Roy tells me the speaker is well known and puts on an excellent presentation. He thinks we would learn something from it. He also wants Joan to go along. He said his department will pay for it, so I figure it'll be worthwhile if you pick up a few points." He handed the seminar brochure to Dan from behind the desk.

Dan thumbed through it and handed it to Brian. As Brian opened the four-page spread, he remembered the last seminar that he had attended. The speaker had spent the whole day talking about things that had little relevance to Brian's immediate needs. He could tell

Ralph was intent on sending him to this one, so he resigned himself to another lost day.

The seminar was being held in a local hotel. The four members of the Hayes party found seats, and filled out their name cards with their company name. Brian was seated next to a woman from Missile Systems, a large local defense contractor. He looked around at the names of the other companies in attendance. There were people from Good Health Vitamins, Precision Air Components, Dorman Chemical, Beartone Manufacturing, and several other companies. Brian wasn't sure he could understand how all of these different companies with different products and different processes could use the same capacity planning techniques.

The speaker arrived at the front of the room. He was a man in his late forties, casually dressed. He placed a transparency on an overhead projector, flipped it on, and moved to the front of the group. "Our topic today is capacity management. As they say on the airlines, if this is not your intended destination, now would be a good time to deplane." The assemblage laughed. "We're here to talk about getting control of your manufacturing operations through capacity management."

Brian was ready. He listened as the speaker offered his manufacturing credentials and explained the areas that he planned to address that day. When the introduction was over, Brian looked across to Joan and nodded his approval. He could see that she agreed with his early assessment.

The speaker then stepped in front of the overhead projector and said, "The first step to planning capacity is the development of reliable production routings. These are the documents that describe the manufacturing process and contain the data necessary for capacity planning. When I was employed at Calber Manufacturing, one of the first things we had to do was to get our routings to accurately reflect what was actually happening on the production floor. How many of you here know how accurate your routings are?" The only people who raised their hands were from Missile Systems. "Well, we have a few, and all from the same company. That is unusual. Normally, no one raises their hand."

Brian felt that this man was talking right to him. "I wonder how accurate our routings are," he thought.

At the first break, Brian and Joan looked at each other and shook their heads. They knew what they were hearing made more sense than they had ever imagined. By the second break, they had begun talking to some of the people sitting around them. The vast majority of them were in situations similar to the one at Hayes. They all had lots of problems. There were differences, however, in how they felt about what they were hearing. Some of these people had very positive attitudes and were excited about going back to their companies to begin fixing things up. Others weren't sure things would ever change in their companies. Still others felt that the techniques that were explained just didn't fit their company. Unfortunately, Dan and Mickey fell into this last category.

By the end of the seminar, Brian could see that there were a lot of things that had to be fixed at Hayes besides the routings, but that seemed to be the best place to start. The seminar had also shown him that there were companies that were doing some things right. It gave him hope.

After the seminar, Brian pulled Joan aside. "You know, Joan, this stuff is starting to make a little sense to me. The speaker talked about the same things that a buddy of mine in the Midwest told me they were using successfully. Can our computer do Capacity Requirements Planning?"

"Sure. The MRP software we bought has that capability," she said.

"Then why don't we use it?" Brian asked the obvious question.

"As far as I can see, because no one has taken the initiative to get it running," Joan answered. "I guess it looks like something we should pursue. It shouldn't be a big problem. Information Systems has asked several times if we want to use it. I've said no, because of a lack of time on my part."

"I think we should get going on it," Brian said, ready to start as soon as he got back to the plant.

"Sounds fine to me," Joan said, "but first we'll have to do something about our data accuracy. You heard what the speaker said. 'Dispatch lists and Capacity Requirements Planning are useless without accurate data.'"

"Right. My buddy said the same thing," Brian said. "He also said that the information coming out of MRP needs to be accurate. Let's make a deal. I'll take the responsibility for the routings and scheduling data, and you work on the MRP stuff." Joan agreed.

The next day, back at Hayes, Brian was motivated. He got on the phone with Elliot in Manufacturing Engineering. "I know you guys are busy. So am I. But how am I supposed to get things under control if the routings are wrong? Elliot, we're not talking about changing the production methods, just correcting the documentation. . . . Well, for instance, on this drive shaft, there's a second turning operation and a deburr missing. . . . I'm telling you, they're not on the routing. . . . They are *so* needed. We do them every time we run this job. We just write them in."

"All right, Brian, all right," came Elliot's response. "We'll get around to looking at them as soon as we get a chance."

"When will that be?" Brian asked.

"I don't know. Just give me a break," Elliot said as he hung up.

Brian's frustration level was rising. It seemed like such a simple thing. The shop was supposed to follow the steps that were on the routing. In order for them to do that, however, the routings needed to contain every step of the process. That shouldn't be so difficult to get right. Everyone at Hayes agreed that the routing should be accurate, but no one ever did anything but talk about it.

One of the primary messages Brian and the others had received at the seminar was that accurate routings were a prerequisite to doing a good job of planning capacities and executing schedules. How was he supposed to get the routings correct when everyone seemed to have a different opinion of what was correct? Brian rechecked his notes from the day before. He wanted to be certain he was using the same terms he had heard.

The speaker at the seminar had said that the routings were a vehicle for communicating the manufacturing process to the shop floor as well as a foundation for the planning and scheduling processes (see Figure 2.1). Both uses were equally important. He had said that the routings needed to contain the following minimum information.

- THE PART NUMBER: identifies the unique item to which this particular routing pertains.
- THE PART DESCRIPTION: the commonly used description of the part. Since the part number is merely an identifier, this element makes it easier for the user to know what the part actually is.

FIGURE 2.1 Typical Routing

173	LEG, TABLE	
PART NUMBER	PART DESCRIPTION	

OPN. NO.	DEPT.	WORK CTR.	OPERATION DESCRIPTION	SETUP	RUN
			RELEASE PICK		
10	M	01	SAW	0.1	.01
20	M	04	TURN	1.0	.15
30	S	07	FORM SAND	0.5	.20
			STORE		

- OPERATION NUMBER: identifies the sequence in which the operations are to be performed within an item's routing. The number should not be used to describe the operation in any way. The convention is to use increments of five or ten to allow for easy additions or alternate operations, although this is not a problem with today's modern computers.

- THE DEPARTMENT: a collection of work centers that are usually combined to reflect the organizational structure. It is often the cost center.

- THE WORK CENTER: one or more people and/or pieces of equipment that can be considered as one unit for purposes of capacity planning and detail scheduling.

- THE OPERATION DESCRIPTION: a simple description of the work to be performed. The key word here is "simple." In some environments, instructions regarding part dimensions, tooling, and operation detail may be included. If this information is lengthy, it is better to place it on a separate text or specification sheet than to include it in the operation description. This will help keep the routing itself simple.

- SETUP TIME: the length of time required to convert a specific piece of equipment or work center from the production of one specific item to the first good piece of the next item.

- RUN TIME: the length of time required to produce one unit of an item at an operation. This information represents what it should take a typical operator to perform the operation under normal circumstances. This is usually expressed in standard hours per unit (such as piece, feet, pound, etc.) or in standard hours per 100 or 1,000 units.

Standard hours should always be used on the routings for both setup and run times because it eliminates the variabilities of part size, process difficulty, operator experience, and other factors. Standard hours assume an average worker following prescribed methods and allows time for rest to overcome fatigue. This information is usually collected either through some analytical means such as time study or from operator input.

Brian compared this information to the routing they used at Hayes (see Figure 2.2) and found it was almost identical. His next task was to determine how accurate the routings were.

Brian got a random sampling of 20 machine shop routings printed out from the computer file. He sat down with his supervisors and went over each routing in detail to see if they were correct. The main problems the supervisors found were in the standards, although they

FIGURE 2.2 Routing Used at Hayes Tractor Company

163726	HUB, FRONT WHEEL	
PART NUMBER	PART DESCRIPTION	

OPN. NO.	DEPT.	WORK CTR.	OPERATION DESCRIPTION	SETUP	RUN
			RELEASE		
			PICK		
10	FAB	16	SAW BLANK	0.5	.10
20	MACH	24	TURN	3.0	.20
30	MACH	22	DRILL	2.0	.10
40	MACH	19	TAP	1.0	.20
			STORE		

also identified several other areas, including missing operations, unnecessary operations, wrong work-center callouts, and wrong sequences. After the review was finished, they realized that only 12 of the 20 routings were completely correct. Brian quickly calculated that the routing accuracy of this sample was 60 percent, far from the minimum of 95 percent that the seminar leader had said was necessary for good capacity planning.

Brian knew that he would have trouble convincing Elliot that the routings were this bad. First, he realized that his sample might not be representative of the entire routing file, and he didn't have time to do this kind of tabletop review for all the routings. Second, he knew that Elliot would think the results were biased, because they were based only on manufacturing's opinions of what was correct. And, third, he knew that Elliot would stand steadfastly behind the standards; manufacturing was always griping to engineering that the standards were wrong.

There was no question in Brian's mind: the routings needed to be fixed. But how was he going to convince Elliot of that? Brian would have to get an independent audit done.

MEASURING ROUTING ACCURACY

Brian searched through the handouts from the seminar and found the attendance list. He decided to put in a call to Sue Corey-Smith, the woman who sat next to him from Missile Systems. She had indicated that their routings were in good shape. She had even made a few comments to Brian about the way Missile Systems had conducted their routing audits. Brian figured it might be worth his while to get in touch with her since she had offered to give him a tour of her facility and explain to him what they had done. Brian wasn't sure that the process of making defense products really had anything in common with the way Hayes did business. Nonetheless, Sue had said that Missile System's average routing accuracy was 99 percent for the last six months. That statistic alone was enough to make Brian interested in finding out more. Brian gave her a call and Sue was happy to set up the tour.

Two weeks later in her office, Sue explained to Brian that determining routing accuracy began by examining an open order (shop order) on the shop floor and checking to see if the part was actually being made in accordance with the routing. The shop order was then checked against the computer file to make sure there hadn't been a change since the order was released. The operation number, the sequence of operations, and the work center needed to be verified, as well as the identification of any missing or unnecessary operations. The setup and run hours also needed to be verified.

She cautioned Brian not to get caught up in the debate over the accuracy of standard hours. There were times when people believed that standards were too loose or too tight. What was important at the start was relative accuracy—a sense of reasonableness. Of course, standards have to be reliable and sufficiently accurate so that people will believe the schedules and capacity requirements that are based on them.

Sue told him that for the purposes of capacity planning and shop scheduling, having standards that are within plus or minus 20 percent of the actual performance is good enough. She explained how the use of a load factor (see Chapter 4) can compensate for the effect of actual-to-standard variance on capacity plans and schedules. In many cases, companies can get as good as plus or minus 5 percent, but most are in the range of 10 to 20 percent.

Sue took Brian out onto the factory floor. He was introduced to an auditor from the Accounting group and the supervisor of the area. Sue emphasized that even though Accounting performed the audits, Manufacturing Engineering was still responsible for creating and maintaining routing accuracy and Production was responsible for reporting any known or suspected inaccuracies. "We just wanted an unbiased group to report the accuracy level as it was actually being performed. The audit is intended to have Accounting report the accuracy level of a significant sample. It is Production's responsibility to identify the problems and Manufacturing Engineering's responsibility to fix them. The audit process makes sure the procedures that have been established to identify and correct routing errors are working. It is up to Manufacturing Engineering and Production to assure the 95 percent minimum accuracy, not the auditor. The auditor's only job is to verify the accuracy level in much the same way that a bank auditor verifies the accuracy of the bank's records: No matter what, it's still the bank's responsibility to assure its accuracy. The focus of the audit is to find out if the feedback and correction process is working."

Brian followed the auditor as she went through the process of checking the routings. Although Missile System's parts, machines, and manufacturing operations were completely different from those at Hayes, Brian could see similarities in the way that the overall manufacturing process could be scheduled and managed. He realized that Hayes could probably learn a great deal from the successes of other companies.

Brian noticed that the auditor was checking only one operation and questioned Sue about it. "It's impractical for the auditor to follow a work order and catch it at every operation. So, we have her verify only that one operation," Sue told him.

"But the speaker said the 95 percent minimum objective was for the whole routing," Brian said.

"We did some comparisons on that," said Sue. "We found that the operation audit caught a lot more errors than just having someone review the routing from memory. We are doing a random sampling of the operations. By doing these audits periodically, over time the probability of uncovering any errors that exist is quite high." Her reasoning made perfect sense to Brian.

Brian also questioned the practice of just asking the operator. Maybe the operator doesn't know the process as he should. Sue responded that they are careful about the operators they interview. They make sure the operator is qualified and avoid new operators. The auditor always checks with the supervisor prior to the audit to assure the operators are qualified.

On the way home, Brian thought about who could do the audit at Hayes. He knew Accounting would not be a good choice, because they didn't have the staff to do it. Besides that, they would probably complain, "It's not our job to check your manufacturing documents." He also figured that Elliot in Manufacturing Engineering wouldn't want to cooperate; and if one of his machine shop people performed the audit, no one would believe it. "Who else is suffering from these bad routings as much as me?" he wondered. It suddenly dawned on him—Carol Barrow, Manager of Quality Control. Carol was constantly taking the heat for the low quality of the parts being produced. Both Carol and Brian were well aware that the real problems were in the manufacturing processes themselves. Getting Quality Control to audit the routings would allow them to focus the proper attention on those real problems.

The next morning, Brian explained the situation to Carol. Even though Carol was hard-pressed to spare an inspector, she was quick to realize the benefit of what Brian was proposing. This approach would not only help him fix some of his scheduling problems, it would also help her efforts to improve quality.

Brian's initial fear about conducting the audit was whether or not the operators would tell the truth. Sue had told him that Missile Systems had worried about that, too, but found that, almost without exception, the operators were all very cooperative. They even devised a form to handle the operator's input. She dug one out of a file and Brian stuffed it into his briefcase. "The reality is," she said, "once people understand the need, all you have to do is ask for their help." When Brian eventually did ask his operators, he got plenty of feedback.

The audit process started the next day. The auditor went into each work center and picked up the routing sheet for the job that each operator was working on. He asked the operator if he performed his operations exactly as specified on the routing. Had he done it in listed sequence? Did the job come to him from the work center listed immediately before his operation on the routing? Did it go to the next work center on the routing when he was done with it? Were there any missing operations? Were the standards reasonable? If the answer to any of the questions was no, the auditor recorded the operation as a "miss". If the answers were all yes, the operation was considered accurate.

When the auditor finished the audit in the work centers, he compared the routing sheets with the routings in the computer file. If the computer file was the same as the routing sheet for the operation recorded as a miss in the floor audit, it remained a miss. If the error had been corrected, then the operation was considered accurate. The auditor then calculated the accuracy percentage by dividing the number of accurate operations by the total number of operations that had been audited.

Technically, an accurate routing is one which has no errors at any of its operations. This method of calculating routing accuracy by sampling operations is acceptable. Ultimately, however, the entire routing must be verified before it can be declared accurate.

The results of Carol's first audit were worse than Brian's earlier sample. It indicated 36 percent accuracy on the routings. However, prior to showing the results to Ralph and Pete, Brian asked Carol to sit on them for a while. He wanted to do a little investigation.

Manufacturing methods had changed over time. Improvements were made, technology changed, new equipment replaced outdated machines, and new tooling was introduced. But the routings had not been kept up to date with those changes.

Brian tracked down Jim, the supervisor of the grinding area, to ask him about one of the erroneous routings. "Listen, Jim," he said, thumbing the audit in his hand, "the auditor indicates here that you're not following the routing on the part #96458 gear shaft."

Jim shook his head from side to side with a smile. "Not for the last three months. We aren't able to get the required finish Manufacturing Engineering says we're supposed to get, so we had to add a second grind operation."

"Since it isn't called out on the routing, how do you remember that kind of thing?" Brian asked.

"Usually, it's not a problem if it's a job that runs frequently. If it's not, the operators try to keep notes. Sometimes when we put a new operator on a job or one of the more experienced operators forgets or there are no notes, we run into some problems. The last time we ran this job, it was originally set up on second shift by a new operator who spent the whole night trying to figure it out. After making lots of scrap, he gave up, even though it was on the hot sheet. When Cecil Nickerson, who has been here at Hayes for 35 years, arrived in the morning, he immediately knew what the problem was, and he simply did the second grind."

"Did you ever tell anyone that the routing's wrong?"

"We told them several times, but they never got around to fixing it, so we quit trying. Now, we just do what we have to in order to get the parts right and write in the operations on the work order."

Brian called Elliot in Manufacturing Engineering and asked him if he would come down and review the problem. Elliot reluctantly agreed.

Elliot asked Cecil, "Can you get that finish on the first grind operation if you're really careful?"

Cecil gave Elliot a disgusted look. "We used to be able to when the machine was new. But now it's worn beyond ever holding that finish requirement."

Elliot relaxed. "Well, there's your problem. It's not my fault. Go talk to Maintenance."

Brian headed down to Maintenance and asked Ivan, the Maintenance Manager, why the grinder hadn't been fixed.

"It's on the schedule," was Ivan's reply.

Looking over Ivan's shoulder at the schedule, Brian noticed the original request date and blurted out, "It's been on the schedule for three months!"

Ivan just shrugged his shoulders. "I'm trying to get to it, guy. It's the best I can do."

Brian stomped away in frustration. Everyone was putting the blame on someone else. No one was willing to assume the responsibility for the problem, so it got dropped in his lap. It appeared that the only way he could protect himself at Hayes was to be as good at finger-pointing as everyone else.

Brian returned to his office disgruntled and discouraged. How was he going to get the support departments to respond more quickly? He began thinking about Missile Systems and its 99 percent routing accuracy. Then he remembered the feedback form that Sue had given him that he had stuffed into his briefcase. He immediately retrieved it. It was a three-part form called "Request for a Bill of Material/ Routing Change" (see Figure 2.3). At the top of the form was a place to state the problem and offer recommendations for action. There was a place for the originator to sign it, which could be anyone in the company but was usually a shop supervisor. The bottom third of the form was for the reply. Bill of material problems were to be sent to Design Engineering, and routing problems were to be sent to Manufacturing Engineering. Each group would investigate their respective requests and the solutions would be implemented.

Brian went to Elliot's office and talked to him about using the form. Elliot was less than enthusiastic until Brian showed him the results of the audit done by Carol's inspectors. Elliot almost jumped out of his seat. He knew as well as Brian that Pete would go through the ceiling if he saw those results. Elliot immediately realized Brian was right. Their only salvation would be to install a corrective action plan as soon as possible. They quickly agreed on some minor changes to the form and Elliot arranged to have it printed right away.

When the new forms were ready, Brian brought his supervisors together and explained how to fill them out. He emphasized that they

FIGURE 2.3 Typical Form for Requesting a Bill of Material or Routing Change

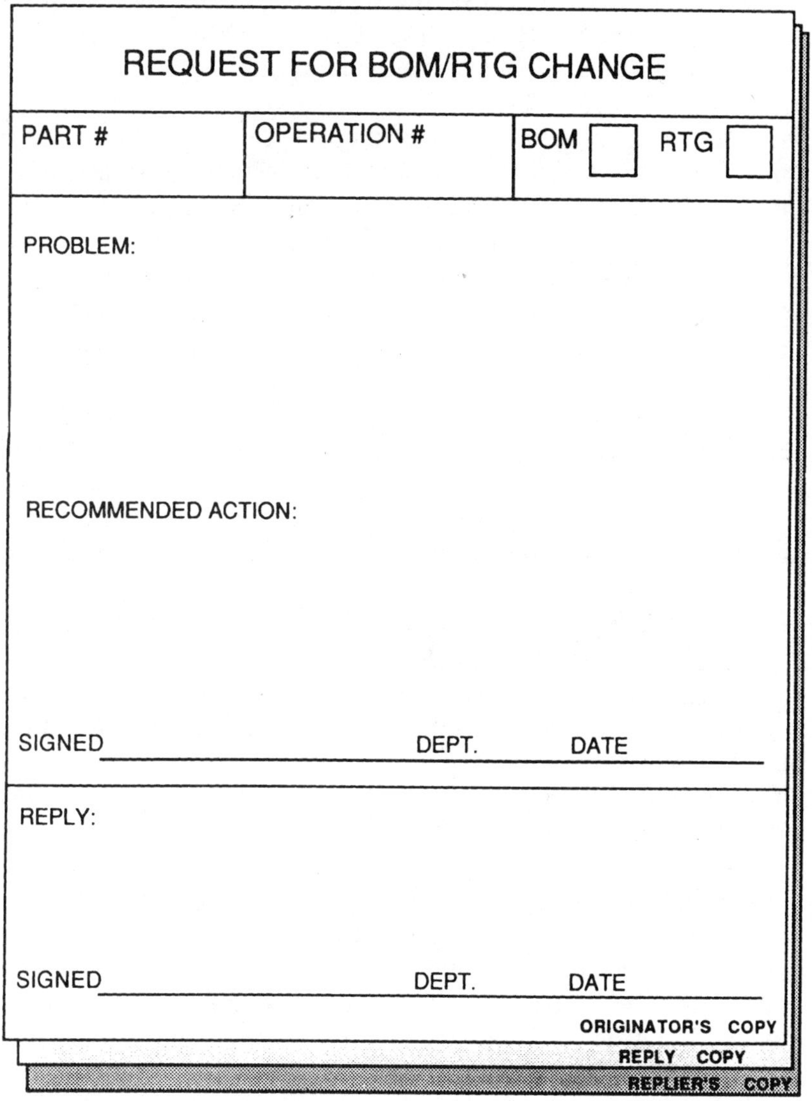

REQUEST FOR BOM/RTG CHANGE

PART #	OPERATION #	BOM ☐ RTG ☐

PROBLEM:

RECOMMENDED ACTION:

SIGNED _____   DEPT. _____   DATE _____

REPLY:

SIGNED _____   DEPT. _____   DATE _____

ORIGINATOR'S COPY

REPLY COPY

REPLIER'S COPY

were to make sure that these forms were filled out whenever there was a problem. "This is how things get better," he promised. Nothing else had worked yet, and they were all ready for a change.

Over the next several days, the supervisors filled out 27 forms, keeping one copy and sending the other two to Manufacturing Engineering. Elliot had alerted his manufacturing engineers to expect the incoming forms.

Later, Elliot brought a stack of requests to Brian. One of them concerned part #96458, the gear shaft that Brian had previously discussed with Elliot. "Look, Brian," Elliot said in his most conciliatory voice, "I'll agree that we should add a second grinding operation until Maintenance gets the machine fixed. But adding an operation for deburring is ridiculous. There's enough time while the machine is running on automatic cycle for the operator to deburr the part that was just finished."

"It makes sense to me," Brian said. "See how easy I am? All you need to do is add a note on the routing so we'll know we're supposed to do it."

"That's simple enough," Elliot said. Both men smiled at how truly simple things could be when they worked together to resolve their problems. "There's one more thing, though," Elliot said, holding up the stack of forms. "The supervisors could help reduce the number of requests."

"How are they supposed to do that?" Brian asked.

"Several of these requests are for relaxing the standards. Instead of jumping to the conclusion that the standard is wrong every time they don't achieve it, have the supervisors get to the bottom of the problem. If it really is a problem with the routing, then send us the feedback form and we'll fix it."

"You got some idea how to convince them of that?"

Elliot had already anticipated Brian's question. "Explain to them that the standards are used to do much more than just measure operator performance. They're also going to be used to plan the operational priorities, to plan capacity, and to calculate the cost of the tractors. Realistic standards are required if we are going to accomplish that accurately," Elliot said to reemphasize his point.

"So I suppose you expect me to turn them around overnight," Brian said, realizing the enormity of the task. "What about Pete's insistence on productivity improvements?"

Fully understanding Brian's dilemma, Elliot answered, "I know you have a big education job ahead of you. The real problem lies with Pete and Ralph. We've got to get them to understand that the standards impact more than just productivity."

In spite of the work ahead, Brian was becoming enthusiastic. For the first time real progress was beginning to happen. He gathered his supervisors and explained the situation. They pledged their support and help, even though a number of them were still skeptical about the standards.

Slowly, working together as partners on the same team rather than as adversaries, Production and Manufacturing Engineering began establishing rapport. They were also gradually documenting their actual manufacturing processes as well. During the subsequent audits, Carol's auditors asked the operators and supervisors if the routings were correct. If they said no, they were asked if an action request had been turned in. By following this procedure, accountability was established. If the form had been turned in, but the computer file had not been updated, it was Manufacturing Engineering's responsibility. If there were still mistakes in the routings and no action request had been written, it was Production's responsibility.

The results of the first audit showed 78 percent of the misses had not been reported by Production. When Brian saw the results, he called his people together on each of the three shifts and explained the situation. He let it be known how unhappy he was that they had been complaining about the routings being inaccurate, but then, when they had been given the chance to fix the problem, they hadn't responded. "What are we?" Brian asked, challenging each of them with his disappointment. "Are we a bunch of crybabies or are we people who can get things done around here?" Brian must have hit home, because afterward, the machine shop people started identifying problems and sending the reports to Manufacturing Engineering in floods. Elliot appealed to Brian for help. Working as a team, the supervisors and some of the lead operators came in on several Saturdays to assist the manufacturing engineers.

One of Brian's supervisors suggested that Brian should post the results of the audits on a big board right by the time clock so everyone could see the results. Another of the supervisors commented that, if they were going to do that, it needed to be kept up-to-date. Everyone agreed that it was a good idea, and Brian committed to an updated board.

When Brian and Elliot showed the results of the first audit to Pete, he reacted with a burst of anger just as they had expected. Fortunately, their plan for solving the problem calmed him down.

As things improved, Pete began to brag about their routing accuracy to some of the other Hayes plants. "It would never have happened without that visit with Sue at Missile Systems," Brian thought.

Now, whenever Production calls Engineering, they come right down and look at the problem in process and take care of it immediately. The 99 percent routing accuracy that Sue had talked about was gradually becoming a reality at Hayes because if anything was wrong, both sides were communicating and both sides were feeding back the information necessary to make the process work. They all realized that if the feedback/fix-it process was working properly, they should find no errors because as fast as the factory found the problem, Manufacturing Engineering would fix it. They agreed that the ultimate goal was 100 percent, and everyone agreed not to slack off when they reached the 95 percent minimum threshold.

Once he had recognized the need for data accuracy and had seen how the routing data accuracy effort had rallied his staff together, Pete started making the reporting of data accuracy a regular part of his monthly performance review meeting.

ALTERNATE ROUTINGS

Brian knew that there are times when the specified routing cannot be followed. The desired machine may be overloaded or broken down. The tooling may be damaged or in use on another job. At times like these, an alternate process often can be used. Rather than changing the master routing, however, which would reroute all future jobs to the alternate process, a one-time change can be implemented for a particular order.

One of Brian's supervisors approached him about a job that was scheduled to run on the multi-spindle drills the next week (see Figure 2.4). The supervisor told Brian that the drills were already overloaded with past-due work, and it was unlikely that this job would get done on schedule. Brian decided to run the job on the single-spindle drills, even though he knew it would take longer and increase the cost. He then needed to get the routing to reflect this. In the past, Brian would have just told the supervisor to go ahead, and

FIGURE 2.4 Original Routing for Part #56832

568321	BRACKET	
PART NUMBER	PART DESCRIPTION	

OPN. NO.	DEPT.	WORK CTR.	OPERATION DESCRIPTION	SETUP	RUN
			RELEASE		
			PICK		
10	FAB	57	WELD	0.1	2.00
20	MACH	36	MILL	1.0	.05
30	MACH	22	DRILL, MULTI-SPINDLE	1.5	.02
			STORE		

he would not have worried about changing the routing. Now, however, since Brian wanted the routing in the shop to represent what the work centers were really expected to do, he went to the expeditor and asked him to delete the multi-spindle operation from the routing on the released order only and replace it with the single-spindle operation. The expeditor immediately updated the routing, using operation add-and-delete transactions (see Figure 2.5).

FIGURE 2.5 Alternate Routing for Part #56832

568321	BRACKET	
PART NUMBER	PART DESCRIPTION	

OPN. NO.	DEPT.	WORK CTR.	OPERATION DESCRIPTION	SETUP	RUN
			RELEASE		
			PICK		
10	FAB	57	WELD	0.1	2.00
20	MACH	36	MILL	1.0	.05
30	MACH	21	DRILL, SINGLE-SPINDLE	1.0	.06
			STORE		

FIGURE 2.6 Master Routings for Part #56832

568321	BRACKET	
PART NUMBER	PART DESCRIPTION	

OPN. NO.	DEPT.	WORK CTR.	OPERATION DESCRIPTION	SETUP	RUN
			RELEASE		
			PICK		
10	FAB	57	WELD	0.1	2.00
20	MACH	36	MILL	1.0	.05
30	MACH	22	DRILL, MULTI-SPINDLE	1.5	.02
30A	MACH	21	DRILL, SINGLE-SPINDLE	1.0	.06
			STORE		

The software being used at Hayes had the capability of storing multiple routings for each part. Although Hayes had not been utilizing this feature, Brian recognized that he could put the primary routings into the file and also load in some commonly used alternates (see Figure 2.6). Whenever a problem was realized, Production Control could select which routing path they wanted to use based on the circumstances at the time with the approval of Manufacturing and Manufacturing Engineering. That way, orders would be routed the way the shop was really planning to run them, and Brian could hold his people accountable for following the routing.

REWORK ROUTING

There are times when rework is required. If it's not going to be done immediately, rework should be handled on a work order so that it will get onto the schedules and the capacity plans. In this situation, a standard rework routing or a customized rework routing will be necessary for the proper rework steps to be scheduled and communicated. A rework routing can be created in one of two ways. The rework operations can be added to the existing routing (see Figure 2.7). If a portion of the order does not need to be reworked, the parts can be moved on to the next standard operation, as the rest of the order continues on for rework. Another option is to split the rework

FIGURE 2.7 Routing with Rework Operations Included for Part #373904

373904	PLATE, ADAPTER		
PART NUMBER	PART DESCRIPTION		

OPN. NO.	DEPT.	WORK CTR.	OPERATION DESCRIPTION	SETUP	RUN
			RELEASE		
			PICK		
10	FAB	16	SAW	0.5	.01
20	MACH	36	MILL	2.0	.03
30	MACH	19	DRILL	1.0	.02
40	MACH	19	TAP	0.5	.02
50	FAB	54	PLUG	0.1	.01
60	MACH	19	RE-DRILL	1.0	.02
70	MACH	21	RE-TAP	0.5	.02
			STORE		

pieces away from the original order and issue a new order for rework using a separate rework routing (see Figure 2.8). Both choices allow the additional capacity requirements to be generated and the rework to be scheduled. Rework routings can be stored as an alternate routing and selected as needed.

FIGURE 2.8 Separate Rework Routing for Part #373904

373904	PLATE, ADAPTER		
PART NUMBER	PART DESCRIPTION		

OPN. NO.	DEPT.	WORK CTR.	OPERATION DESCRIPTION	SETUP	RUN
			RELEASE		
			PICK		
10	FAB	54	PLUG	0.1	.01
20	MACH	19	DRILL	1.0	.02
30	MACH	21	TAP	0.5	.02
			STORE		

WORK-CENTER IDENTIFICATION

The machine shop at Hayes was making great progress toward increasing the accuracy of its routings. One area that had not been considered was the impact that work-center identification would have on capacity planning. Unfortunately for Brian and Elliot, they did not uncover the work-center identification problem until they had already started to do capacity planning (see Chapter 4). They made the mistake of assigning work centers without understanding the role work centers played in the whole planning and scheduling process.

There are four basic reasons for work centers to be on the routing:

1. To direct the work to the proper place
2. To apply the appropriate move and queue time to the schedule
3. To generate capacity requirements for the appropriate resource (people or machines)
4. To allow appropriate cost calculations

A work center is the smallest unit for planning and measuring capacity. Each machine, work station, or person can be established as a work center, but this is usually an unnecessary level of detail. It can result in voluminous data and reports.

When establishing work centers, there are several considerations that must be taken into account. All of the work stations assigned to a work center must, in general, be interchangeable; that is, they must be able to process any work that comes to the work center. A work center can be composed in three different ways:

1. A machine or a group of machines that perform similar operations

When specifying a group of machines as a work center, it must be determined if: (a) most of the work directed to the work center can be performed on any of the machines included in the work center group and (b) the work center contains the necessary capabilities to do the work as defined on the routing. It is acceptable if a small percentage of the work must be done only on one specific machine in the group.

For example, turning machines and grinding machines should be in separate work centers because they do entirely different operations, unless they are grouped together in a manufacturing cell (see item 3 below and also Chapter 9). It is less obvious, however, that single-spindle turning machines should be separated from multi-spindle turning machines or that machines that accommodate various work-piece sizes should be separated. Other considerations might include different output rates, capacities, colors, or materials. Again, the key issue is interchangeability.

2. A person or group of people that perform similar tasks

Manual operations (e.g., assembly, inspection, and packaging) can be grouped into work centers based on the interchangeability of the skills, where most people assigned to the work center can perform most of the work scheduled for it. Also, if the people in a group are cross-trained on the various steps of the work to be performed, a single work center is appropriate.

3. A group of machines or people that perform a sequence of operations

The tractor assembly line at Hayes fits this criterion, with different operations performed along the line in a prescribed sequence. On Hayes's transmission casing (see Figure 2.9), various stations perform their operations simultaneously. The transmission casings move on a conveyor from the milling station to the boring station and on to the drill and tapping station. As one casing is being milled, another is being bored and another is being drilled and tapped.

Brian recalled a conversation he had with an engineer from Castlebend Ceramics, a company that made china. The engineer described a work center that consisted of four different operations linked together in a continuous process (see Figure 2.10). A ribbon of glass was produced by the melting furnace, fed into a press where plates were formed, and passed to a shear where the plates were trimmed to a clean edge. They then went to an annealing furnace, which hardened the glass. Castlebend had arranged all four of these pieces of equipment into a single work center.

These examples are called flow lines because the product always moves down the line in the same way, one piece at a time in a continuous flow. None of these situations requires a detailed routing to

---

FIGURE 2.9 Production Line for Transmission Casings at Hayes Tractor Company

---

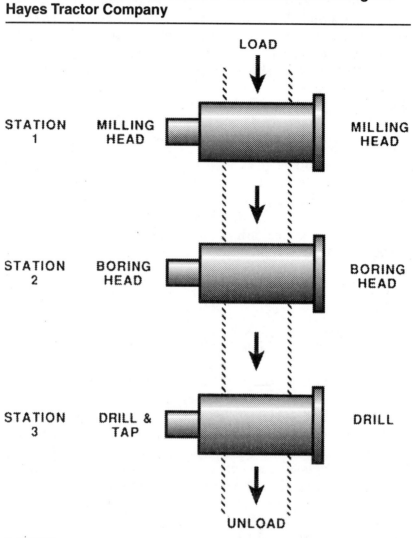

identify the capacity or priority at any individual operation. From a priority standpoint, whatever starts at the first step determines the priority at the rest of the steps. The capacity of the line is determined by the slowest step. Plan the capacity of the bottleneck operation, and the capacity of the entire line has been planned. Schedule the

FIGURE 2.10 Process for Manufacturing China Plates at Castelbend Ceramics Company

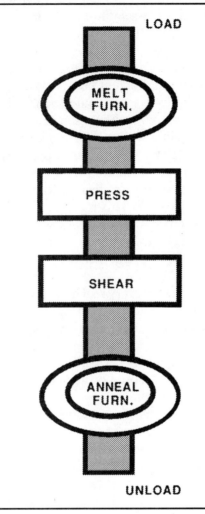

starting or gateway operation, and all other steps on the line will be scheduled appropriately.

Automated flow lines are not the only cases where a group of dissimilar machines can be called a work center. Any grouping of machines or people, however large or small, can be considered a work center. These are often called manufacturing cells and should be considered as one work center, as long as the flow of work always follows the same path inside the cell for an established group of similar products. Individual operations are not performed within the cell on other products. Mickey's assembly line is, in reality, a cell, even though at this time he doesn't realize it. Brian will also discover that cells can be set up in other areas relatively easily (see Chapter 9).

There are situations in some companies where operators are capable of running several different kinds of machines, for example, surface grinders, OD grinders, and centerless grinders, or where several packaging lines are manned by a single crew. When the equipment has been placed in a work center based on its capability, the planning of the capacity for the group of operators can be done by setting up a separate resource center for the operators and aggregating the capacity requirements for the individual machine work centers into that resource center. This requires a software feature that provides for the assignment of work centers to resource centers and the capability to aggregate the capacity requirements. This issue will be discussed in more detail in Chapter 4.

Brian considered making every machine a work center. When he tallied the number of machines, he realized that he would have more than 150 work centers. Recalling what the speaker had said at the seminar, Brian knew that meant he would have to deal with 150 capacity plans and dispatch lists—what a nightmare! Brian was also aware that a lot of his work could be done on any of several similar machines; that is, the machines were interchangeable. He really needed to know the total capacity requirements and priorities on that group of machines.

The first problem regarding work centers in the machine shop appeared in the turning operation. Manufacturing Engineering had assigned two different sizes of lathes to the same work center. Two of the machines could perform work on bar stock up to two inches in diameter, and the third could perform work up to a three-inch diameter. It was possible to lump the capacity of the three machines together, as long as no more than one-third of the work was over two inches in diameter and their total capacity wasn't exceeded.

The trouble started when a mix change occurred and the amount of work over two inches in diameter exceeded the capacity of the larger machine. At that point, the three-inch machine became so overloaded that the work center fell behind schedule, even though the total workload on the work center had not changed. It became evident that this work center had to be reorganized. The solution was to set up the two-inch machines as one work center and the three-inch machine as a separate work center. This gave Brian the advantage of grouping the two-inch machines together and, at the same time, provided him with visibility of the requirements for the larger machine alone.

Dan ran into a similar situation with a group of four punch presses. The newer presses in the group were capable of producing at nearly twice the rate as the two older models. The newer models were obviously the preferred machines, and production was directed through them whenever possible. Manufacturing Engineering had set the standard times based on the capability of the new machines.

Unrealistic information immediately surfaced. The machine-load system used the higher machine output rate and showed that plenty of capacity was available. Unfortunately, when the new presses were completely loaded and the old presses had to be used, they could not produce at the scheduled rate. It didn't take long for Dan to realize that if he planned his labor to the scheduled rate, he would quickly fall behind schedule, even though the Manufacturing Engineering standard indicated everything was all right. This was the perfect excuse for Dan to blame the computer system when in fact it was the data—the improper grouping of work centers—that created the problem.

Once Elliot started digging around in the details of Dan's problem, the solution was clear. "I think we should subdivide these machines based on their output rates," Elliot told Dan. The new presses would make up one work center, and the two older presses would be set up in another. Once this was done, Elliot's people saw that the new presses were overloaded: They needed to reroute some of the work from the faster new machines to the slower older ones. The work orders to be scheduled on the older presses would have their routings changed to reflect the slower process. Everyone recognized that the production costs would be higher on the slower machines, but it was necessary to reschedule the overload to the slower machines just to get the parts made.

In properly identifying and defining the work centers, we have to consider the machine's capabilities. In Brian's case, this meant that because of the mix, the two- and three-inch lathes had to be separated. The output rate of the machines in a work center also must be considered. In Dan's case, by separating the new presses from the old and setting the time standards based on the individual machine capabilities, we can identify any capacity constraints.

A final factor in the assigning of work centers is the issue of supervisory control. If two supervisors each had the same types of machines, those two still may not be combined into one work center. For example, a prototype shop may have an identical piece of equipment as a production area. Although they pass the test of "identical capability", they must be assigned different work centers. The reason is accountability. When two supervisors try to manage one work center, neither is accountable.

In a multiple shift situation where different supervisors manage different shifts, the accountability for the work center needs to be accepted at the next level up in the organization. This can present a problem in large companies where single accountability for all shifts is located several levels up in the organization. If located too high in the organization, the person will not take the time to review the capacity plans for each work center every week. This was not a problem at Hayes because Mickey, Dan, and Brian had responsibility for the three shifts.

The morale at Hayes started to improve. People throughout the plant were recognizing that things were getting better. First, Manufacturing Engineering was responding to the problems on the routings. Second, the production people were reporting any discrepancies in the routings, and they were also building a great deal of confidence in their accuracy. There were fewer delays because the routings reflected what really had to be done and no work had to be sent back. It had become clear to everyone on the production floor why accurate data mattered so much: The reliability of their planning and scheduling information was only as good as the data upon which it was based.

Brian was also pleasantly surprised when Sharon Levy, the Controller, complimented him on the work he had done to clean up the routings. She explained that the Accounting department had always been concerned about how the routings were structured because they used that information to calculate product standard costs by "rolling up" the cost of each operation into the total cost. The roll-up process consisted of applying the labor and overhead rates for each work center to the setup and run times on the routings. The standard cost calculations would be wrong if there were missing or unnecessary operations on the routings, if the setup and run times were wrong, or if the work center assignments were incorrect. Sharon also pointed out that the actual costs were also more accurate since Brian was changing the routings on open work orders whenever a change in the process was necessary or rework had to be done. She wanted Brian to know how excited her department was about the cleanup effort Brian was implementing because they knew that their cost data would now be a lot more accurate.

With accurate routings, the door was also opening for Brian to take the next step into operation scheduling. It would be at this point that he would begin to gain control. Finally, he would be able to correctly establish what was expected from his department so that he could produce what was really needed next.

Chapter Three

Mastering Dispatching
and Scheduling

The factory was never really quiet, but there were times when it was at least calm. At 6:00 A.M., toward the end of third shift and an hour before the first shift started, Brian liked to walk through the nearly deserted machine shop. He wasn't always looking for something specific, just getting a feel for the shop and for the day ahead. It was as if he hoped that somewhere, hidden in the smell of that distinct machine-oiled air, a magical solution had been found that would straighten out the problems in his factory.

The answer, of course, was neither in the air nor in some miracle. It was, however, already present in his factory. As Brian was slowly discovering, his solution lay in understanding the basic elements of running a production area, learning what tools were available, and then using those tools to better manage his operations.

He'd walk into his office after one of these moments in the shop and the reality would come rushing back. The reports piled on his desk seemed insurmountable. There was a time in the not-too-distant past when the majority of the information in that pile of paper was simply wrong. Prior to improving the accuracy of the routings, data integrity had been a joke.

Brian recalled a typical recurring situation. A call would come in from a customer who wanted a tractor delivered in four weeks when the normal lead time was ten weeks. Sales and the customer would

41

compromise on a six-week delivery date. After the tractor assembly order was jammed into the master schedule, the parts orders would be sent out by the material planner onto the shop floor. No one was really sure if the shop could deliver the product in six weeks or not, but everyone knew that all the stops would be pulled out in an attempt to do so. The complaints from the shop about orders already being late when they finally got them were generally ignored. If the shop could do it in six weeks, everyone looked good. That often meant either working overtime or pushing other work aside. Brian and his colleagues were just expected to "work around or through the problems," and "do the best you can."

COMMUNICATING PRIORITIES

The role of the shop schedule is to provide information for the short-term (a few days to a few weeks) control of shop operations. It communicates the priorities required to convert the planned Master Production Schedule into deliverable product. Priority is the position a production order should take in the queue (waiting line). Priority in and of itself does not imply that an order should necessarily be expedited, but merely in what sequence the orders are needed to support the master schedule.

Hayes used the due dates assigned to the work orders to establish priorities in the shop. The order due dates were assigned by the material planners to coincide with the need dates calculated by the MRP system. These dates were then used by the scheduling system to establish due dates for each of the manufacturing operations. The trouble was that most of the shop orders were either already past due or had been released with less than the full planned lead time available. Consequently, many of the operations were also past due. In many cases, the order due dates did not reflect when the jobs were really needed. Of course, the past-due dates were particularly meaningless. Since nobody knew when the work was really supposed to be done, the shop would prioritize their work from the hot list.

One of the groups of parts for which Brian was responsible was the gears. The process to produce a gear began with Dan's Fabrication department sawing 20-foot steel bars in half so they would fit in Brian's bar lathes. The 10-foot bars would then be sent to Brian's machine shop. Since most of the scheduled dates were past due, Dan would decide the priority on the saws based on the Assembly hot list. If a part didn't appear on the hot list, Dan wouldn't saw the bars until he had some open time, which was when nothing on the hot list was waiting for the saws.

Since Brian's scheduled operation dates were also meaningless, Brian didn't know which orders he should be working on first. By the time Dan moved the sawed bars to Brian, the job was often more than 30 days into the total 60-day planned lead time for the gears, with the result that it was nearly impossible for Brian to complete the job by the time it was needed in Assembly. Then, it wouldn't be too long before those gears showed up on the hot list, and the machine shop would have to jump through hoops to get them done. The fact that Dan had consumed 30 days instead of the 2 days allocated in the schedule was now irrelevant.

Without having valid schedules for operations in his department, Dan had only the order due-to-stock date to go by. Jobs that were not past due or near their due-to-stock date didn't get much attention. Since all jobs don't have the same lead times, the same routings, or go through the same processes, the stock date alone doesn't prioritize the early operations. To really know what to work on, the supervisor needs to see the priorities by operation.

Brian knew that if he was ever to get his jobs from Dan in time to complete them on their scheduled due date, Dan needed a valid schedule that told him when he should have *his* operations completed. Brian also realized that a valid schedule by operation would be a great help to him in his own shop to help settle the conflicts over priorities with his own supervisors.

As he was going home one night, Brian drove by the airport. He had always loved watching the airplanes as they lifted off—the power thrust, the coordination of so many complex systems that seemed to defy all earthly boundaries. As a large commercial airliner cruised in for its landing, Brian wondered how in the world airline manufacturers ever scheduled parts for something as complicated as an airplane. Then he remembered John Hall, the general supervisor from Precision Air Components whom he had met at the seminar.

The next morning he pulled out the seminar attendance list and gave John a call. John told him he would be pleased to show Brian and some of his colleagues around Precision Air, provided Brian would return the favor and show him around Hayes at some later date.

Brian immediately contacted Joan to see if she wanted to go. She thought it was a great idea. They also agreed it would probably be worthwhile to take Tony, the machine shop expeditor.

When they arrived at Precision Air, John took the three of them out onto the shop floor to show them how Precision's scheduling system worked. They walked to the closest work center, where John picked up a computer printout, which he called a dispatch list. Brian noticed that it looked similar to the schedule he had seen in the expeditor's office earlier at Hayes.

"Does this thing really work for you?" asked Brian.

"Sure," John said, "once we got the routings cleaned up and the MRP due dates correct."

Brian looked at the operation due dates and the order due dates. There were a few jobs behind schedule, but, by and large, they were in good shape. He looked over to Tony and waved the dispatch list. "This looks pretty similar to our shop schedule, doesn't it?"

Tony shrugged, "Yeah, except for one thing. They obviously have dates the supervisors believe in."

Brian turned to Joan. "How are you doing in fixing the MRP data? Are our order due dates reliable?"

"For the most part, " Joan said. "I'm not sure how overloaded we are, but then neither is anyone else. There also could be some jobs in there that aren't needed when they are scheduled. But unless someone can help identify them, the material planner probably wouldn't catch it. Accurate dates can only be calculated by MRP if it has accurate data to begin with. We just haven't been able to ferret out all the problems yet. And there are a lot of them."

John chimed in. "You'd better have good routings."

Brian smiled. "At least we have that under control," he said.

"Well, I'll tell you," John said, "the most difficult thing about a dispatch list is getting people to use it and not rely on the hot list. I found that the only way to do that was to return to the basics and teach all the supervisors and operators how the whole scheduling system works. It was only after that they really started using it."

Brian once again turned to Joan. "You think you can put together that kind of program at Hayes and teach everyone?" he asked.

"Sure," said Joan.

"Hold on a second here," John jumped in. "That won't work unless you lead the training sessions in your department yourself, Brian. The words and actions have to come from you."

"Why's that? Joan knows more about this stuff than I do, and she's more capable of teaching it than I am," Brian said.

John shook his head. "We tried having the education and training department come out and teach everyone about how the dispatch list works. Our problem was that the general supervisor and superintendent only gave it lip service. Whenever there was an emergency, they reverted right back to their old ways. It was the same old behavior. It wasn't until they really understood how the system worked that they took ownership of it. And only then did the shop people buy into the new system and start following the schedules. Let me tell you, having to teach it to others forces you to understand it yourself. It also sends a clear message to the troops when the boss says it. The second time around, when we used this "boss-teaches" method, we got the behavioral change we were looking for."

"There's something I'm not getting here," said Brian. "If you're doing things as well as it appears, why did you bother going to the seminar?"

John smiled. "Two reasons. First, we haven't gotten capacity planning working as well as we would like, so we thought we might pick up some pointers. Things may look good around here right now, but if we get any sizable change in business, we could end up right back where we were. Then, we would have to work our butts off to get back on schedule. The second reason we went was to find out how to schedule those work centers where there are capacity constraints. We don't have the luxury of overtime or adding people in some work centers. What about you?" John asked. "Are you doing any capacity planning?"

"We've got the software," Brian said, "but we can't get the numbers to come out right. The truth is, we really haven't had the time to look into it seriously until now."

As Brian, Joan, and Tony drove home, they discussed the strategy that would be necessary to accomplish the education process that John had recommended.

"I have some training materials already," Joan said, "but I need some help to put them all together. If I could use Tony for a couple of weeks, we could probably pull it off."

"You have to be kidding," Brian replied. "I'd never survive without him out in my area."

"Hey, Joan," Tony piped up from the backseat, "you remember that four-week vacation I asked for and you said 'No problem'? Well, maybe you and Brian should start training my replacement now. I don't want Brian talking you out of letting me have that time off."

"You have someone in mind?" Brian asked.

"How about one of your shop supervisors?" Tony suggested. "You can replace them with one of the leadmen. After all, Brian, you should be training them anyway."

As Brian was about to agree, Joan jumped in. "You may have to help me convince Roy. He's undoubtedly going to be reluctant to let me work on this full time for two weeks."

"Wonderful," Brian thought. "Wait until Ralph hears about this—he'll be furious." Brian knew, however, that he was going to have to step up to this issue sometime. He remembered something he had heard at a supervisor's training class: "Great leaders provide a vision and then move the obstacles so the task can be accomplished." Now he understood why great leaders were so hard to come by. He knew he was up against some real obstacles.

As they pulled into the Hayes parking lot, they put the final touches on their plan. Brian waited until after the shortage meeting the next morning to talk to Ralph. His timing couldn't have been better: Not only did Brian have fewer shortages than anyone else, but Ralph was in a hurry to catch a plane to Hayes's Midwest plant and was only half-listening to Brian's plan. Without giving it a second thought, he gave Brian his okay.

Later that same day, Brian sent Larry, one of his second-shift shop supervisors, to assist Tony. After a few days, Larry was handling the scheduling routines with only minor guidance from Tony. This allowed Joan and Tony to begin putting together Hayes's education and training sessions. In two weeks, they were able to complete the training material. During that time, Brian had spent his evenings going over what they had developed so that he and Joan could start the process of teaching the supervisors and expeditors at once.

SHOP SCHEDULING

The educational material created by Joan and Tony began with an explanation of shop scheduling. They wrote:

> The way to determine shop priority is to employ an operation-scheduling system. The objective of operation scheduling is to com-

municate to the shop what jobs they should be working on and when those operations should be completed in order to meet the demands from Material Requirements Planning and, in turn, the Master Production Schedule. A prerequisite for shop scheduling is a valid—accurate and attainable—Master Production Schedule. An invalid master schedule will result in invalid Material Requirements Planning. Invalid Material Requirements Planning will then result in shop schedules that are unattainable. It is simply not possible to hold a shop supervisor accountable for meeting schedules under these circumstances.

The training material went on to explain that operation scheduling establishes start and completion dates for each operation necessary to meet the material plans and provides a foundation to monitor the progress of work. The method by which the schedules are calculated is a process called backward scheduling. In this process, start and finish dates for each operation are calculated by offsetting activities backward from the order due date to arrive at the initial order release date.

The start date of an order that has been planned by MRP is determined by offsetting the total lead time from the MRP Item Master File. This is not necessarily the same number as the lead time obtained by the backward scheduling process. The MRP lead time is a fixed number, whereas the backward scheduled lead time is calculated from the order, routing, and work center data. In reviewing the training material, Brian thought that a major effort would be required to get the lead time data right. Whenever the parts weren't delivered to the stockroom on time, the prevailing reason given was that there wasn't enough time provided to do the job. The typical response was to increase the lead time.

THE LEAD-TIME LOOP

Brian remembered an encounter that Dan had had earlier with Joan over lead times. "I obviously don't have enough time to complete my jobs," Dan said, "because they're always late." This had become a continuing gripe of his at the morning meeting. "I need more lead time," he complained. He became relentless in his pursuit of this issue. His arguments with Joan continued for several weeks before she went against her better judgement and finally gave in. "I'll add a week to the lead times on all your parts," Joan told him.

One reason Joan had been reluctant to increase the lead times was because she didn't want to move all of the customer orders out a week. Dan understood that. It was agreed that Joan would increase Dan's lead times by one week, but the order due dates would remain the same. Unfortunately, because of the system's lead-time offsetting process, when Joan put that added week into the computer, all the orders that were scheduled to be released were now scheduled to be released a week earlier. All of the planned orders in Material Requirements Planning were impacted — their recommended start dates were all moved one week earlier than before.

Suddenly, a week's worth of work had become past due in respect to its start date, plus there was a new week's worth of work scheduled to be released. Increasing the lead time by a week caused the release of two weeks' worth of work. When the two weeks' worth of work hit the shop floor, the situation became even more confused: No one was really sure which job to work on.

At the next shortage meeting, Dan said, "My schedule is even worse than it was. Work is backing up, and I'm going to have to add more capacity if it doesn't improve soon. I tell you, Joan, I need more lead time."

Joan tried to explain that the week that she had added was compounding the problem, but Dan wouldn't buy it. Joan gave in and added another week to the lead time. Again, two weeks' worth of work went out and again things got worse on the floor. After the next week, when Dan once again pleaded for more time, Joan smiled and, without any further argument, said, "Sure, Dan, I'll fix it."

Joan knew that continuing to increase the lead times would only make things worse. So, without telling Dan, she went into the database and deleted one week of the additional weeks of lead time. Consequently, all the start dates for the orders planned to be released that week were scheduled out a week, so there were no new orders to be released. Since no new work was released, the jobs already at the work centers got all the attention. They began to catch up to the schedule and the number of shortages went down. The following Monday, Dan came into the shortage meeting smiling. "You know, Joan," he said, "I think we're finally on to it here. I think we hit the magic point. Maybe what we should do is add another week."

Joan, still not letting on that she had decreased the lead time instead of increasing it, said, "Sure, Dan, I'll take care of it."

For the next two weeks the charade continued. Since only small amounts of work were being released, the load level was dropping rapidly. This gave Dan time to catch up on his late jobs. After Joan had cut out all the lead time she had added, she kept cutting until the total lead time was two weeks less than it had been originally. She knew that through the years Dan had been padding his lead times. She also knew that by taking out the additional two weeks, she had reached the point where most of Dan's unnecessary padding had been removed. Had she tried to subtract more, Dan really might not have enough time to do the jobs. From this point on, Joan understood that any further reduction should continue one day at a time, and only with Dan's approval. The question was how to let him know what she had already done.

Sometimes, patience has its own rewards. The next morning in the shortage meeting, Dan said, "Joan, I have to tell you things are running great. We have fewer late jobs than we have ever had before. That extra lead time really did the trick."

Joan broke the news. "Dan, it's not quite what you think." After Joan had explained what she had done, there was dead silence. Ralph could see that Dan was about to explode, and so he spoke before Dan could say anything. "Dan, don't knock it if it works, and you just said things were getting better."

"It was the only way I could get you to understand," Joan said. "The issue isn't lead times, Dan; it's whether or not you have the capacity to do the job. And you can't solve a capacity problem by increasing the lead time. Increasing the lead time simply increases the backlog of work."

One way to explain this is to use an analogy of a hose. Compare the planned lead time to a garden hose. If there's water (work) running through the hose, it doesn't make any difference how long the hose is. Only a certain amount of water can flow out at any one time. To get more water to go through, the hose has to be made bigger, not longer.

Does that mean the shorter the hose the better? The answer is yes, if adequate time is given for the work to get done. Making the hose too long causes the water (work) to be released earlier than is necessary. With constantly changing priorities, the wrong jobs are often worked on first, thus consuming capacity that should have been used on another job with a higher need. Also, if engineering or customer changes are made when there are long lead times, scrap or rework may result. Long lead times confuse the issue of whether there is a priority problem or a capacity problem.

It was this encounter that made it clear to Brian and Dan how important it was to have realistic lead times. Joan and Tony explained in the training material that the best way to accomplish this was to take the total lead time for each part number and break it down into the individual operations that were performed by a work center. The lead time needs to include the functions of releasing the order to manufacturing, picking the required components from the stockroom, and storing them in the stockroom when the order is complete. The time for each operation should be divided into queue, setup, run, and move times (see Figure 3.1). These elements could all be added together to calculate the total lead time for that part number. Since these calculations were based on the data in the production routings, Brian further understood why it was so important to have routing accuracy.

ACTUAL LEAD TIME

Tony and Joan's description of actual lead time was the amount of time taken from order release until a specific job was completed and arrived in the stockroom. This was fairly straightforward. However, when they went on to say that the actual lead time on the same part number might vary significantly from one order to the next because of many factors, particularly priority, Brian was puzzled.

Then he thought about when Pete, the General Manager, was pushing a product through the shop. Pete's particular order might take only 5 days to complete, but that same part might take 25 days if not expedited. Brian had to laugh when he thought about how an order might stay open forever if it was never expedited.

PLANNED LEAD TIME

Another subject that Tony and Joan outlined for their training course dealt with planned lead times. They defined planned lead time as the elapsed time *expected* to get a production run from order release through to order completion, including all of the anticipated elements of production. In Figure 3.2, there are two operations. The

FIGURE 3.1 Lead-Time Elements

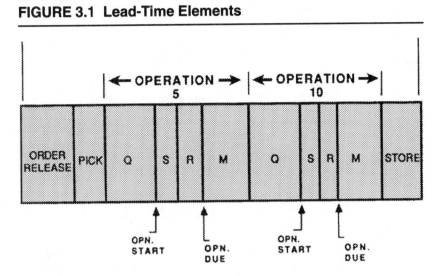

QUEUE (Q) - the queue time is the amount of time a job waits at a work center before setup or work is performed on the job.

MOVE (M) - the amount of time it takes work to move from one operation to the next.

SETUP (S) - the changeover time required to go from making one product to making another product. This is most often stated in standard hours.

RUN (R) - the amount of time required to make one part. to determine the amount of time to make multiple parts the quantity is multiplied by the time to make one. As with setup time, this figure is often stated in standard hours.

STANDARD HOURS - the length of time it should take to set up or run a product. This time can be determined from time studies, estimates, or any other method that represents a realistic value.

ORDER RELEASE - the time normally required to prepare the order (gather drawings, specifications, print the paperwork, add special instructions) and transport the order to the stockroom or production floor.

PICK - the average time required to gather the raw materials or parts and move them to the production area.

STORE - the average time required to verify the job completion and put the completed parts into stock.

planned lead time is calculated by starting with the amount of time it takes for the order release process. Then, the standard pick time is added. Next, the standard queue time, the standard setup time, and the standard run time for the first operation are added. Then, the standard move time to the second operation is added. Following that, there is queue time, setup time, and run time for the second operation. Finally, the move time to the stockroom and the time required to put the parts away are included. The result is the total planned lead time.

At Hayes, Dan never knew what the real priorities were among the

---

FIGURE 3.2 Calculating Planned Lead Time for a Two-Operation Order

---

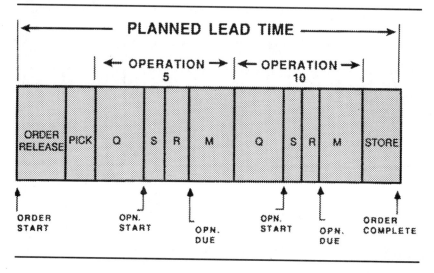

jobs on the floor. It seemed to him that he was always being pushed to complete a job in less than the normal amount of lead time planned for the job. In an effort to assure that he had enough lead time to do a job, Dan had wanted to pad his planned lead time. As Dan learned, this didn't solve the problem, but made it worse. Joan had discovered the right solution: minimize the amount of work-in-process, communicate valid priorities, and work to the schedules.

There are two aspects to valid schedules. First, a valid schedule should reflect what is really needed to support the Master Production Schedule. Secondly, a valid schedule needs to be one that can actually be met. If the schedule reflects the need, but can't be executed, it is invalid. Conversely, if the schedule reflects something that can be done, but is not needed, it is also invalid.

To maintain valid schedules for production operations, the Master Production Schedule must be relatively stable. If the Master Production Schedule is continually changing, the priorities in the factory also will be continually changing. When a master schedule change is considered, the question must be asked: "What will making a change to the Master Production Schedule cost in terms of working overtime, finding alternate operations, inefficiencies, and increased purchasing problems?" A master schedule that is not a true representation of what can be accomplished in the shop is not realistic.

OPERATION SCHEDULING

The process of operation scheduling is based on the concept of backward scheduling. To perform backward scheduling, the Manufacturing Resource Planning system needs some specific information. First, it needs data from MRP: the order number, part number, quantity, and due date for planned orders and the scheduled receipts from MRP (see Figure 3.3). The second factor is the routing, which defines

FIGURE 3.3 Operation Scheduling Process

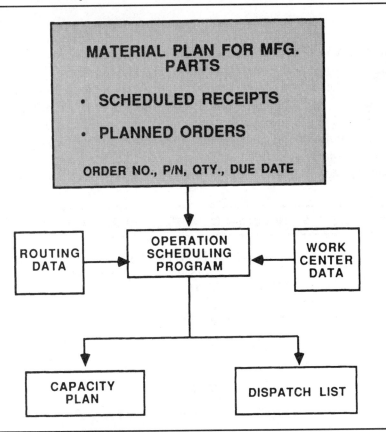

FIGURE 3.4 Routing Data for Part #163726

163726	HUB, FRONT WHEEL	
PART NUMBER	PART DESCRIPTION	

OPN. NO.	DEPT.	WORK CTR.	OPERATION DESCRIPTION	SETUP	RUN
			RELEASE		
			PICK		
10	FAB	16	SAW BLANK	0.5	.10
20	MACH	24	TURN	3.0	.20
30	MACH	22	DRILL	2.0	.10
40	MACH	19	TAP	1.0	.20
			STORE		

the steps necessary to produce the product, the operation sequences, the standard times required, and the work centers where the operations are to be performed (see Figure 3.4). The third set of data is the work-center information, which includes planned queue times (see Figure 3.5) and scheduling rules (see Figure 3.6), such as shift length, number of shifts, move time, pick time, store time, and release time.

A manufacturing calendar aids in backward scheduling. It identifies regularly scheduled workdays. Days such as weekends and holidays are not used to plan work schedules. Overtime, such as

FIGURE 3.5 Work-Center Data: Planned Queue Times

PLANNED QUEUES

DEPT.	WORK CENTERS	QUEUE (DAYS)
FAB	16 SAW	1
MACH.	19 TAP	1
MACH.	24 LATHE	2
MACH.	36 MILL	2
MACH.	22 DRILL	1

FIGURE 3.6 Work-Center Data: Scheduling Rules

ALLOW:

- 8 HOURS/SHIFT

- WORK CENTER 19 & 36 : 1 SHIFT
    ALL OTHER WORK CENTERS : 2 SHIFTS

- MOVE TIMES:
    2 DAYS BETWEEN OPERATIONS IN
        DIFFERENT DEPARTMENTS FOR MOVE

    1 DAY BETWEEN OPERATIONS IN
        DIFFERENT WORK CENTERS FOR MOVE

    0 DAYS BETWEEN OPERATIONS IN
        SAME WORK CENTER FOR MOVE

- 1 DAY TO PUT AWAY IN STORES

- 2 DAYS TO PICK COMPONENTS & MOVE
    TO FIRST WORK CENTER

- 1 DAY FOR RELEASE

- ALWAYS ROUND HOURS UP TO A FULL DAY

weekends that are used to resolve a problem of being behind schedule or to solve a temporary capacity problem in a particular work center, should not be considered in the calendar as scheduled workdays. In Figure 3.7, weekends are not included as scheduled days, nor are holidays such as July 4.

We can now do the backward scheduling for a planned shop order: 40 pieces of part #163726 (see Figure 3.8). This shop order contains the routing information, the order number, the quantity to be completed, and the scheduled due date. This quantity and due date information is obtained from MRP. Using the graphic representation in Figure 3.9, we can put in the planned queues from Figure 3.5, which would be one day for operation 10, two days for operation 20, one day for operation 30, and one day for operation 40. Looking at the scheduling rules in Figure 3.6, we would include the order release time of one day, pick time of two days, and the time to put away into stores of one day. (These numbers are for example only, and are not

FIGURE 3.7 Manufacturing Calendar

			JUNE			
S	**M**	**T**	**W**	**T**	**F**	**S**
					1 _371_	2
3	4 _372_	5 _373_	6 _374_	7 _375_	8 _376_	9
10	11 _377_	12 _378_	13 _379_	14 _380_	15 _381_	16
17	18 _382_	19 _383_	20 _384_	21 _385_	22 _386_	23
24	(25) (387)	26 _388_	27 _389_	28 _390_	29 _391_	30

JULIAN DAY   M. DAY

			JULY			
S	**M**	**T**	**W**	**T**	**F**	**S**
1	2 _392_	3 _393_	4 _HOLIDAY_	5 _394_	6 _395_	7
8	9 _396_	10 _397_	11 _398_	12 _399_	13 _400_	14
15	16 _401_	17 _402_	18 _403_	19 _404_	20 _405_	21
22	23 _406_	24 _407_	25 _408_	26 _409_	27 _410_	28
29	30 _411_	31 _412_				

FIGURE 3.8 Work Order No. W109 for Part #163726

163726	HUB, FRONT WHEEL		40		W109
PART NO.	DESCRIPTION		QUANTITY		ORDER NO.
OPN. #	DEPT.	WK. CTR.	OPERATION	SETUP	RUN
10	FAB	16	PICK RELEASE SAW	0.5	.10
20	MACH	24	TURN	3.0	.20
30	MACH	22	DRILL	2.0	.10
40	MACH	19	TAP STORE	1.0	.20

to be taken as recommendations. Most scheduling systems permit the use of fractional days or hours. We are using full days in order to keep the arithmetic simple.)

Next we calculate the setup and run times (see Figure 3.10). For operation 10, we multiply the run time to produce one piece by the order quantity of 40 pieces, which results in a total run time of four hours. If we add to that the setup time of .5 hours, we have a total setup and run time of 4 .5 hours. We do the same calculation for each operation, 10 through 40.

Since the scheduling will be done in days (or fractions thereof) rather than hours, setup and run times must be converted into days for the backward scheduling. To convert to days, we find out how many hours per shift there are and how many shifts per day (see Figure 3.6). In the case of operation 10, we have 8 hours per shift and 2 shifts per day, because work center 16 works 2 shifts, for a total of 16 hours. Since 4.5 hours can be accomplished in 16 hours, we schedule one day (see Figure 3.10). Fractional days can either be rounded up or down. In some cases, they can be scheduled as fractions. In this example, fractional days are rounded up per our scheduling rules. For operation 20 in work center 24, we again work 8 hours per shift and have 2 shifts per day for a total of 16 hours. The 11 hours we require also will fit in one day, so we schedule it as such. Work center 22 is also a 16-hour day. Operation 30 has 6 hours of work required, so we also schedule it as one day. However, operation 40 in work center 19,

FIGURE 3.9 Scheduling Diagram: Adding Queue Times

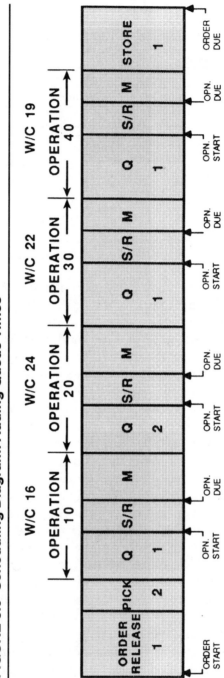

FIGURE 3.10 Calculating Setup and Run Times for Work Order No. W109

163726	HUB, FRONT WHEEL	40	W109
PART NO.	DESCRIPTION	QUANTITY	ORDER NO.

OPN. #	DEPT.	WK. CTR.	OPERATION	SETUP	RUN
10	FAB	16	SAW	0.5	.10
20	MACH	24	TURN	3.0	.20
30	MACH	22	DRILL	2.0	.10
40	MACH	19	TAP	1.0	.20

ORDER DUE DATE: 7/31			
LEAD TIME			
HOURS		DAYS	
R	S&R	S&R	
4	4.5	1	
8	11.0	1	
4	6.0	1	
8	9.0	2	

is scheduled for only one shift, so there are only 8 hours available. Since 9 hours of work are required, two days will have to be planned.

When we add our setup and run times to our graphic presentation, we have one day each for operations 10, 20, and 30, and two days for operation 40 (see Figure 3.11).

To determine the move time, once again we return to our scheduling rules (see Figure 3.6). The move time from operation 10 to operation 20 is two days, because the work is moving between different departments. For operation 20 to operation 30, the move time is one day, because it's moving between work centers, but staying in the same department. The same is true between operations 30 and 40. Between operation 40 and the stockroom, the move time is two days because the work moves between different departments (see Figure 3.11).

To calculate the operation start and completion dates (see Figure 3.12), we begin with the order due date of July 31 (see Figure 3.8), which is the date the order is scheduled to go to stock. We locate that date on the manufacturing day (M-day) calendar (see Figure 3.7), which turns out to be M-day 412. We subtract one day for stores and two days of move time between operation 40 and stores. We have an operation due date of 409. Subtract two days of setup and run time, and we have an operation start date of 407. Subtract one day of queue and one day move time, and we have a due date for operation 30 of 405. Subtracting one day of setup and run time gives us a start date of 404. Two days of combined move and queue time between operation 20 and operation 30 provide a due date of 402. One day of setup and run time means a start date of 401. Subtracting four days of combined move and queue between operation 10 and operation 20 gives a due date of 397. One day of setup and run time gives us a start date of 396. Subtract one day of queue and the pick complete date is 395. Subtract two days to pick and the pick start date is 393. Finally, we subtract one day to release and the planned order release start date is 392.

As Brian read through the backward-scheduling exercise, he nodded his head in understanding. It made perfect sense. It was how he had always scheduled everything else in his life. For example, he would talk to his wife about going to a friend's house for dinner and

FIGURE 3.11 Scheduling Diagram: Adding Setup/Run Times and Move Times

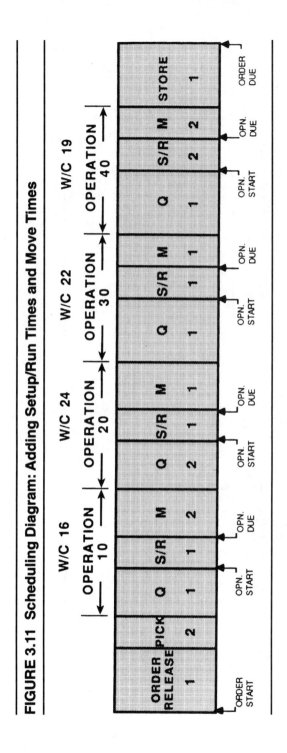

FIGURE 3.12 Scheduling Diagram: Adding Dates Using Backward-Scheduling Logic

	W/C 16			W/C 24			W/C 22			W/C 19		
	OPERATION 10			OPERATION 20			OPERATION 30			OPERATION 40		
ORDER RELEASE	Q	S/R	M	Q	S/R	M	Q	S/R	M	Q	S/R	M	STORE
1	1	1	2	2	1	1	1	1	1	1	2	2	1

PICK: 2

| ORDER RELEASES 392 | PICK START 393 | PICK COMP. 395 | OPN. START 396 | OPN. DUE 397 | OPN. START 401 | OPN. DUE 402 | OPN. START 404 | OPN. DUE 405 | OPN. START 407 | OPN. DUE 409 | ORDER DUE 412 |

playing cards. They were expected at 8:00 P.M. Brian knew that it took 35 minutes to drive there. So, in order to be on time, they had to leave their house by 7:25. It took him 10 minutes to dress and 20 minutes to shower and shave. This activity had to begin by 6:55. The drive from Hayes to his home took 15 minutes: 6:40. To allow for traffic delays and bathroom-access delays, he would add 15 minutes buffer time. This meant that if he and his wife were to arrive at 8:00, he had to leave the factory by 6:25. This was backward scheduling.

It became evident to Brian that if the supervisors participated in the development of the information used in backward scheduling (order release, picking, queue, setup, run, move, and store), the schedule dates would have a good deal of credibility. All Brian needed to do was explain the simple logic the computer used to calculate the operation start dates and due dates. Then, assuming that the order due date from Material Requirements Planning was correct, he could allow his supervisors to participate in setting the queue and move times—they already had a say in setup and run times through their routing-accuracy efforts—and they would then believe the operation due dates. Brian knew that both education and participation would be absolutely critical in order to bring his supervisors into the process so that he could hold them accountable for the accuracy of the data.

Brian's only concern about using backward scheduling at Hayes was that they were always accepting orders inside of lead times. One day, while reviewing the backward-scheduling logic in the training material with Joan, Brian asked her about the problem. She told Brian that there was also another method of calculating operation dates called forward scheduling. She explained the difference between backward and forward scheduling. Backward scheduling starts with the need date that is derived from MRP, and, by moving backward in time, calculates the dates by which all the operations need to be completed in order to meet that need date. Forward scheduling begins with the expected start date and calculates the operation dates by moving forward in time. If the available lead time equals the planned lead time, forward and backward scheduling will produce the same results. There are times, however, when a job needs to be completed in less than the full lead time, a situation that Brian had experienced more than once.

Brian realized that if the backward scheduling logic were used when he had to complete a gear that should have a five-and-a-half-week lead time in the middle of week 4 (see Figure 3.13) and today was the start of week 1, operations 10 and 20 would be past their due dates before the job was released. If this were done often, the first or second operations would constantly be getting work that was already past its operation due date, and the last operations would be given the full amount of lead time. This was not a fair distribution of the total time available to produce the product and could be very discouraging to the work centers at the beginning of the manufacturing process. Should this happen, those in the beginning would be inclined to give up on the credibility of the schedule and revert to working only on the hot items. Of course, as soon as they reverted back to the hot sheet, nothing would get done on time and the last operations would suffer.

However, if forward scheduling is used when an order is received two weeks inside of lead time (see Figure 3.14), the system would start with today and schedule each operation forward at its planned lead time. As Joan explained this logic graphically, Brian quickly identified the flaw. The original customer order was promised in the

---

FIGURE 3.13 Backward Scheduling for Orders with Shortened Lead Times

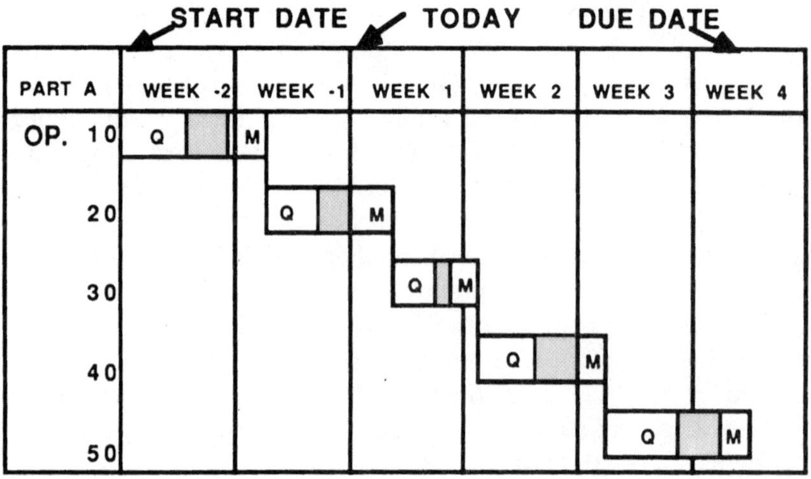

FIGURE 3.14 Forward Scheduling for Orders with Shortened Lead Times

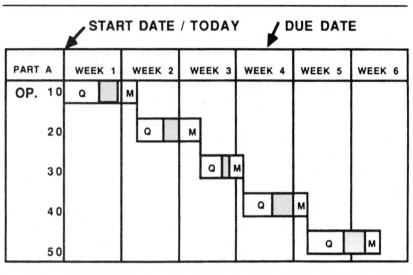

middle of week 4. If the scheduling system forward schedules, the operational priorities would show operation 40 and 50 completion dates due after the order was due.

Given the two choices, Brian recognized that since forward scheduling could cause the operation due dates to be later than the need dates, it was totally unacceptable. It was also clear to Brian that if the available lead time is greater than the planned lead time, forward scheduling will likely provide completion dates that are earlier than necessary. In doing so, it has established erroneous priorities. Yet, in Joan's example, backward scheduling would produce dates for the first two operations that were past due. It was obvious that he could not complete work yesterday. However, Brian also realized that if the scheduling had been done properly, the older dates would indicate that he was behind schedule and would tell him the sequence in which to work (relative priority). Although he couldn't tolerate everything being late, a small number of past due operations signaled to Brian that he had to do something to get caught up. Backward scheduling would tell him the *absolute* priority, which would not only tell him the priority sequence, but also when the work must be completed. Being able to see absolute priorities would give Brian the information he needed to manage his department properly. However, a lot of scheduled past-due operations are a signal that there is a problem that needs to be addressed.

Brian knew, as does any experienced shop manager, that there are five fundamental techniques that can be employed to schedule products in less than the full lead time. The first is to compress the queue and move times. Hot jobs don't sit around for long periods, because the expeditor is constantly pushing them and can manually override the schedule. This can be accomplished in the computer by determining the difference between the planned lead time and the actual time available and subtracting that from the move and queue times. For instance, if an order with a normal lead time of six weeks had to be done in four weeks, and its queue and move times were three weeks, we could subtract two weeks from that and have one week of queue and move to be distributed based on the distribution of the original move and queue times. Figure 3.15 shows how the compression would work. In this example, we are able to meet the MRP need date without showing the order past due at the first operation. Setup and run times should not be compressed.

Another way to compress queue and move times is for the planner to override the scheduling logic and adjust the scheduled operation start and completion dates to fit the situation. For instance, perhaps one operation needs its entire queue time, but several others don't need any queue time at all. The planner can manually override the operation dates to reflect what is desired. Caution should be exercised when choosing to manually adjust the dates because it is a labor-intensive process. It should only be used when really necessary.

A second technique that can be used to compress lead time is to overlap operations. This involves the moving of pieces ahead to the next operation before the entire run quantity has been completed at the previous operation (see Figure 3.16). With this technique, lead time can be compressed even more than with the queue/move compression process. The disadvantage of this technique is that multiple moves must be made rather than waiting for the whole job to move all together. By overriding the operational start dates calculated by the computer and inserting an earlier start date, even though the previous operation hasn't been completed, we have accurately simulated what needs to happen in order to meet the order due date.

FIGURE 3.15 Short Schedule Techniques: Compressing Queue and Move Times

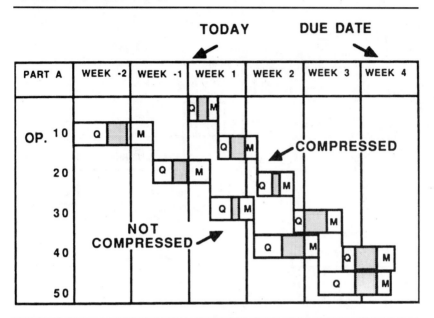

A third way to compress lead times is to split the order into smaller lot sizes (see Figure 3.17). Production can then run fewer parts than normal, thus getting the first pieces through more quickly. The disadvantage of this approach is in the multiple setups that are necessary to complete the original order quantity, as well as the additional handling and transactions.

A fourth approach is to run parts on a multiple number of machines in a work center simultaneously (see Figure 3.18). Running a job over three machines that would normally be produced by only one machine obviously cuts the run time by two thirds. Again, the disadvantage is that multiple setups and multiple sets of tooling are necessary.

Finally, additional shifts could be added either as a temporary solution or on a longer-term basis. This reduction in lead time is illustrated in Figure 3.19. For example, if we are running one shift and have a job that has 3 hours of setup and 13 hours of run time, we

FIGURE 3.16 Short Schedule Techniques: Operation Overlapping

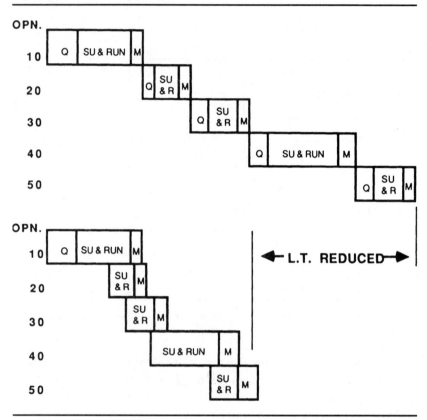

FIGURE 3.17 Short Schedule Techniques: Order Splitting

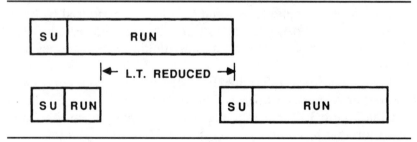

FIGURE 3.18 Short Schedule Techniques: Operation Splitting

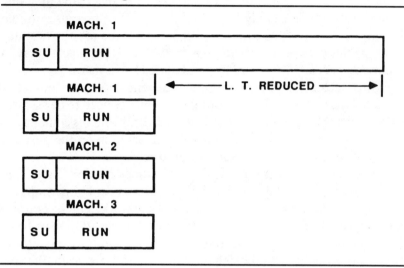

FIGURE 3.19 Short Schedule Techniques: Additional Shift

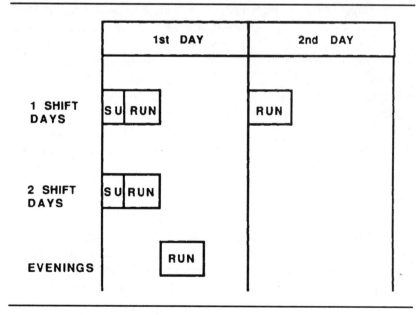

would set up and run the piece for 5 hours on the first day. The piece of equipment would sit idle until the next day when we returned to complete the job. If a two-shift operation is in place, the first-shift operator would do exactly as we had done in the previous example, but the second-shift operator would complete the job the first day. Once again, there is a disadvantage in that additional costs may be incurred, such as shift premiums and added supervision.

Which technique should be used? It depends upon the individual circumstances. The added costs or inconvenience need to be assessed and weighed against missing the schedule. Brian and his comanagers used a combination of these techniques depending on the part and the status of the machines and/or operators.

We should note at this point that sometimes circumstances exist that make some or all of these techniques impractical or perhaps impossible. Many companies are running some work centers 24 hours a day, seven days a week, in order to shorten the lead time or to increase equipment utilization. In such cases, the additional shift option is not available. If all machines are being fully utilized, the split operation option is not available. In these circumstances, a technique called finite capacity scheduling can be used. This technique will be discussed in Chapter 6.

It is important to realize that controls must be established regarding the release of orders with less-than-full lead times. Material planners should be permitted to compress queues up to a previously agreed upon percentage throughout the process. But if that compression does not alleviate the scheduling problem, they should not release an order inside of lead time without the approval of the supervisor. It is up to the supervisor to tell the planners that they could compress the process more by utilizing these other techniques. This is essential to maintaining the accountability necessary to control the factory's operations.

The important factor to remember is that this is not a question of whether or not an order can be completed inside of lead time. The Brians, Dans, and Mickeys of the world have all learned how to do that in order to survive. The real question is how many times it can be done without losing control. To protect themselves against the constant influx of hot parts, companies have traditionally factored lots of cushion into lead times. This, as might be expected, has caused its own share of confusion, since no one is really sure what can be accomplished and what can't. In such an environment, all anyone ever remembers is how quickly a hot part made it through the last time. The expectation is that all parts can move that fast.

How much work can a company accept in less-than-full lead time? This varies considerably depending upon the company environment. If overtime is an option, perhaps as much as 15 to 20 percent can be accepted. In other situations, experience has shown that anything over 5 percent causes problems. In some cases, a production order with as little as 50 percent of standard lead time available can be accommodated, while in other cases, much less lead-time compression can be tolerated before a major impact is felt. An excessive number of short-lead-time work releases are likely to have a highly unfavorable impact on production schedules.

As Brian will discover when he looks into the process and philosophy of Lean Manufacturing (see Chapter 9), the various techniques for shortening lead times can be a precursor to Lean Manufacturing. When Hayes began compressing queue times, it became obvious that queues were inherently wasteful. It also became obvious that they needed to initiate some major programs to reduce them. The motivation should be to drive queue times down as a matter of course. This was ultimately turned into a significant competitive advantage at Hayes. With a shorter lead time, an order that was formerly inside lead time and had to be thoroughly investigated to see if it could be done now could be accepted with no investigation and with complete confidence that it could be delivered on time. As lead times are shortened, the 5 to 50 percent guideline above will become tighter. Getting people in manufacturing to participate in reducing lead times is contingent upon the adherence to the established lead times. Violating them will cause manufacturing to revert to its old behavior of padding lead times, because they know that the lead times will be violated.

DISPATCH LIST

The work-center schedule (called a "dispatch list") that John Hall, General Supervisor at Precision Air Components, showed Brian provided a priority tool for his supervisors that was accurate and allowed them to plan their work. The schedule at Precision Air Components and the one in the new software at Hayes contained the same information (see Figure 3.20). That information is as follows:

1. WORK CENTER NUMBER: defines the work center. The computer selects the scheduled orders for operations to be performed in this work center for inclusion on the dispatch list.
2. DATE: the date the computer generated the dispatch list. It is used to determine the most current dispatch list.
3. ORDER NUMBER: unique order number assigned to every individual open work order.
4. PART NUMBER: item number. This identifies each part or item.
5. QUANTITY: the number of remaining parts scheduled to be completed on this order number at this operation.
6. OPERATION NUMBER: the specific operation that is scheduled to be performed.
7. OPERATION START DATE: the date that the specified operation is to be started. This date is developed by the backward-scheduling logic.
8. OPERATION DUE DATE: the date that a specific operation is to be completed. This, too, is developed by the backward-scheduling logic.
9. ORDER DUE DATE: the date the order has been scheduled to be completed by the material planner (i.e., the MRP due date).
10. SETUP HOURS: The standard setup hours remaining on this order.
11. RUN HOURS: the standard run time remaining (pieces times standard hours per piece) on this order.
12. NEXT OR PREVIOUS WORK CENTER: if the order is currently in this work center, this information indicates where it is to go after this operation is completed. If the order has not yet reached this work center, this information indicates the work center immediately prior to this one on the routing. This information enables the supervisor to contact the other appropriate work centers regarding delays, expediting, and scheduling problems.
13. OPERATION STATUS: the latest reported status. Is it running, being set up, or waiting in queue?

FIGURE 3.20 Dispatch List for Work Center 24

WORK CENTER NO.: 24					DESCRIPTION: LATHES					DATE: 7/2	
ORDER NO.	PART NO.	PART DESCRIPTION	QTY.	OPN. NO.	OPN. START DATE	OPN. DUE DATE	ORDER DUE DATE	SET UP HRS.	RUN HRS.	NEXT/ PREV. WC	OPN. STATUS
JOBS CURRENTLY AT THIS WORK CENTER											
W123	144398	SHAFT	200	20	6/26	6/27	7/19	0	7.0	04	R
W123	144398	SHAFT	200	30	6/29	7/2	7/19	1.0	10.0	07	Q
W124	428876	BOLT	3000	30	6/29	7/3	7/24	2.0	30.0	07	Q
W110	330246	GEAR	500	20	6/28	7/3	7/18	1.0	15.0	07	Q
W120	407211	BOLT	4000	30	7/2	7/5	7/20	2.0	50.0	07	Q
W112	163726	HUB	40	20	7/3	7/5	7/23	3.0	8.0	07	Q
W128	118132	GEAR	400	20	7/5	7/10	7/24	2.0	40.0	07	Q
							TOTAL	11.0	160.0		
JOBS COMING TO THIS WORK CENTER											
W129	186846	SHAFT	20	20	7/3	7/5	7/12	1.0	4.5	01	R
W138	258721	SPACER	2000	20	7/9	7/11	7/25	0.5	20.0	05	S
W140	321406	HUB	50	30	7/10	7/12	7/27	1.0	30.0	01	H
							TOTAL	2.5	54.5		

In addition to this information, the list of jobs must differentiate between what is currently at the work center and what has not yet arrived. This can be accomplished through either of two options.

First, the jobs can be identified and divided into different sections, as shown in Hayes's dispatch list. The work in queue or actually being worked on would come under the heading "Jobs Currently at This Work Center." Under operation status, it would show the status at this work center. The bottom section, "Jobs Coming to This Work Center," would list all the jobs that haven't arrived yet. In this section, the operational status column would indicate the status of the job at its current work center.

The second option would be to put all work in operation due-date order and indicate through a code whether or not the job was at the work center. This could be as simple as putting an asterisk (*) next to the job(s) that are not yet available to be worked on. The status column would remain the same as in the first option.

It is not important which option is chosen as long as the work that hasn't arrived yet is noted on the dispatch list. There are three reasons for this:

1. It allows the supervisor to see what work is currently available for assignment.
2. It allows the supervisor to see what's due to arrive in order to perform daily scheduling.
3. If the work is past due to its operation start date, it allows the supervisor to be proactive in finding out why it hasn't arrived and expedite the work through.

The information necessary to determine priority is also contained on the dispatch list. The order number, the operation start date, the operation due date, and order due date are displayed for each order. Running only by work-order due date provides no milestones to schedule the time that each order should spend in each operation. If those in the beginning take too much time, the operations at the end have to scramble to catch up. By identifying scheduled priority by operation, priorities can be provided for each work assignment at each work center. If each operation due date is met, the order due date will be met consistently. The operation due date is what the supervisor is held accountable to meet. The order due date is included simply to give the supervisor visibility in case he can't meet an operation due date. If a supervisor can't meet an operation due date, then he or the expeditor must contact the downstream work centers (later operations) to see if they can make up the lost time. If they can't and subsequently the order due date will be missed, the material planner must be advised and given the expected new completion date. It should be emphasized that the order due date is used for informational purposes only. The operation due date is what the supervisor is measured against.

Once Brian, Tony, and Joan had finished educating and training the supervisors in the machine shop, they started a cleanup process. The supervisors, capacity planners, and material planners were going to review all the past due orders to ensure they were needed. Everyone knew the results wouldn't be perfect, but they also knew things would become a lot better than they had been. Working as a team, they all agreed to come in over the weekend to get the work done.

Monday morning, Brian was looking over some dispatch lists. When he picked up the bar-lathe list, which was the next operation after Dan's bar-sawing operation, he couldn't believe his eyes. The work-coming section showed there were 48 jobs that were past due at the bar lathe and were sitting in Dan's saw department. They ranged from 1 to 28 days past the operation due date.

That morning in the shortage meeting when they came to the first late gear, Brian spoke up. "That's late because I didn't get it from the saws." Brian pulled out the dispatch list, looked at Dan, and said, "That's not all. Unless I get these 48 jobs, they'll also be late."

Dan grabbed the dispatch list and stared down at the sheet. "This is garbage and you know it, Brian."

"I'm afraid it's not. We cleaned the data up over the weekend, and now it's accurate—I'd bet my bottom dollar on it," Brian said.

"He's right," Joan said, supporting Brian.

After the meeting, Dan went straight to the saw supervisor. "I want you to saw every job around here for Miller. I want his raw-material storage yard chuck full when he arrives in the morning. You understand?"

The supervisor knew enough not to say a word. He nodded his head and called his operators over. Day shift sawed bars. Second shift sawed bars. There was an explicit message for third shift, "Dan wants every bar sawed." The next morning Brian had his bars.

Because Brian had a dispatch list that showed jobs that were coming to the work center, he was able to pull the work through the previous operations.

After using the dispatch lists for a few weeks, Brian found they were surprisingly effective. The number of shortages he had to deal with was decreasing because the supervisors were working to valid dates. They had visibility of the jobs that were about to come due and could work on them prior to their appearance on a hot list. Joan and

Brian agreed that they would give the supervisor only one list and that would be the dispatch list. If Mickey, in Assembly, identified something as being hot, the material planners would investigate it immediately. If needed, they would change the schedule in MRP to put it on the top of the dispatch list, even if it meant having to write it in by hand temporarily.

Ralph, however, continued to make his own rounds throughout the factory. After reading Tom Peters and Robert Waterman's book *In Search of Excellence*[1], he called it "management by walking around" (MBWA).

One evening Ralph walked into the frame-weldment area, supervised by Hank Jones. As soon as Hank saw Ralph, he pulled him over. "I'm afraid this frame isn't going to make it to the assembly line by tomorrow morning, Ralph, and this is the special for Nebraska Implement that Pete promised."

Ralph wasn't pleased with this news and asked why. The problem was that Hank was short two brackets. The inventory count had been wrong. Realizing he would miss the schedule without the brackets, he had immediately tried to track the parts down. What he found was that there was an open order in the machine shop. "Did you tell them you had to have it?" Ralph asked.

"I sure did. But they told me the brackets weren't due yet, and consequently they were way down on the dispatch list. They also told me that unless the material planners changed the operation due date, they were going to work on the jobs that were due ahead of the brackets."

"Well, hell, if you have to have the parts, someone has to get them." Ralph immediately went to Larry, one of the supervisors of the machine shop. "Did Hank call you about those brackets that he needs?" he asked.

"He sure did," Larry replied.

"Did you start working on them yet?" Ralph asked.

Larry said, "No. Brian told us to work the priorities per the operation due dates on the dispatch list."

"Let me see that thing." Ralph's concern was more than evident.

Larry handed Ralph the dispatch list. "This doesn't mean a damn thing." Ralph fumed. "What means something is that Hank needs those brackets and he had better get them."

Now, Larry knew who the boss was, and when Ralph spoke he

moved or else, even if it was contrary to Brian's instructions. Larry went over to the radial-drill operator and told him to break down the setup. He then hurried to the other end of the shop to talk to Roger, another supervisor. "Ralph wants those brackets right now," he said, "and I'll have one ready for you to start on in about 45 minutes."

"I knew it as soon as I saw him," Roger said. "I just got the milling machine set up and now I have to break it down. A three-hour setup down the tubes. I thought we had something going for us when Brian told us to work to the dispatch list. I was just caught up, too, and was going to be able to save another three hours on the next job because it was just like the one I have in now. Well, there goes that dream."

"Yeah, I know what you mean," replied Larry. "For the first time, I thought we were actually going to be able to spend our time on something other than chasing hot parts. I knew it was too good to last."

About an hour later, after completing his rounds, Ralph went back to Hank and told him, "You'll get the brackets in a couple of hours." As they stood there talking, the planner walked in and put two brackets on the table.

"Boy, that was fast," Hank said. "Where did those come from?"

The planner looked at him oddly. "Didn't the first-shift supervisor leave you a note?" He shook his head no. "Well, he called me earlier in the day," the planner said. "Are you sure he didn't leave you a note?"

Hank checked again. "Oh, yeah, here it is. I didn't see it. I got in a few minutes late. . . ."

The planner nodded. "He told me he couldn't finish the frame without those brackets. So when I saw that the next order for the brackets was number 25 on the radial-drill dispatch list, and then it had to go through the mill operation, which already had a heavy load, I knew I had to do something. In order to get them done tonight, the machine shop would have to break a setup on the radial drill and the mill, which would take a considerable amount of time. I figured we'd lose too much productivity that way, so I called up the service-parts warehouse, and they had them. I borrowed these two and promised to return them next week when the open order is done."

As Ralph listened to the conversation, he recognized the problem that he had created by reacting as he had instead of using the tools available to determine the best solution.

The next morning, Joan told Brian about the incident and decided that they needed to act quickly or they never would get Hayes's operations under control. They sat down and came up with some dispatching rules.

RULE 1: Honor only the Dispatch List for priority.

The dispatch list is intended to reflect the real priorities of the shop schedule. If a scheduled order due date needs to be changed, it's the material planner's job to communicate that to the supervisor either directly or through a shop liaison. The material planner is responsible for maintaining the priorities in the schedule and the supervisor is accountable for meeting the schedule. If anyone else is allowed to change the order due date, the material planner has lost all his or her accountability. If the problem can be resolved by rescheduling some of the operations without changing the order due date, then the capacity planner/shop scheduler should do so. There would be no need to communicate with the material planner in that instance. There is no question that management has the authority to change the schedule if they wish to do so. It must be done, however, through a formal procedure that investigates all the alternatives first in order to choose the best one.

RULE 2: If a work center is behind schedule, work on the shop orders in operation due-date sequence.

This rule says, "Get on schedule as soon as you can." To accomplish this, the oldest job must be worked on first. There are situations where working out of sequence might get the work center back on schedule more quickly than by working in sequence. If that is the case, by all means do it. There are also times, however, when a setup can be saved, but it will cause other jobs to fall behind schedule. For example, we have seven jobs listed in priority sequence (see Figure 3.21). Jobs 1 and 2 are behind schedule. Job 7 uses the same setup as job 1, but it's not due for four days.

Running job 7 right after job 1 might save two hours by minimizing changeovers, but it would do nothing to get job 2 on schedule. Besides, job 3 would then also be past due, and that would still leave two jobs behind schedule. Job 7 would be ahead of schedule, but that wouldn't benefit anyone. Although this may seem like a good decision from this work center's point of view, it may have a major impact on many other areas that are expecting these jobs on time. What

---

FIGURE 3.21 Dispatch List Data Showing Operations behind Schedule

---

TODAY = MANUFACTURING DAY 100

JOB #	OPERATION DUE DATE	SETUP	RUN TIME
1	98	2 HOURS	4 HOURS
2	99	3 HOURS	7 HOURS
3	100	1 HOUR	5 HOURS
4	101	2 HOURS	7 HOURS
5	102	4 HOURS	12 HOURS
6	103	1 HOUR	3 HOURS
7	104	2 HOURS	6 HOURS

---

this work center must do first is to assess the impact downstream. It must then determine what extra resources need to be applied to get this work center on schedule with the minimum amount of impact on the following work centers. In almost all situations this means performing the jobs in accordance with the dispatch list and applying the additional resources as needed.

A high level of discipline is needed to make this rule work. The key is to use the operation due dates to make the right decisions for the overall good of the company, even when the temptation is to do what is best in the short term for an individual work center.

RULE 3: If the work center is on schedule or ahead of schedule, work on the shop orders in the most productive sequence that will still maintain the schedule. Rules 2 and 3 are saying that it is more important to meet the schedule than to improve productivity. The notion here is that you can be very "productive" by making the wrong stuff.

This rule gave José, a machine shop supervisor, the opportunity to improve his work center productivity. It allows him to use his knowledge and ability when he is on or ahead of schedule. The dispatch list is a list of priorities, not a dictate of sequence. If today were manufacturing (M) day 97, it would make good sense, because of setups, to run job 7 and then job 4. This rule permits that. If the work center falls behind schedule, the supervisor must assess the downstream impact prior to working jobs out of sequence. Unless the downstream situation allows for jobs to arrive late, the supervisor, in accordance with Rule 2, must return to the top of the dispatch list and get back on schedule. It is far more cost-effective overall for the company to concentrate on keeping on schedule than to emphasize productivity. One small area operating late can create inefficiencies in many other areas.

RULE 4: Do not release an order with a past-due start date without shop approval.

Launching an order with a past-due start date doesn't do any good if the shop cannot meet the final due-to-stock date. If the order is going to be late, it is best to know it at the time of release, so that a valid date can be established. That will allow everyone to have valid priorities. It also keeps one work center from working to meet a schedule that another work center can't possibly meet.

RULE 5: Do not break setups in response to a newly issued dispatch list, unless it has been previously agreed upon.

This is common sense. Occasionally, errors are made by the planner inputting a date or analyzing situations that result in the dispatch list showing inaccurate information. Since Rule 4 is in place, a job should not show up as past due without the supervisor's prior knowledge. Therefore, it is wise for the supervisor to check before breaking a setup. Had Ralph understood this rule, he would not have been so quick in ordering a setup to be broken.

RULE 6: Notify planner of any shop order that will miss its order due date.

The sooner a problem is reported, the better chance there is to react to it with the least amount of disruption to the process. Once a supervisor realizes that waiting until after the fact to advise the planner of a delay only puts him further behind, he becomes quite comfortable with this rule. The tool used to communicate such a problem is called an Anticipated Delay Report. It can be a specific document, as in Figure 3.22, or it can be handled by using the previous day's dispatch list, noting on it the jobs that are in trouble and all other pertinent information. There is any number of methods, including verbal communication. The important point is that such information should be communicated as early as possible.

Initially at Hayes, using the Anticipated Delay Report was something of a joke because so much work was past due. Brian, Tony, and

FIGURE 3.22 Anticipated Delay Report

WORK CENTER 04 DATE 7/2					
WORK ORDER	PART NO.	DUE DATE	CAUSE	NEW DATE	ACTION

Joan knew there was a lot of cushion in the schedule, so they decided to use the Anticipated Delay Report only if a job would miss the order due date by more than ten days. Gradually, they worked to reduce that grace period.

They accomplished this by having Tony go around to each work center every day. He would check with the supervisors to see where they stood in relationship to their operation due dates. To reinforce the importance of Tony's task, Brian randomly checked work centers later in the day, after Tony had made his rounds.

If Tony and the supervisor agreed that a work center was so far behind in regard to its operation due date that the order due date would be missed by more than the prescribed tolerance, Tony would communicate that to the downstream work-center supervisor to see if that time could be made up. If it couldn't, Tony and the supervisor whose work center was behind would work together on the anticipated delay report. What Tony really needed was the supervisor's commitment on when the order would be completed.

Normally, Tony started this process with the first operations. By the time he reached the downstream operations, the majority of the problems had been found and resolved.

Once the new completion date was determined, Tony would communicate that to the material planner to figure out what needed to be done. Sometimes, it was as simple as having Assembly work around the past-due part. Other times, it meant that an order would have to be split or the schedule compressed at all costs. There were also times when the delay would impact the delivery of a tractor. These times, however, were now occurring with less frequency. Equally as important, they were getting early warnings when a tractor delivery might be delayed. This gave them the time to take the appropriate action to ensure the delivery would not be missed. The supervisors also recognized that the closer they stayed to the schedule, the more flexibility they had to react to emergencies when they occurred.

As time went on, the tolerance on those items that were late continued to tighten. Eventually, the process improved to the point where supervisors were dissatisfied if a job went even one day past the operation due date.

Again, it is important to emphasize that the dispatch list is not a job sequence mandate; it's a priority list. Although priority is arguably the most significant input to the assignment of work, there are other considerations. A good production supervisor is aware of these. A good supervisor knows more about how to achieve the highest levels of productivity than a material planner or a computer does. A good supervisor will know which operator and/or equipment is best suited to each particular job. These rules give the supervisor the flexibility to improve productivity and at the same time, preserve the integrity of the priority process. The most difficult part of this process is to reduce the load to no more than a few past-due jobs. Once that has been accomplished, it is relatively easy to maintain it.

It is no secret that working behind schedule is expensive. Costs begin to mount as soon as overtime work commences or money is spent on alternate operations. The effort should be made to meet the scheduled operation dates initially rather than reacting after the work is late. The emphasis should be on every work center meeting the schedule rather than worrying about the performance of an individual area. If the schedule is consistently met by all work centers, it will result in each area being productive. This allows all areas to operate in a least-cost environment.

Once the dispatching rules were completed, and all the machine shop personnel understood them, Brian and Joan agreed that it was crucial for Ralph and Pete to sign off on these new rules. Ralph gave in more easily than Brian anticipated. Maybe it was Brian's well-timed example of productivity losses that softened up Ralph, especially when he used a bracket for an example.

"Okay, okay, you guys," Ralph exclaimed, "I'll sign the thing. But just don't tell me I have to give up my shop tours. I really believe that stuff about MBWA—you know, 'management by walking around.'"

Pete was easy. His only comment was, "I'll do anything to get this place on schedule."

DISPATCH LIST SEQUENCING CONSIDERATIONS

When Brian introduced the dispatch list, there had been some fear that by adopting a formal scheduling system, supervisors would be reduced to following orders from a computer and no longer direct their own departments. Implementation of the dispatch list proved there was no basis for this fear. Once the work center was on schedule, the supervisor was free to decide the proper sequence in which to do the work. The difference the supervisors found was that the schedule was now their first consideration, and they were to concentrate on that. Productivity was a natural extension of this process.

When a work center finishes a job, the supervisor goes to the dispatch list to see what is at the top of the list. Once the priority has been established, he has to take into consideration the capabilities of the machine. For example, the machine that just opened up could be one of the older machines in the work center, unable to hold the tolerance necessary for the top job on the dispatch list. It would be foolish for him to put that job on that machine and produce poor-quality parts. He could also run into a problem with an operator who has never before run a specific job—one with very definite idiosyncrasies. The supervisor must take such matters into consideration and would most likely decide to run a different sequence from that on the dispatch list.

Other factors that could prompt alternate sequencing decisions are preventive maintenance activities, the late arrival of a job coming from an upstream work center, or a priority need from a downstream work center. This list can go on to include as many different variations as there are companies or people in them. It's always best to leave the decision up to the supervisor to consider the impact on his ability to meet the schedule. The supervisors must use their experience and good common sense to make their decisions.

What Brian learned through experience was that the dispatch list provided valid priorities by operation. It allowed him to know where he stood against the schedule, so if necessary he could adjust. It helped him identify potential problems and resolve them before they caused trouble. Whenever an operation couldn't be finished on time, that delay was communicated and the problem highlighted. But, most important, it provided him with vital data in a simple and direct format.

The dispatch list is not a replacement for supervision, nor does it dictate the sequence for running jobs. It is a tool for the supervisor. It depends upon accurate data and reliable information from MRP, as well as accurate and timely reporting of activity from the shop floor. It does not self-correct when data or reporting is wrong. Therefore, it is important to properly maintain the integrity of the information. Otherwise, the supervisor will be given a dispatch list in which he has little confidence, with the result that he will regress to the informal system.

Things were beginning to show some improvement at Hayes, and Brian decided he needed to do a little "management by walking around" of his own to make sure everything was all right. He went to José's desk to check on the dispatch list. He couldn't find the dispatch lists anywhere. Brian immediately tracked down José. "Where are all your dispatch lists?" Brian asked, fearing that they had been thrown away.

"They're at the machines," José replied. "The operators are figuring out what has to be done next, unless, of course, they have a question. Then they come to Tony or me."

"The operators?" Brian couldn't believe what he was hearing. "You mean you're leaving those decisions up to the operators?"

José smiled. "Calm down, Boss. We don't want you having heart failure just as things are looking up. Let me ask you, Brian, how are we doing in this department?"

Brian considered José's question a moment. "Well, I guess you've probably got the least past due of any of the supervisors."

"There's no guessing about it," José said proudly. "Ask the operators why."

Brian did just that, and what he found surprised him. He was amazed how informed and knowledgeable the operators were about the schedules and their function within the process. More importantly than that, he was astounded by how much more enthusiastic they were about meeting their schedules. Time and again he heard, "When the information's right, it makes my job easier."

GETTING THE INFORMATION RIGHT

One morning at the shortage meeting, Mickey was all over Brian. "I've just been told we are short the four yokes for the last two special loaders. If we don't get those yokes out of the shop and into Assembly, I'm never going to complete those two loaders due on the 8th." This shortage, and Mickey's outburst, caught Brian completely by surprise. There was nothing he hated more than getting called down for something he didn't know about.

Within minutes of the end of the meeting, Brian was out on the floor talking to his supervisor. "So, tell me, why are these late?"

"Late?" came the reply. "I just got the order and it was past due when I got it."

Brian looked at the order and headed up to Production Control to talk to Joan. "All right, Brian, calm down. Let's see why this puppy's late." Joan quickly discovered that on the previous order the shop had scrapped 4 out of the original 20 pieces. "Those 4," Joan told him, "are the 4 needed for those last two loaders. Mickey was supposed to be covered." Joan dug a little further, "Hey, wait a minute here," she said. "These yokes were scrapped out in the first operation, and that was five weeks ago. Come on, Brian, if you'd reported that when you scrapped it out, I could have gotten you another order for those 4 parts five weeks ago."

Brian knew he'd just paid the price for his department's lack of good reporting. If they had told Joan the parts were scrapped in a timely manner, they would have gotten the replacement order much sooner. Unfortunately, this wasn't the only bad news he got from Joan. It seemed there was also a good deal of bad reporting going on in a number of Brian's operations. Brian realized it was time for a little more MBWA.

Brian picked up a dispatch list and ran a check. Joan wasn't exaggerating. There were some transactions getting reported properly, but many others were being ignored.

Brian immediately headed off to talk to one of his supervisors. "I'm sure there's an explanation for the errors in these reports," Brian said, trying to be as diplomatic as possible.

"The truth is, Brian," the supervisor said, "it takes too long. I can't seem to get all the jobs done and do all this reporting, too. It just takes up too much of my time."

The rest of the supervisors gave Brian basically the same answer. José, however, said he didn't have any trouble getting his reporting done and done right. "What I want to know," Brian said, "is how come you've got the time and all these other jokers are too busy?"

"It's really pretty simple," said José, "Every day when I get the reports and I find errors, I take them back to the operators and have them fix the problem. All I did was get these guys to understand that this stuff is important and that they had to fix their own errors. After I went back to them a couple of times and made them correct the reports themselves, they learned."

"Don't the other supervisors do that?"

"Are you kidding? They just try to get through the reports as fast as they can. Getting them out is all they're after. Listen, if an operator is consistently making an error on something, and I get it back the next day, I've got two choices. Either I can take it back to the operator and figure out what happened or I can take the shortcut and guess what probably went wrong and try to fix it myself. That's the fastest way. Maybe 60 to 70 percent of the time I'm actually right. If I'm not, it comes back the next day and I can just take another guess. Of course, that doesn't solve the problem."

The fact that the rest of his supervisors would be making this second choice had never occurred to Brian. "All I do, Brian, is spend a little more time with my guys up front, show them the mistake, and ask why it was made. Once you understand why you're making a mistake, you stop doing it. They also know I'm serious because I'm out there until they get it right."

Brian was no dummy. He got the point. The next day he was on the floor talking to the operators and supervisors, asking questions and then asking some more questions. "Why was this operation late? What action is it going to take to catch up? If you're not going to make the due date, whom have you told?" Brian now understood the importance of being out on the floor on a daily basis, walking, talking, listening, and asking questions. It was exactly like the supervisor had said, "The truth is people respond to the consistency and repetition of your actions, not just what crosses your lips in passing."

The key message that Brian had to communicate to his people was accountability. He also had to make them understand the need for accuracy. If they didn't report their information correctly, they were going to get bad information out of the system. And, in the end, they would all pay the price for bad reporting.

Brian's lesson and responsibility, however, went a step further. He had to accept that he could be pleased with his shop's progress, but he never again would be able to be merely content with maintaining the status quo of the shop. He now understood that the only way to effectively compete in today's marketplace was to push and strive for continuous improvement.

Once the dispatch list has been implemented, the typical daily shortage meeting should be replaced by a daily dispatch meeting which should last only 5 to 10 minutes. Although this new meeting is similar to the shortage meeting, the emphasis is put on avoidance of shortages by focusing attention on operations that are lagging behind schedule rather than waiting until the actual shortage occurs.

This is also the opportunity to discuss jobs that need to be released with less-than-normal lead time, as well as any other situations where action is necessary. A set of rules for this meeting should also be established, such as the following:

1. Monitor the number of jobs that are being written onto the dispatch list. Most software systems provide ample on-line updating capability, and handwriting jobs onto the schedule should not be necessary. If there are more than a few jobs being written in—the number may vary depending on the quantity of jobs that flow through a work center—there is a problem with the planning and scheduling process that must be fixed.
2. Emphasize that the shop supervisors will honor the dispatch list, with a commitment from management that all jobs will be handled through the formal scheduling system.
3. No chairs, no coffee, and no BS.
4. Adhere strictly to the notion that "silence is approval."

Since the machine shop was the only area using dispatch lists, the standard shortage meeting was continued. However, Brian and Joan decided to hold another meeting in the machine shop prior to the official one in Ralph's office. There were some rough times in the beginning, but it didn't take long and the meeting went quickly and smoothly. Brian was pleasantly surprised when these meetings ended up taking significantly less time than his previous conversations with Tony to update the shortage list. In fact, it was taking less than ten minutes. Not only were the solutions to the problems they encountered in this meeting better, but each week it seemed there were fewer and fewer problems because the shortages themselves were becoming fewer.

As Chapter 8 will show, other possibilities for dispatching occur in areas other than production such as order picking, inspection, order release, design engineering, tooling, maintenance, and numerical control programming. There might be times when, partway through the manufacturing process, a product has to go to an outside supplier for an operation and then return to the factory for further processing. In such instances, the dispatch list could be used to communicate priorities to the supplier, as if the outside operation were another operation in the shop.

Though the shop schedule and the dispatch list made life easier for Brian, he noticed that several of his critical work centers were becoming less critical. What he didn't realize was that by working on the wrong priorities he had been wasting capacity. He would have to break setups, make parts that weren't needed at that point in time, and, worse still, make parts that ended up being scrapped or reworked because of an engineering change. That savings in capacity would be enough in several work centers to assure that a job would be completed on time. What he still needed was accurate and reliable capacity plans. To obtain those, he had to understand what his required capacities were, and what he was actually capable of producing to assure the capacity was in place when it was needed. The key was to plan instead of react. This is exactly what he will learn next.

Chapter Four

Understanding Capacity Planning

As Brian stared down at the most recent capacity planning report lying on his desk, his mind shot back to one of his early meetings with Ralph. It was still during that time when Brian felt under the gun to prove himself. He had tried to show that he was willing to stand up for what he believed was right, but he couldn't tell if Ralph appreciated it or not.

Right in the middle of trying to get the routings accurate, but before Brian had started to use the dispatch list, Ralph had waved Brian into his office and motioned for him to sit down as he finished a call. After placing the phone back on the hook, Ralph turned to him. "Brian, my boy," he said in a tone Brian had previously heard him use only with Dan and Mickey. It wasn't just that it was friendly. Ralph was smiling. "I just want to tell you, I've noticed the reduction in the shortages from your departments. That's good work. The only problem is your productivity numbers have been lagging. Now, I want to be clear about this. I don't want people getting hurt out there or making junk. I want your first concerns to be safety and quality. That's a given. But I don't want to see the emphasis put on on-time delivery one month and productivity numbers the next. I want them both every month."

Brian remembered how confused he had been by what Ralph was

asking. There had been a pile of work to get out. Brian had worked every operator he could get his hands on overtime for two weeks, running every machine available to get it done. What Ralph was saying, however, was that anybody could run lots of machines, use lots of people, and spend lots of money in order to deliver on time. It was also true that just about anybody could use nothing but the best people in the shop on the best machines and improve their productivity. Ralph wanted them both. What neither of them really understood at the time was that they needed better tools and techniques to accomplish both of these objectives. In addition to valid schedules, they needed the tools that would be provided by capacity planning and input-output control.

Brian's first response to Ralph's demand was to head up to Elliot's office. Elliot was in the process of finishing off a glazed doughnut when Brian walked in. "You didn't save a bite for me?" Brian asked. "That's just like you, Elliot. I come up here to talk turkey and you're downing dessert."

"What can I do for you, Miller?"

"You have to help me get Ralph off my back."

"What does he want now?"

Brian explained the situation. "We're busting our butts down there, and he's telling me productivity is lagging. Elliot, good buddy, you could do me a real favor here."

"Why does this sound like trouble?"

"All you have to do, Elliot, is relax your standards a bit. They're really unrealistic, and there's no way I can meet them. They're just killing my productivity."

"You must be kidding, Miller. I mean, you have to understand my position. I get measured around here on keeping the standard cost of the part down. If I increase the standard times, the standard cost goes up. I don't need to pull out the bottom line for you, do I? Besides, I think you can make the standards if you just put your mind to it."

"Can't you relax them just a tad . . . give me a little breathing room?"

"Sorry, Brian. I can't just go out and loosen all the standards. We agreed a few weeks ago that we were after realistic standards and I really believe it's starting to work."

"Well, it doesn't show in the productivity numbers," grumbled Brian.

"Come on, Brian. Give it a chance. We just got started," Elliot said with a smile. "Use some of your Midwest charm to soften up Ralph a little bit."

"I tried that. I tried being as charming as they come, but it didn't work. What you're asking me to operate on right now, Elliot, is blind faith."

The memory of those earlier times was still fresh with Brian. Now, he picked up the report on his desk and smiled. Within a couple of months of that meeting, they had implemented the dispatch list, and last month they had turned on the Capacity Requirements Planning module of their MRP software. What he had discovered was that with Capacity Requirements Planning, he could arrange in advance to get the right number of people and the right amount of equipment that would enable him to get both on-time delivery and productivity. In addition, the scrap and rework that was created by rushing to make the numbers was also being greatly reduced.

In the beginning, however, Brian would walk onto the shop floor and see the full boxes that held the work orders and know it was already too late to effectively react to his capacity needs. If he was going to get the work out, he was going to have to get more capacity, but forward visibility into his capacity requirements was nonexistent. He had no idea how much of each resource he would need to line up in the future or, if the work order volume declined, whether he had to lay anyone off. It also meant that he couldn't tell the two guys who had asked for a few days off next month for the opening of trout season whether they could have the time or not.

Then there was the call Brian got from the Maintenance Department to schedule the refurbishing of one of his machines. A number of Brian's machines were old and frequently breaking down. They simply couldn't hold the necessary tolerances demanded of them. Not only were these conditions causing a good deal of scrap and rework, they were also contributing to a loss in productivity. Finally, Maintenance received the parts and had the time to overhaul the Warner-Swasey 4AC. The problem was that they wanted to do it right away. Brian, however, had a full load of work ahead of the machine. He tried to explain to Ivan, the Maintenance Manager, that there were bound to be times in the future when the load would be lighter. Unfortunately, he couldn't tell him exactly when that might be. Without this information, Brian was reluctantly forced to let Maintenance have their way.

The problem was compounded after Brian finally had his 4AC back, and was starting to catch up. Maintenance called him again and told him they were taking his 2ACs off-line to refurbish the spindles. Brian had to go through the whole exercise one more time.

Since, as Chapter 1 showed, the "gut feel" that Mac, the former machine shop supervisor, employed was truly an ineffective approach to planning capacity, Brian had to find something better. In desperation, he went back to Elliot.

Brian showed Elliot his machine-load report. As usual, it showed a large overdue load in his work centers and a future load that tapered off to nothing very quickly (see Figure 4.1). Brian explained to Elliot that he knew he was going to get more work in the future in spite of what the report said. He needed a way to predict what these work loads were going to be so he could deal with conflicts such as maintenance schedules and people asking for time off. Elliot reminded him that the machine-load report included only the actual orders that had been released to the shop by Production Control. Brian stared woefully at the report and wondered, "Why can't you tell me more about the future?"

FIGURE 4.1 Machine-Load Report

WORK CENTER NO. 24		WEEKLY CAPACITY: 240 HRS.
WEEK	LOAD	OVER/UNDERLOAD
PAST DUE	824	+824
WEEK #1	286	+ 46
WEEK #2	150	- 90
WEEK #3	90	- 150
WEEK #4	39	- 201

He turned back to Elliot. "You know, the truth is, Elliot, even if I knew what my future workload was, I'd still have problems. I don't know how much capacity I really have."

"What do you mean?" Elliot asked. "I calculate the available capacity for all the departments, including yours."

"But I don't think it's right," Brian said. "At least, I never seem to be able to produce what you say I should without working overtime. Something is obviously not adding up."

Elliot tried to explain the process of calculating available capacity for Brian. He told him how he used the traditional industrial engineering method of figuring what is called the rated or nominal capacity. "It's simple," he said. "I multiply the number of machines by the number of hours per shift times the number of shifts per day times the number of workdays per week. That's your "gross capacity" if everybody worked at 100 percent efficiency and utilization. But since we know that's not going to be the case, I multiply that gross capacity by the target efficiency and utilization factors for the work center to get how much you should be able to produce."

"Okay," Brian said, "theoretically, I should have that much capacity. But my actual output rarely reaches that level without working a lot of overtime. I've got the machines you say I have, but I don't always have the operators to run them, and those I do have on the payroll aren't always there. Where in your calculations do you figure in absenteeism? Besides, Elliot, as I keep telling you, I haven't been reaching the efficiency levels you think are possible, and my utilization is a joke.. You know what shape some of my machines are in."

"We've all got problems, Brian, but that's the way we've always figured our capacity. Look back over the reports and you'll see for yourself that you've been able to produce it."

"Right, but only with plenty of overtime and terrible productivity results. I got Ralph on my case not only to get my work out on time to the schedule, but he also wants improvements in my productivity. I need some help, Elliot. I just can't seem to do it with the tools I've got."

On his way back to his office, Brian remembered a conversation that he had previously had with Joan. She had mentioned the name of Hal Beckman, someone she'd met at a meeting of the American Production and Inventory Control Society (APICS). Hal was from the Good Health Vitamin Company, and had mentioned something to Joan about recently implementing Capacity Requirements Planning. Brian hurried back to his office to give Hal a call.

Hal was happy to hear from Brian, and he sympathized with his dilemma because it had also been his own. What Hal explained to Brian was nothing more than a great deal of common sense that neatly linked things together. Hal outlined the ideas and tools he used to manage capacity.

He told him how Good Health determined their required capacity. This was the capacity he needed to meet his schedules. He then developed a plan for making that amount of capacity available. "The challenge," Hal said, "will be to get your management to understand that this capacity plan is the work-center supervisor's operating budget. In fact, our accounting group takes the hours by work center, applies the labor costs, and that gives them the direct labor operating budget by work center. They add it up by department to get the department operating budgets. Once you know how much capacity you really need in terms of people and equipment, you can put together a plan to make that capacity available, and the supervisor can be held accountable for executing that plan."

TERMINOLOGY

Capacity is the ability to move work through a work center in a given time period. There are, however, several aspects of capacity. The capacity planning process begins by establishing a common understanding of the terminology.

The first step in capacity management is taken when the company decides—through the business plan, production plan, and the master schedule—what they want to make. The *required capacity* is the capacity necessary to support those plans; in other words, if a company wants to produce a given product, this is how much capacity it will take. In calculating required capacity, no consideration is given as to whether or not that much capacity is actually available or can be obtained. Clearly, that issue has to be dealt with, and this chapter will show how.

The *demonstrated capacity* reflects what each work center has produced in the recent past. This is a true reflection of what the work center is capable of producing under current conditions and circumstances, such as product mix, work schedule, staff levels, efficiency, and utilization. It is a proven capability, and it represents what the work center can be expected to produce in the near future without intervention.

Actual output capacity, however, is not always fixed. Machines and people can be added or deleted. Machines deteriorate or are overhauled to increase their productivity. New people with less training are hired and, in some instances, labor efficiency improves. Therefore, it is up to the work-center supervisor to blend anticipated changes (decreases as well as increases) with demonstrated capacity to determine what the work center can be expected to produce in the future.

Planned capacity is the amount of capacity that is expected to be available during a specific future time period. It is based on the demonstrated capacity adjusted by any changes expected by the work-center supervisor. This means adding or deleting shifts, people, machines, overtime, or productivity improvements.

The planned capacity is the capacity expected to be available if operating under normal conditions and a regular schedule (e.g., an 8-hour shift and a 40-hour week). The *maximum planned capacity* establishes a higher level of capacity that could be accomplished if a supervisor were to work the maximum overtime, add a shift, or hire people to run all of the machines. It is the maximum amount a work center is able to produce without capital expenditure for equipment or facilities. A company would prefer to operate at the planned capacity level because it is the most cost-effective, but the maximum planned capacity establishes an upper limit to the available capacity.

CAPACITY PLANNING OBJECTIVE

The purpose of capacity management is to identify and solve capacity problems in a timely manner, which means before an emergency arrives or the work load becomes unmanageable. The objective is to maintain a balance between the capacity that is available and what is required. If more capacity is required than is expected to be available, only two things can be done:

1. Get more capacity
2. Reduce the requirements

If less capacity than is available is going to be needed, management must once again make adjustments to balance the two.

It is essential to plan the level of available capacity by considering the required capacity, which is determined by the planning and scheduling system. If the required capacity exceeds the current planned capacity, that planned capacity must be increased. There is, of course, some practical limit beyond which we cannot conveniently nor economically increase capacity. When the required capacity exceeds this maximum level, some decisions have to be made, such as adding capital equipment, building an addition to the plant, or putting a limit on how much business to accept. These are major decisions that require the attention of top management.

CAPACITY UNITS OF MEASURE

To properly manage capacity, it is important to establish a consistent unit of measure. Some companies are accustomed to dealing with capacity in terms of product units. At the seminar Brian had attended, a company that made ball bearings, Beartone Manufacturing, planned its capacity in terms of bearings per day. Good Health Vitamins planned its capacity using tablets per day. And Samson Tires planned capacity in units of tons of molded rubber per week.

There are problems with this approach, however. Beartone Manufacturing, for instance, makes a broad range of bearing sizes and the resources vary with the size. They also produce special bearings, which require more resources per unit than the standard products do. At Good Health, there are different sizes of tablets to contend with and complex multiple vitamin tablets, as well as simple tablets. And at the Samson Tire factory, similar variations exist. The point is, if it takes different amounts of resources and capacities to produce specific items on a schedule, planning capacities in gross product terms is inadequate. If there are variations in the product mix and resource requirements, another method must be used. Also, the incoming and outgoing work must be expressed in the same units. For example, Good Health would have a difficult time effectively planning input in pounds of tablet mix and output in numbers of tablets.

Planning in units of standard hours is recommended. Standard hours can be used as a common denominator for all products. It's measurable. It allows input and output figures to be expressed in the same units. It also eliminates product variables, such as size and complexity. This is particularly important when work centers produce different products and components. Using standard hours also makes it easier to convert required capacity into the quantity of people or machines needed—the ultimate objective.

With Capacity Requirements Planning, the Manufacturing Resource Planning system calculates capacity requirements for the orders that are already released, as well as for the future planned orders that have not been released. It was these planned orders that enabled Hayes to generate capacity requirements plans beyond what the machine-load report was showing.

It is important to understand the logic of this approach. In Chapter 3, the process of backward scheduling was explained using a shop routing (see Figure 4.2). On that shop order, the supervisor would need to plan an order release for 40 of part number 163726 shafts in the week of 7/2. That planned order can now be used to calculate the shop's capacity requirements.

This example returns to work center 24 and operation 20, which is a turning operation. This particular work center is under José's supervision. The routing shows José that his setup time is three hours and his run time is .20 hours per piece. He multiplies the .20 by the 40 needed pieces, adding in the setup time, and he finds that he needs 11 standard hours to produce those 40 pieces in work center 24 (see Figure 4.3). What he must now establish is when that capacity is required.

The total lead time for this part is four weeks. José knows that it is due in stock on 7/31. The question he needs to answer is when during that four weeks does operation 20 need to be performed? The answer is obtained via the backward-scheduling logic as explained in Chapter 3. Beginning with the due date to stock obtained from MRP, offsetting it by the amount of time it will take to put the parts into stock, the move time, and the time for operation 40, and continuing that process on back to operation 20, José can see that operation 20 needs to be performed in week 7/9 (see Figure 4.4). He knows that it will take 11 hours in week 7/9 to produce those parts.

By going through every released and planned order in the system scheduled for work center 24, the standard hours required can be loaded into the capacity plan. The planned capacity requirements for work center 24 are shown in Figure 4.4. By walking through this

FIGURE 4.2 Backward Scheduling Diagram

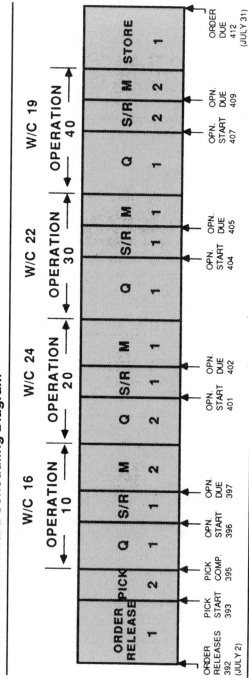

FIGURE 4.3 Calculating Required Capacity

PART NO. 163726	DESCRIPTION HUB FRONT WHEEL		ON HAND 18	LEAD TIME 4	ORDER QTY. 40		
WEEK BEGINNING		PAST DUE	7/2	7/9	7/16	7/23	7/30	8/6
PROJECTED REQUIREMENTS			12	16	14	8	12	16
SCHEDULED RECEIPTS				40				
PROJECTED AVAILABLE		18	6	30	16	8	36	20
PLANNED ORDER RELEASE			40					

OPN. NO.	DESCRIPTION	SET UP HRS.	RUN HRS.	WORK CENTER
20	TURN	3.0	.20	24

WORK CENTER - 24

OPN.	HOURS	WEEK
20	11.0	?

FIGURE 4.4 Weekly Capacity Scheduling

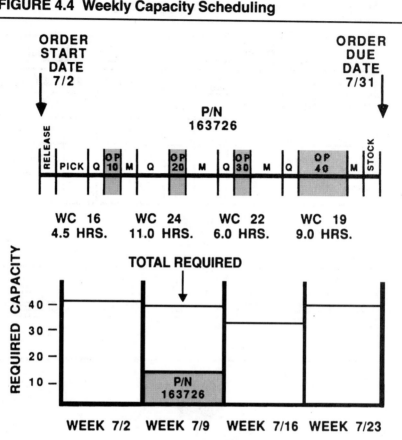

calculation, José understood how the dates were derived. He was also glad that the computer would do all these calculations for him.

In the example above, the required capacity hours were loaded into the weekly bucket (period of time) that contains the operation due date. There are four ways in which required capacities can be spread across the calendar.

1. Load all hours into weekly buckets containing the operation *due* date.

2. Load all hours into weekly buckets containing the operation *start* date.

3. Back load from the operation due date into daily buckets.
4. Forward load from the operation *start* date into daily buckets.

The first two methods work well for many companies. On the other hand, planning capacities in weekly requirements is inadequate in some circumstances. Situations that require the use of the daily-bucket approach (methods 3 and 4) follow:

1. When there are long-running jobs, the weekly-bucket approach distorts the week-to-week picture. In work centers that have a small number of jobs going through, this picture could be distorted by as little as a two-day run time. However, if a large volume of jobs is going through the work center, run times of more than a week could be tolerated if the scheduled completion dates are randomly distributed throughout the week.
2. As companies move along the Lean Manufacturing journey (see Chapter 9), the shortening of lead times and reduction of order quantities will mean that weekly capacity buckets won't be sufficient to guarantee daily delivery schedules.

In some situations, it is desirable to schedule operations within some finite capacity constraints. This will be discussed in Chapter 6.

Figure 4.5 shows the results of loading the required capacity into daily buckets. Operation 20 requires 50 hours in work center 24 and must be completed on Monday, 7/23. José knows that he can schedule only 7 hours per day. Back loading from the due date, he would put 7 hours into Monday, 7/23; 7 hours per day into 7/16 through 7/20; 7 hours into Friday, 7/13; and the last 1 hour would be loaded into Thursday, 7/12. The final result is that 8 hours will be required in the week 7/9, 35 hours in week 7/16, and 7 hours in week 7/23.

The choice of which alternative to use depends upon the requirements of the individual company. Whichever method is used, however, it is important that the users—the capacity planner and shop supervisor—understand the logic of the process.

AVAILABLE CAPACITY

The objective of planning is to balance the available capacity with the required capacity. But how much capacity is really available? Sev-

FIGURE 4.5 Daily Capacity Scheduling

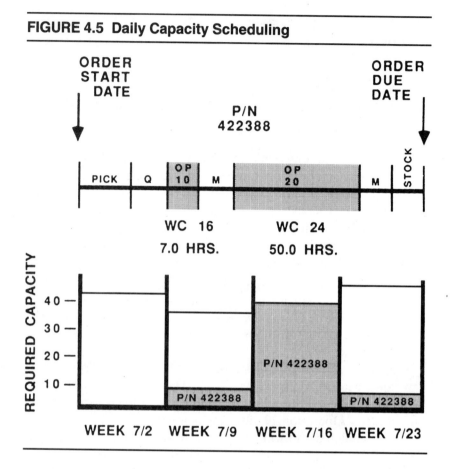

eral ways to look at available capacity have already been defined. There is the nominal capacity as determined by Elliot's calculation explained earlier. There is the demonstrated capacity, representing what was available in the past and what can be expected to be available in the future if nothing changes. And there is the planned capacity and the maximum planned capacity. Which one should be used? Actually, all of them play a role in managing capacity.

To begin with, there are some fundamental decisions that senior management will have to make regarding how they typically want to run the facility. At Hayes, Pete and his staff have decided to schedule the plant to work two shifts per day, eight hours per shift, five days a week (see Figure 4.6). They have also chosen to place an upper limit on the scheduled working hours of two shifts per day and ten hours per shift, thus authorizing two hours of overtime per shift. They have decided against scheduling the factory to operate more than six days a week on an ongoing basis. These are the guidelines that Pete gave to the staff. The supervisors were expected to do whatever was needed, within these guidelines, to get the work done. This is not to say that in a real emergency a Sunday can't be worked as well, but it will not be scheduled on an ongoing basis.

It is then the responsibility of Brian, Dan, and Mickey, working with their supervisors, to translate these guidelines into specific operating schedules for each work center. If the guidelines have to be exceeded in a work center, it needs to be brought to Pete's attention so that he may consider the necessary short- and long-term solutions. If, on the other hand, the guideline level is not required in other work centers, only the amount of time needed to fulfill the requirements should be scheduled.

Basically, the guidelines represent Pete's overall management

---

FIGURE 4.6 Work-Center Guidelines

DESIRED CAPACITY:

__2__ **SHIFTS PER DAY**

__8__ **HOURS PER SHIFT**

__5__ **DAYS PER WEEK**

MAXIMUM CAPACITY:

__2__ **SHIFTS PER DAY**

__10__ **HOURS PER SHIFT**

__6__ **DAYS PER WEEK**

---

strategy for the way the factory will be run. The individual work-center planning provides the detail by which Brian, Dan, and Mickey can plan their different resources.

Calculating Capacity Requirements

Brian, Dan, Mickey, and their supervisors were accustomed to monitoring their efficiency and utilization quite closely. To learn how to balance these, they needed a good understanding of what each is. Utilization is a measure of the use of available resources, usually machinery and people, in a productive capacity. It determines the percentage of the hours when a person or machine was available (attendance hours) that were actually spent producing parts (charged hours). Efficiency is a measure of performance against the standards. In other words, during the time a person or machine was being used, how efficient (or effective) was that use. Efficiency is the earned hours (at standard) divided by the charged hours. When combined together, utilization and efficiency provide the commonly used measure, productivity.

The calculation of these factors is explained in Figure 4.7. For example, the Hayes milling department has 320 labor hours per week available. On average, absenteeism has reduced that to 300 attendance hours per week. If the average total time that the operators spend on productive work is 270 hours per week, the utilization is 90 percent (270 divided by 300). If the standard hours of output are 240 per week, the average efficiency is 89 percent (240 divided by 270). To calculate productivity, the supervisor can either multiply the efficiency times utilization or divide the standard hours of output by total attendance hours, giving us 80 percent (240 divided by 300).

Load Factor

Load factors combine the effect of efficiency, utilization, and absenteeism. Unlike productivity, which does not account for absenteeism, load factors are equal to the ratio of the output of a work center in standard hours to the gross available clock hours of a resource. This allows the supervisor and capacity planner to translate standard hours of required capacity into resources required at a work center. It also provides a convenient means of converting available people or

FIGURE 4.7 Calculating Efficiency, Utilization, and Productivity

AVAILABLE HOURS = 320
TOTAL ATTENDANCE HOURS = 300
ACTUAL HOURS SPENT ON PRODUCTION = 270
STANDARD HOURS OUTPUT = 240

$$\text{EFFICIENCY} = \frac{\text{STANDARD HOURS OUTPUT}}{\text{ACTUAL HRS. SPENT ON PRODUCTION}}$$

$$\frac{240}{270} = 89\%$$

$$\text{UTILIZATION} = \frac{\text{ACTUAL HRS. SPENT ON PRODUCTION}}{\text{TOTAL ATTENDANCE HOURS}}$$

$$\frac{270}{300} = 90\%$$

$$\text{PRODUCTIVITY} = \frac{\text{STANDARD HOURS OUTPUT}}{\text{TOTAL ATTENDANCE HOURS}}$$

$$\frac{240}{300} = 80\%$$

machines into expected standard hours of output (i.e., available capacity).

To calculate the load factor, the gross available hours of machine time and/or manpower that exist in a given work center must first be calculated (see Figure 4.8). In this case, Brian has decided to run this work center only one shift per day, because that is sufficient to complete the work that is required to be done. The next step is to determine how many operators and machines there are. In this example, Brian has four operators and four machines available at 8 hours per shift. One shift times four operators times 8 hours equals 32 available hours. He multiplies that by five days per week and he gets 160 hours available per week. That is the gross available capacity. Brian knows, however, that the work center actually produced an average of only 120 standard hours per week during the past four weeks. That has been the work center's demonstrated capacity. Therefore, the

FIGURE 4.8 Calculating Load Factor

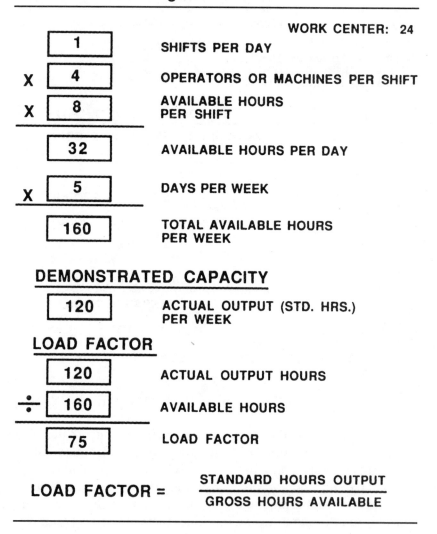

WORK CENTER: 24

| 1 | SHIFTS PER DAY |

X | 4 | OPERATORS OR MACHINES PER SHIFT

X | 8 | AVAILABLE HOURS PER SHIFT

| 32 | AVAILABLE HOURS PER DAY

X | 5 | DAYS PER WEEK

| 160 | TOTAL AVAILABLE HOURS PER WEEK

DEMONSTRATED CAPACITY

| 120 | ACTUAL OUTPUT (STD. HRS.) PER WEEK

LOAD FACTOR

| 120 | ACTUAL OUTPUT HOURS

÷ | 160 | AVAILABLE HOURS

| 75 | LOAD FACTOR

$$\text{LOAD FACTOR} = \frac{\text{STANDARD HOURS OUTPUT}}{\text{GROSS HOURS AVAILABLE}}$$

demonstrated load factor is equal to 120 (the actual output in standard hours) divided by 160 (the available hours), or 75 percent. In other words, out of the total time this work center has budgeted every day, Brian can only expect to produce 75 percent of that amount in actual standard hours of output. This means each operator can be expected to produce 6 standard hours of output for each

8-hour day that he is on the payroll. Each work center, of course, will have its own load factor.

Using a load factor in planning capacity can help supervisors get a better handle on what output to expect from their work centers under given circumstances. Demonstrated capacity represents what the supervisor can expect to produce in the future unless something changes. If any element affecting the load factor is expected to change, it is important that the planned load factor be adjusted to reflect that change. The adjustment should be the result of the supervisor's commitment to certain improvements in efficiency, utilization, or absenteeism—not merely the result of management edict or arbitrary adjustments. It is important to get the supervisor to take ownership of the new number. Other more detailed measures, such as efficiency, utilization, or absenteeism can be helpful in determining where problems are, but in planning capacity they should all be considered collectively, which is what the load factor does.

PLANNING AVAILABLE CAPACITY

When the Master Production Schedule changes, either up or down, it is obviously going to have an impact on how much capacity will be needed. Demonstrated capacity reflects how much capacity was used to meet the earlier schedule. The question now becomes how much capacity will be available to meet the future schedule? Brian must have a way to figure out how many machines or people will be needed to produce the required output.

What happens when José is informed, via Capacity Requirements Planning, that 300 standard hours of capacity are required in work center 24? He needs to translate the gross available hours into the expected output in standard hours, which is the planned capacity (see Figure 4.9).

According to the operating guidelines, José is authorized to run two shifts per day. Four machines and four operators are available on each of the two 8-hour shifts, which means there would be 64 gross labor hours available per day. Since the work center works five days a week, the gross available hours per week equals 320. Will 320 hours satisfy the schedule that Pete has approved? No, because some of those hours will be lost to absenteeism, nonutilization, and ineffi-

---

FIGURE 4.9 Calculating Planned Capacity

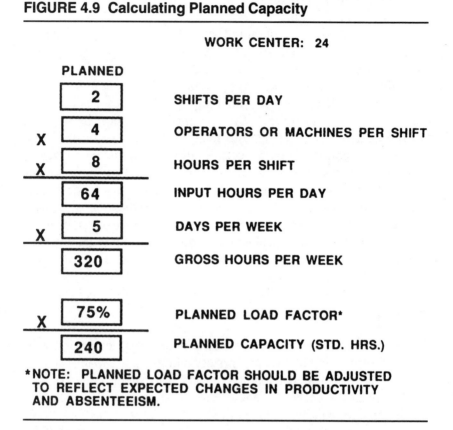

WORK CENTER: 24

PLANNED		
	2	SHIFTS PER DAY
X	4	OPERATORS OR MACHINES PER SHIFT
X	8	HOURS PER SHIFT
	64	INPUT HOURS PER DAY
X	5	DAYS PER WEEK
	320	GROSS HOURS PER WEEK
X	75%	PLANNED LOAD FACTOR*
	240	PLANNED CAPACITY (STD. HRS.)

*NOTE: PLANNED LOAD FACTOR SHOULD BE ADJUSTED TO REFLECT EXPECTED CHANGES IN PRODUCTIVITY AND ABSENTEEISM.

---

ciency. Once the load factor of 75 percent is applied, José knows that only 240 standard hours of output can be expected. He'll need to gain some capacity, by either extending his operating hours or changing some of the elements affecting his load factor, such as improving utilization, efficiency, or reducing absenteeism. The load factor that the supervisor uses to calculate future available (planned) capacity is called the planned load factor.

The same process can be used to calculate maximum capacity (see Figure 4.10). Using the figures from the work-center guideline established earlier—two shifts per day multiplied by the four available machines, times 10 hours per shift, times six days per week—indicates to José that his available hours would be 480. Multiplying that

---

FIGURE 4.10 Calculating Maximum Planned Capacity

WORK CENTER: 24

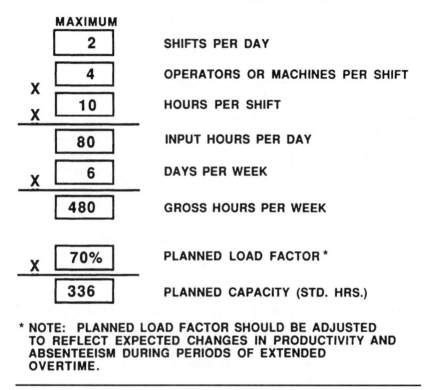

MAXIMUM

2	SHIFTS PER DAY

X

4	OPERATORS OR MACHINES PER SHIFT

X

10	HOURS PER SHIFT

80	INPUT HOURS PER DAY

X

6	DAYS PER WEEK

480	GROSS HOURS PER WEEK

X

70%	PLANNED LOAD FACTOR *

336	PLANNED CAPACITY (STD. HRS.)

* NOTE: PLANNED LOAD FACTOR SHOULD BE ADJUSTED
TO REFLECT EXPECTED CHANGES IN PRODUCTIVITY AND
ABSENTEEISM DURING PERIODS OF EXTENDED
OVERTIME.

---

by the 75 percent load factor would tell him that his maximum planned capacity in standard hours is 360.

Both Brian and José were well aware that during times of extended overtime, such as 10-hour days or six-day weeks, productivity was likely to slip because of increased fatigue, absenteeism, or machine downtime. They adjusted the planned load factor during these periods down to 70 percent, thus making the maximum planned capacity 336 standard hours.

Ultimately, supervisors like José must make the commitment for output by the work center. It is imperative that he has the proper information available to him to manage his resources.

RESERVING CAPACITY

After going over all of the data with Brian and seeing that his planned capacity in work center 24 should be increased above the current 240 hours, José pushed back his chair and looked at Brian quizzically.

"What's wrong?" asked Brian. "You understand all the calculations, don't you?"

"Yeah," replied José. "But I'm worried that if I set my staff level to these new numbers, I'm going to get caught short when the inevitable emergency hits. You know, the hot job that Sales wants us to push or the replacements for the parts scrapped at Assembly. Even though our planning has improved a lot, we still get a fair share of unplanned emergency work. I think I should plan a little more available capacity so that I'll be able to handle it without overtime."

Brian admitted that José had a good point. They weren't out of the woods yet, and they probably never would totally eliminate the need for that little extra capacity for the emergencies. Brian knew that Ralph wanted him to keep a little in reserve as well. But what was the best way to do that?

Brian knew that he could simply understate his available capacity on the CRP reports and keep a little in his back pocket, so to speak. But he also knew that giving false data was playing the game the way Dan used to do with his padded lead times and others would soon figure out that he could do more than what he was stating. That would destroy all the hard work that had been done to build integrity into the information.

José piped up. "Why don't we just lower the load factor a little bit. That would permit me to put on a few more people to meet the planned requirements, and then I could cover the emergencies."

Brian thought about José's suggestion for a minute before he realized that it was just another way of understating his true available capacity. What he needed to do was to reserve some capacity, but make it visible. Then everyone would know how much capacity he had for the emergencies, and when the workload exceeded that as well, he would feel justified in asking Ralph for more people.

Brian knew there had to be a way. And then it dawned on him! Why couldn't the material planners put some work orders on the system for reserved capacity? They could set up some dummy part numbers and create routings that would place planned capacity requirements on the work centers which he would designate. They had enough history to be able to figure out where the emergencies were most likely to hit and how much capacity was usually required. The information wouldn't have to be exact, just good enough to cover his average emergency work.

Brian called Joan to talk about his idea. It would be extra work for her planners because they would have to manage these special orders very carefully.

After she and Brian batted the notion around, Joan said she couldn't think of any reason why it wouldn't work. "You know, Brian," Joan said, "it seems like a great way not only to reserve the capacity, but to make it visible to anyone who wanted to know. Those special orders would show up in my material plans as well as in your capacity plans. Then, as the actual emergency work hits us, we can simply replace one of the dummy orders with a real order. We might even consider doing this at the master schedule level."

Brian told Dan and Mickey about the new idea. As expected, Dan rejected the notion and said he would continue to do the emergency work on overtime. "After all," he mused, "if Sales and Production Control can't tell me what to plan for, then they can't gripe when I have to work overtime to do it. Besides, I keep a little in reserve anyway through my own means."

Mickey, on the other hand, thought it was a great idea. He felt that if Joan just put a couple of these orders a week into the master schedule, that would cover him.

Brian called Joan and told her that he would help her gather the data for the machine shop and that Mickey had promised to do the same for the Assembly Department.

It should be noted that the notion of reserving capacity, though a common practice, should be treated with caution. It is easy to fall into the just-in-case trap and use reserved capacity rather than addressing the real problems. As Chapter 9 will show, many of the techniques that are used to manage schedules and capacities will be modified or eliminated as the concepts and practices of Lean Manufacturing are implemented. Reserving capacity is one of those.

CREATING THE CAPACITY PLAN

What follows is an example designed to illustrate how the computer generates the capacity requirements. Since this example pushes a lot of numbers around, a work sheet has been set up to help understand the process (see Figure 4.11). Each column represents a one-week period ending on the dates indicated. By looking at the calendar (see Figure 4.12), we can see that each of the numbered days—391, 395, 400 . . .—corresponds to the Friday of each given week. For this example, we will use the timing alternative 3, explained earlier, which loads all hours into daily buckets starting from the operation due date. This example uses six shop orders (see Figure 4.13).

Let's look at work center 02. Beginning with work order 125, we check to see if that work order goes through work center 02. It does

---

FIGURE 4.11 Capacity Requirements Work Sheet for Work Center 02

WORK CENTER: 02

WK. END. W/O #	6/29 391	7/06 395	7/13 400	7/20 405	7/27 410	8/03 415
W125	8		5	8		
W133			10		16	
W116				9		
W152					9	
W134				1	16	
W108						17
TOTAL	8	0	15	18	41	17

FIGURE 4.12 Manufacturing Calendar

JUNE						
S	M	T	W	T	F	S
					1 371	2
3	4 372	5 373	6 374	7 375	8 376	9
10	11 377	12 378	13 379	14 380	15 381	16
17	18 382	19 383	20 384	21 385	22 386	23
24	(25) (387)	26 388	27 389	28 390	29 391	30

JULIAN DAY   M. DAY

JULY						
S	M	T	W	T	F	S
1	2 392	3 393	4 HOLIDAY	5 394	6 395	7
8	9 396	10 397	11 398	12 399	13 400	14
15	16 401	17 402	18 403	19 404	20 405	21
22	23 406	24 407	25 408	26 409	27 410	28
29	30 411	31 412				

FIGURE 4.13 Capacity Planning Data from Work Orders Using Work Center 02

PN 264
WO# 125   REL. DATE 382

OPN.	WC.	TOTAL HRS.	START DATE	COMP. DATE
10	01	5	386	387
20	02	8	390	391
30	03	5	395	396
40	02	13	399	401

DUE DATE 404

PN 264
WO# 133   REL. DATE 388

OPN.	WC.	TOTAL HRS.	START DATE	COMP. DATE
10	01	6	392	393
20	02	10	396	398
30	03	6	402	403
40	02	16	406	408

DUE DATE 411

PN 173
WO# 116   REL. DATE 385

OPN.	WC.	TOTAL HRS.	START DATE	COMP. DATE
10	01	4.5	389	390
20	04	11	393	394
30	07	6	397	398
40	02	9	401	403

DUE DATE 406

PN 173
WO# 152   REL. DATE 391

OPN.	WC.	TOTAL HRS.	START DATE	COMP. DATE
10	01	4.5	395	396
20	04	11	399	400
30	07	6	403	404
40	02	9	407	409

DUE DATE 412

PN 268
WO# 134   REL. DATE 382

OPN.	WC.	TOTAL HRS.	START DATE	COMP. DATE
10	01	8.5	386	387
20	05	18	390	392
30	06	9	394	396
40	03	9	400	401
50	02	17	404	407

DUE DATE 410

PN 268
WO# 108   REL. DATE 388

OPN.	WC.	TOTAL HRS.	START DATE	COMP. DATE
10	01	8.5	392	393
20	05	18	396	398
30	06	9	400	402
40	03	9	406	407
50	02	17	410	413

DUE DATE 416

in operation 20 and 40. It requires 8 hours of setup and run time at operation 20 and 13 hours at operation 40. From the backward scheduling rules (see Figure 4.14), we see that work center 02 is capable of producing 8 hours of work per day (one shift). We must now put the 8 and 13 hours into the appropriate buckets on the work sheet. Using timing rule 3, we identify the operation due dates, in this case 391 and 401, respectively. If the operation is already past due, it will be placed in the first weekly bucket. Since operation 20 is due on 391, it would fall into the week ending 391 bucket. Operation 40 is due 401, which by referring to the manufacturing calendar is a Monday. Since our scheduling rules (see Figure 4.14) say this work center (02) works on one shift and each shift is only 8 hours, we cannot schedule any more than 8 hours in that day. Consequently, the other 5 hours would have to go into the previous day, M-day 400, a Friday, which is in the week ending 400 bucket (see Figure 4.11). Work order 133 also goes through work center 02, and it requires 10 hours due on M-day 398 and 16 hours on M-day 408. Since 398 is a Wednesday, 8 hours can be put into Wednesday and 2 hours into Tuesday, so all

---

FIGURE 4.14 Scheduling Rules for Work Center 02

ALLOW:

- 8 HOURS/SHIFT

- WORK CENTER 06 & 02 : 1 SHIFT

- ALL OTHER WORK CENTERS: 2 SHIFTS

- 2 DAYS BETWEEN OPERATIONS IN DIFFERENT DEPARTMENTS FOR MOVE

- 1 DAY BETWEEN OPERATIONS IN DIFFERENT WORK CENTERS FOR MOVE

- 0 DAYS BETWEEN OPERATIONS IN SAME WORK CENTER FOR MOVE

- 1 DAY TO PUT AWAY IN STORES

- 2 DAYS TO PICK COMPONENTS & MOVE TO FIRST WORK CENTER

- 1 DAY FOR RELEASE

10 hours can go into the week ending 400 for operation 20. Operation 40 is due on M-day 408, which is also a Wednesday, so 8 hours can be worked on Wednesday and 8 hours on Tuesday. This way, all 16 hours can go into the week ending 410 bucket. Operation 40 on work order 116 is scheduled on M-day 403 and takes 9 hours. Since 403 is a Wednesday, 8 hours can be done then and 1 hour on Tuesday. Thus, all 9 hours can be placed in bucket 405. Work order 152 has operation 40 due on day 409, which is a Thursday. Therefore, 8 hours can go in Thursday and 1 hour on Wednesday. All 9 hours can be placed in the week ending 410 bucket. Work order 134 takes 17 hours for operation 50, with an operation due date of 407. This is a Tuesday, so we can place 8 hours in that day and 8 hours in Monday, which leaves us 1 hour short. This hour would have to be done on the previous Friday, M-day 405. One hour would then be placed in the week ending 405 bucket and 16 hours in the week ending 410 bucket. And, finally, work order 108 takes 17 hours in work center 02 with a due date of 413. That would make 8 hours on Wednesday, 8 hours on Tuesday, and 1 hour on Monday. All 17 hours can go into the week ending 415 bucket. We then total the hours in each week: 8 in week 391, 0 in week 395, 15 in week 400, 18 in week 405, 41 in week 410, and 17 in week 415.

Once the software has processed all the information for all the released and planned orders going through a work center, it generates a capacity requirements detail report (see Figure 4.15). This report displays all work orders scheduled to go through work center 24 for the weeks 8/6 and 8/13. The header record shows the work-center number, a description of that work center, a department number, the date of the report, the demonstrated capacity of the work center, and the maximum planned capacity.

Each line of the detail report contains the following information for each work order in each weekly period:

- The work-order number
- The part number
- The part description

- The quantity of product remaining to be produced at this operation in this work center
- The operation number to be performed
- The date this operation is scheduled to be completed
- The date this work order is scheduled to be completed (to the stockroom)
- The setup hours remaining to be completed on this work order at this operation

FIGURE 4.15 Capacity Requirements Detail Report for Work Center 24

WORK CENTER NO.: 24 DATE: 8/06
DESCRIPTION: LATHES DEMO. CAP'Y.: 120
DEPARTMENT NO.: M MAX. PLAN CAP'Y.: 336

WEEK	ORDER NO.	PART NO.	PART DESCRIPTION	QTY.	OPN. NO.	OPN. DUE DATE	ORDER DUE DATE	SETUP HRS.	RUN HRS.	STAT.
8/06	W123	144398	SHAFT	200	30	7/2	7/19	1.0	10.0	R
	W124	428876	BOLT	3000	30	7/3	7/24	2.0	30.0	R
	W110	330246	GEAR	500	20	7/4	7/18	1.0	15.0	R
	W120	407211	BOLT	4000	30	7/4	7/20	2.0	50.0	R
	W112	163726	HUB	400	20	7/5	7/23	3.0	8.0	R
	W129	186846	SHAFT	20	20	7/5	7/12	1.0	4.5	R
							TOTALS	10.0	117.5	
8/13	W128	118132	GEAR	400	20	7/10	7/24	3.0	36.0	R
	W138	258721	SPACER	2000	20	7/11	7/25	0.5	20.0	R
	W140	321406	HUB	500	30	7/12	7/27	1.0	30.0	R
		163726	HUB	400	20	7/13	7/30	3.0	8.0	P
		330246	GEAR	500	20	7/13	7/31	1.0	15.0	P
							TOTALS	8.5	109.0	

- The run hours remaining to be completed on this work order at this operation
- The status code of the planned or released work order

This detailed report gives the supervisor a comprehensive picture of all the work that is expected to be produced by this work center over the reported horizon (typically 12 months). As one can imagine, the report is usually lengthy, and therefore typically isn't printed but is available on CRT. What the supervisor wants to know is the total hours required out of a work center in each week and whether that figure is more or less than he has planned. If that figure reasonably matches the supervisor's planned available capacity, he doesn't have to worry. However, if it's greater or smaller, he'll have to initiate some corrective actions.

SUMMARY CAPACITY PLAN REPORT

The software needs to generate a report that is easy to read, like Figure 4.16, which is a summation of the detailed report. In this report, only the total hours of load for each week are shown rather than the individual order detail. It also offers a week's information on one line, so a supervisor can see his capacity needs for a whole year on one or two pages.

The summary report header record contains the following information:

- The date of the report
- The work-center number
- A description of that work center
- The number of machines in that work center
- The number of operators available for that work center
- The ratio of machines to operator (in this case, one operator can run two machines simultaneously)
- The scheduled days per week for that work center
- The scheduled shifts per day for that work center
- The scheduled hours per shift for that work center
- The demonstrated capacity for that work center

FIGURE 4.16 Summary Capacity Plan for Work Center 24

DATE:	8/06	NO. MACH.:	5	HOURS/SHIFT:	8
WORK CENTER:	24	NO. OPER.:	2	SHIFTS/DAY:	1
DESCRIPTION:	LATHES	MACH./OPER.:	2	DAYS/WEEK:	5
DEMO. CAP'Y.:	120	MAX. CAP'Y.:	336	LOAD FACTOR:	75%

MACHINE CAPACITY

WEEK	REQ'D CAP'Y. (HRS.)	PLAN CAP'Y. (HRS.)	LOAD VS. CAPACITY (%) 50 100 150
8/06	128	150	XXXXXXX
8/13	118	150	XXXXXX
8/20	116	150	XXXXX
8/27	126	150	XXXXXXX
9/03	130	150	XXXXXXX
9/10	144	150	XXXXXXXX
9/17	140	150	XXXXXXXX
9/24	150	150	XXXXXXXXX
10/01	166	150	XXXXXXXXXXX
10/08	160	150	XXXXXXXXXX

LABOR CAPACITY

REQ'D CAP'Y. (HRS.)	PLAN CAP'Y. (HRS.)	LOAD VS. CAPACITY (%) 50 100 150
64	60	XXXXXXXXXX
59	60	XXXXXXXXXX
58	60	XXXXXXXXX
63	60	XXXXXXXXXXX
65	60	XXXXXXXXXXXX
72	60	XXXXXXXXXXXXXXX
70	60	XXXXXXXXXXXXXX
75	90	XXXXXXX
83	90	XXXXXXXX
80	90	XXXXXXXX

7/28

- The maximum planned capacity for that work center
- The planned load factor for that work center

Typically, the capacity planner maintains this information in the computer database with the concurrence of the shop supervisor.

In a work center that contains both equipment resources and labor resources, supervisors must plan capacities for both. Some software packages display the capacity plans for both resources on one report as in Figure 4.16. Others have separate reports for each. Having both resources on one page makes it easier for the capacity planner and supervisor to use, but it is not particularly important which approach we use. Other aspects of planning multiple resources are discussed later in this chapter.

Each side of the report has the same data requirements, but, as shown in Figure 4.16, the data itself is not necessarily the same. Let's look at the machine side of the report first. The required capacity is the standard hours of machine output required to support the schedule. This number was generated from the Capacity Requirements Planning system. The person accountable for the required capacity is the capacity planner.

Referring back to Figure 4.15, we can see the breakdown of the 128 hours required in week beginning 8/6. It is made up of 10.0 hours of setup time and 117.5 hours of run time. The total has been rounded up to 128. Further breakdown of the total hours into the individual jobs is also obvious.

The planned capacity represents how much capacity, in standard hours, is expected to be available to apply against the scheduled jobs. The planned machine capacity of 150 hours per week is determined as follows: five machines times 8 hours per shift times one shift per day times five days per week times a 75 percent planned load factor. This is the work-center supervisor's number. The supervisor is the one who is responsible for knowing how much work can be generated from his work center. If the supervisor recognizes that he will need more capacity to meet the required capacity, it's up to him to initiate action to get it. He must also record the updated planned capacity in the database.

Note that the work center in Figure 4.16 has five machines available and two operators who run two machines at a time. This means that the work center can only run four machines at any one time. It may seem that the capacity should be calculated on the basis of only four machines, since that is all we can run. But capacity is defined as the maximum sustainable output for the scheduled working hours. We want to know how much *machine* capacity we have assuming there would be enough operators to run all the machines available and enough work to keep them all busy. The *machine* capacity is calculated on the basis of how many total machines we have. The operator question will be addressed separately.

Let's look at it another way. Suppose that an operator was added to the first shift. Now the work center can run all five machines, although one of the operators would be "inefficient" since he would be working at only half capacity (running one machine rather than two). However, the real *machine* capacity is based on all five machines.

The load-versus-capacity section graphically tells the supervisor at a glance the relationship between the required capacity and the planned capacity. It is the ratio of the required capacity to the planned capacity expressed as a percentage and displayed in bar chart form. Although a welcome supplement, it is not a prerequisite to successful capacity planning. The ability to see this relationship between required and planned capacity out into the future means that decisions can be made as to whether or not to work overtime, to add machines, to move people in from other work centers, to split an order, or whether the schedule itself has to change.

On the labor side of the report, this work center has one operator running two machines simultaneously. The required labor hours, therefore, are one half the machine hours. The planned labor capacity of 60 hours is derived as follows: two operators times 8 hours per shift times five days per week times the 75 percent planned load factor. Notice that beginning with week 9/24, however, the planned labor capacity has been increased to 90 hours. This reflects the supervisor's intent to bring another operator on board at that time.

This report is telling José that he has sufficient machine capacity to meet the plan until the week of 10/01. He does not, however, have enough labor capacity with a straight 40-hour week. He will have to get more labor capacity to meet the schedule. He'll also have to make a commitment to move the work through the work center as efficiently as possible.

The required capacity is not level. It ranges from a low of 58 labor hours to a high of 83. José also knows that the work will not arrive at the work center exactly as planned. To determine his base requirement for people, he averaged the hours over the next 4 weeks and arrived at a little over 60 labor hours. Since the variation from week to week wasn't excessive, he could average the output over the next month and plan his staffing levels accordingly. The amount of variation permissible is dependent on the amount of queue at the lathes and at the downstream work centers.

In this case, José has decided to work overtime for the weeks 9/3 through 9/17. In the week of 9/24, the labor overload is 15 hours (75 required, 60 available). This is more than can be made up with reasonable overtime, so José has decided to bring a new operator on board that week. Since this is only a one-shift operation, José can see from the summary report that he doesn't have enough machine capacity after 10/10. He'll need to put the new operator on the second shift.

As indicated by the required capacity data, José is not going to have enough work to keep this operator busy running two machines. By subtracting the 60 hours for the two first-shift operators from the required capacity, we can see that he only needs 15 additional labor hours in week 9/24, 23 hours in week 10/1, and 20 hours in week 10/8. Since the operator is capable of providing 30 standard hours of output per week, it is obvious that the new operator will be underutilized. What should José do? He can't hire part of an operator. In this case, José is aware that there is an overload situation in the deburr work center. He has decided that he will take some hand-deburr work from that work center and bring it to the lathe work center, where the operator can do that work when the lathe is on automatic cycle. When there is no scheduled work for the operator, José plans to send him to the deburr work center to help out there. That way he will get full utilization of the operator and, at the same time, solve the deburr overload problem.

PLANNING MULTIPLE RESOURCES

There are several instances in which a supervisor needs to plan multiple resources in a single work center. The situation above, where both machine and operator capacity must be planned, is the simplest case. Other situations involve multiple labor skills, labor pools, tooling, fixtures, and test equipment.

There are fundamentally three ways to handle these situations. First, if the second resource capacity is directly proportional to the machine capacity, as in the example above, the required capacity is calculated by multiplying the required machine capacity by a factor that defines the ratio between machine hours and the second resource hours. This factor is stored on the Work Center Master file in the database. In the case where the second resource is labor, it is sometimes called a crew factor. It represents the number of operators required per machine. In the example above, the factor is 0.5, or one operator per two machines. In other cases, the number may be greater than one, as with Mickey's Paint line. In this case, Mickey had two people loading the line and three people unloading it. The machine (line) capacity would be calculated, and then multiplied by five to arrive at the number of operator hours required.

The second situation is where different amounts of a resource are required to perform the operation rather than just multiples or fractions of the machine resource. For instance, operators of different skills may be required, such as a case when an operator, technician, and an inspector are required simultaneously. Another common situation in this category is the planning of tooling capacity in addition to the basic machine capacity. To plan these multiple resources requires that data for each required resource be included on the routing for the operation in question. Each resource would be given its own identifying resource number (i.e., work center). The software can then calculate the required amount of each resource needed and the schedule for when it is needed just as we did earlier for the machine capacity. The difference is that separate calculations are necessary for each resource. A separate capacity planning report is also necessary for each resource.

Brian had several fixtures that consumed a considerable amount of capacity. It was an ability he liked to have, so he went to the system analyst, Laura Sanderford, to see what could be done. "Listen, Laura, I'd like to know if we could add a second resource to the routing so I can plan my fixtures?" Brian asked.

"Just let me take a look first, and I'll let you know in a couple of days," she replied.

True to her word, Laura gave Brian a call two days later. "It's something we can do," she said, "but there's a problem. It's going to take a lot of programming. Are you sure this is something you really need to get the job done?" she asked.

Brian had been down this road before. There were always lots of things the computer could do, and they all required programming. This was another case when he had to make a decision regarding his priorities. He knew this one was far from being on the top of his list, especially after Laura explained to him what it would cost. As it would turn out, he could duplicate the tooling for less than the programming would cost.

The third multiple-resource situation involves those circumstances where operators are capable of running a variety of equipment, such as the use of labor pools or crews. The machine capacity must be calculated separately from the labor capacity since each needs to be planned independently. This involves the work center identification issue that was discussed in Chapter 2.

Brian saw an example of this when he went on the visit to Good Health. Hal took him to the packaging department, where he had five packaging lines, each capable of handling different package sizes and configurations. He only ran four of them at a time, because one line was usually being changed over to the next product by a separate setup crew. This meant he only needed four operating crews. However, he wanted to plan the line capacity separately from the operating crew and setup crew capacities to be sure that he didn't overload either the crews or any single line. Hal did this by assigning each packaging line its own work-center number, at the same time, tying all of them into an operating crew resource center number. He also assigned an operation number to the setup and assigned that to a setup resource center. Then, he modified his software to add up the operating capacity requirements from each line to get the total capacity requirements for the operating crew. He had separate capacity planning reports printed for the operating crew, the setup crew, and for each line.

This was actually a simple modification, and Brian found it could be very useful at Hayes. By having the system add up the standard hours by supervisor, the supervisor could see the total people required. This, in turn, would ensure that if several work centers only needed a partial operator, the supervisor wouldn't plan a full operator for them and thereby overplan the number of people required. We saw this in the example of José sharing a lathe operator with the burr bench. This does mean, however, that people need to be cross-trained. The capacity report can be beneficial in determining where people will need to be shifted from and where cross-training would be required. By adding another summary, then, Brian could see the total people requirements for his department.

INFINITE AND FINITE LOADING

To backtrack a bit, when we first generated the required capacity on the capacity report, we never took into consideration how much capacity we actually had. What we were doing is a process called infinite loading. The concept of infinite loading is to take everything that is scheduled and load it into the work center to an infinite level, without regard for available capacity. The problem with this approach is that work centers do not have infinite capacity.

An alternate concept is finite loading. (Note that finite *loading* is similar but in some ways different from *finite capacity scheduling* that will be explained in Chapter 6.) Finite loading is based upon the notion that we should put no more into the work center than it can be expected to produce. Although this may be exactly what we want to achieve, employing the finite loading process requires some understanding and caution. The finite loading process loads the work center in priority sequence up to a preestablished limit. If the scheduled load exceeds the limit in a given period, the computer automatically reschedules the operation to reduce the load.

The results of these two approaches are shown in Figure 4.17. In the top graph (infinite loading), the load is very erratic and exceeds the available capacity in several periods. Obviously, some action should to be taken to level this load and avoid the overload periods. The bottom graph represents what the load would look like after applying the finite loading technique. The load is level and doesn't exceed the available capacity in any period.

Although the finite-loading concept is valid, and the result appears excellent, there are some significant concerns with the approach. First, it assumes that capacities are fixed, which is often not

FIGURE 4.17 Infinite and Finite Loading Techniques: Comparison Graphs

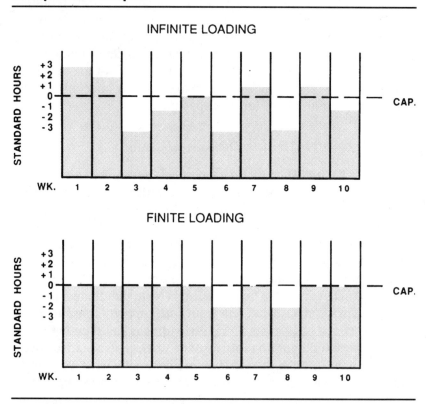

the case. Additional capacity can be gained by working overtime, adding people, adding a shift, or any number of other methods the managers of that area have learned to employ over the years.

Second, with finite loading the computer automatically reschedules the operation due dates, either in or out, whenever the stated load limit is exceeded. Moving the dates out results in the rescheduling of all downstream operation dates. This will invariably cause some of the other downstream work centers to become overloaded, and they, in turn, will need to be rescheduled. This massive rescheduling almost always results in the order due date being rescheduled to a future date. As this chain of events moves up through the bill of material, the master schedule ultimately will be impacted, causing customer deliveries to be missed. This could be devastating to a company.

Automatically rescheduling operations to earlier dates has the opposite effect of moving them out. Instead of going up through the bill of material, the rescheduling goes down. This results in many expedite messages in the Purchasing Department. Since suppliers are often manufacturing companies themselves, asking them to expedite is not always practical. Even if they were able to do it, trying to react to all the expedite messages would be virtually impossible. If rescheduling is to be done, we should have human involvement and not have this duty assumed automatically by the computer.

One of the biggest issues with finite loading is that, since it automatically reschedules capacity requirements, the supervisor is not able to see the actual future capacity required in order for a work center to support the needs of the master schedule. It only loads the shop to the bottleneck work center's capacity, leaving other work centers underloaded. To many, this may not seem like a problem. In reality, however, it is a problem since the non-bottlenecked resources are not being effectively utilized and that drives up operating costs. By temporarily getting more capacity for a bottleneck work center, the other work centers can operate at near full capacity. This not only reduces the cost of operating the facility, but it also allows more product to be shipped.

The greatest problem with the finite-loading technique, however, is that we allow the computer to make the decisions. When the computer makes the decisions for us, there is no accountability, which is the key to successful management.

The alternative to these approaches is Capacity Requirements Planning (CRP). The concept behind CRP, like finite loading, is to put no more into the work center than it can be expected to produce. The first step begins the same way as does infinite and finite loading; that is, to load the work center in priority sequence. However, rather than the computer automatically rescheduling overloads as in finite loading, management balances the planned capacity with the required capacity by changing the equipment availability, the work force, the tooling, working overtime, and so on. It can also be accomplished by changing the required capacity via alternate routings, subcontracting, or make-versus-buy decisions. Usually, rescheduling is only done as a last resort because the existing schedule reflects what is needed to meet the Master Production Schedule. Given a large number of capacity problems, the analysis required to level the load can be overpowering. Therefore, a technique is needed to assure that the capacity is in the ballpark prior to running Capacity Requirements Planning. As we will discuss in Chapter 7, this technique is called Rough-Cut Capacity Planning.

The difference between finite loading and CRP is people. People can consider all the various situations that might arise, such as the skill sets of the available operators, how the machines are running, or the quality of the material, and apply their knowledge and judgement to the situation. What happens when the overload is only slight? Can the order be split? Are there some ways to work around the problem? If there is no resolution and the master schedule must be changed, which item on the master schedule would have the least impact? It is best to have people make these decisions since people can be held accountable for making them and computers cannot. Whatever solution is finally chosen, someone must be accountable to assure it is executed.

Infinite loading is a bad name, because it implies infinite capacity. Obviously, that doesn't exist. Capacity Requirements Planning is a process of using the infinite load concept and using people to adjust the overloads and underloads so that it makes good sense for the company.

Capacity Requirement Planning is a very effective tool when capacity can be flexed (overtime, shift length, additional or fewer resources, etc.). However, in some situations, capacity cannot be flexed. The finite-loading technique is valid in those situations. The process of finite capacity scheduling will be discussed in Chapter 6.

Hayes had started using the dispatch list from their software package in July. They also started printing out the capacity plan. Brian got together with Joan from Production Control, his supervisor José, and his expeditor, Tony. Brian and Joan explained to José and Tony that their task would be to go through each work center and check the capacity report for any possible overloads. If there were no problems evident in a particular work center, they should skip over it. If they found a problem they could solve without the approval of Brian or Joan, they should go ahead and make the adjustments and advise them of what they had done. It would be José's responsibility to review the information with the second- and third-shift supervisors for their concurrence. They would meet every Tuesday at 2:00 P.M. to review the plans. If there was a problem that they did not have the authority to resolve, they should bring it up at the meeting for discussion. Brian and Joan then documented those things that José and Tony were not authorized to do: add a new employee, work overtime, start a new shift, subcontract work, or purchase capital equipment.

José and Tony went to work with the reports. They immediately found there was a three-week period where the operator capacity for the large Hobbs was overloaded. They had plenty of machine capacity but not enough people to run the equipment. José knew that he had some people in the shaper work center that had been cross-trained in the Hobbs work center as well. They looked at the shapers and the load there was fairly light. José figured they could safely move two of the operators from the shapers to the Hobbs and the problem would be solved. Fortunately, because of the operators' cross-training, moving from one work center to another did not present a problem.

Next they looked at the single-spindle drill and found there was only a slight overload for one week. As they scanned the report, they couldn't see any way to relieve the overload other than working overtime on a Saturday. They made a note of it for their meeting with Brian and Joan.

When Tony and José came to the horizontal broach, they found there was a large overload which they referred to as a "bow wave." What that meant was that the broach was constantly behind schedule, because by the time it would finish one job the next would already be late. They called it a "bow wave" because the stack of work resembled the wave pushed up in front of a large ship. This work center had been working two shifts with considerable overtime. It was apparent they would never get caught up just by working overtime. They concluded that they needed to add a third shift to maintain the load that was coming at them and also continue to work the overtime until the "bow wave" was gone. A quick calculation showed that would be in three weeks if they could get another operator for third shift immediately. Another work center to discuss with Brian and Joan at their meeting.

Moving on, they saw that a heavy load was going to hit the large turret lathe in six weeks. They looked at the detailed capacity report and found that they could actually split the job and reschedule part of it out into the future.

Their next decision would not be as easy. When they checked the capacity of the surface grinder, they found a huge overload 12 weeks out that extended through the full year's horizon. There was no possible way they could reschedule it. After some further consultation, it was decided that they were going to have to subcontract that work out. When they reviewed the N/C drills, they found the same situation as with the surface grinder—an overload through the full horizon with subcontracting appearing to be the only feasible solution.

Subcontracting, however, was only a temporary solution because it was expensive and significantly increased the lead time. Beyond those considerations, José and Tony knew that Brian would want to control his own destiny on these parts. The question was what to do? As José and Tony were mulling over this predicament, they flipped through the Capacity Requirements Planning reports. The answer dawned on them. What about the machines where there was excess capacity? Hayes management had learned that making parts just to keep machines busy was bad business. Not only were inventory carrying costs incurred, but also that practice resulted in valuable space being used to store parts that weren't needed. Perhaps even more wasteful when making parts that weren't needed right away was the risk of obsolescence due to engineering changes. As Tony and José scanned through the Capacity Requirements Planning reports, they found five machines in various work centers for which there was absolutely no foreseeable need. Why did this extra capacity exist? When Hayes had purchased some newer, faster machines, the old machines were kept around just in case they were needed. But they had not been used in months. Tony and José figured the best solution would be to trade the five excess machines for a used N/C drill and surface grinder. Tony and José made note of the problem and their suggested solution for their meeting with Brian and Joan.

On Tuesday at the conclusion of the capacity planning meeting, Brian and Joan were amazed at how fast Tony and José picked up on the process. In fact, they agreed with all of their recommendations. They quickly concluded that they needed to expand the process to the rest of the supervisors who work for Brian. The only problem Brian and Joan had with Tony and José's recommendations was their idea to trade the excess equipment for a used N/C drill and surface grinder. This was not something Brian or Joan had the authority to approve. That would take Ralph's approval.

When Brian approached Ralph, he was flabbergasted by the idea. "You can't do that!" he said, shaking his head from side to side.

"Why?" Brian asked, holding his ground.

"You just can't," Ralph said, not too convincingly. "I mean, it's never been done before."

Brian smiled as Ralph walked right into the position Brian had planned. "Don't you remember what you told me, Ralph? 'Cause it to happen.' If I get Elliot to go along with it, will you work on Sharon in Accounting?"

"How do you talk me into these things, Miller?" Ralph complained.

"Because you know I'm right or you're beginning to like me," Brian suggested with a grin.

"All right. You got your way," Ralph said with a laugh. "Now, get out of here."

It wasn't easy, but Brian pulled it off. Five old unneeded machines for two used, but nonetheless good, ones. "Not bad," Brian thought to himself, "and moving those five machines out has left me some open space. Maybe now's the time to get Elliot going on that rearrangement of equipment that he's been talking about." Brian laughed as he thought about Ralph. He decided it would probably be wise to hold off telling Ralph about that idea for the time being.

The point is that the capacity report itself didn't make the problems go away. Rather, it pointed directly to them and let management know, in advance, that there were problems that needed to be fixed.

After a capacity planning meeting, Tony, José, Joan, and Brian were talking in Brian's office. "You know," Tony said, "planning may be a lot more effective than expediting, but sometimes I miss the thrill of chasing a part through the shop and the satisfaction of getting it to Assembly. Now that we're working all these problems out early, expediting just isn't required. My job as expeditor has changed."

"You probably want a title like Capacity Planner now," Brian said.

Tony shrugged. "That might not be a bad idea. It just might send the right message to people."

Joan agreed. "Tony, I think you got something there."

"We probably should change the pay range, too," Brian said, giving Tony a wink.

"Thanks," growled Joan. Changing Tony's title was no problem. Getting a pay-range change was always a problem.

As we will see in Chapter 7, if Rough-Cut Capacity Planning has been done properly by senior management during the sales and operations planning process and at the master schedule level, major capacity constraints should have been dealt with already. When done properly, Rough-Cut Capacity Planning will level the capacity to the point that the majority of the capacity problems can be relatively easy to solve by the supervisor and the capacity planner.

MEETING THE CHALLENGE

At Hayes, after several months of diligently working with his supervisors and the capacity planners on capacity planning, Brian got a call from Ralph. Brian went up to Ralph's office as requested.

"I have to tell you, Brian, " Ralph said, taking a drink of coffee from his double-sized, "I'm-the-Boss" coffee mug, "I didn't think all this capacity planning you've been doing would work. I really didn't. But the reports have been a help in getting the right capacity at the right place at the right time. Your shortages are down and you're starting to show some real productivity improvements. Even Sharon and the rest of her cohorts in Accounting are pleased that a production manager seems concerned about costs. You were absolutely right about capacity planning." Brian couldn't help but smile. All his efforts were beginning to pay off. "Now all we have to do," Ralph added, turning his back on Brian to check a schedule on his desk, "is go to work on Dan and get him to do the same. And I want you to help him do that."

Brian was amazed at how fast his good feeling could evaporate. Getting his shop running well seemed like child's play compared with the assignment he'd just been handed. Then Ralph laughed. "Don't worry, Brian. I'll get Dan to listen. You just show him how to use the new system to plan his capacity."

A couple of days later, Brian had the perfect opportunity. Dan tracked him down and told Brian that they were going to install a new plasma burner, a project that would basically shut that area down for about two weeks. The capital request finally had been approved for the purchase of this new burner to replace the three old ones that were crammed into the shop.

"We have to take two of the old burners out first," Dan said, outlining the plan, "but I can leave the small single-torch burner down in the corner for emergencies. This means we'll only be able to do a small amount of burning for those two weeks. So, I'm going to need you to help me figure out how we can meet the schedule without subcontracting."

As it turned out, this wasn't such a difficult task. Brian, Dan, Joan, and the capacity and material planners all got together. They looked at the detailed capacity reports for the weeks when the changeover would take place. Taking the total hours for those two weeks, they found the work could be spread over the preceding three week period by adding people to the second shift, adding a temporary third shift now, working overtime, and rescheduling some jobs. They could build up stock in advance and just shut the burners down for two weeks.

Joan's planners used MRP to pull the planned orders forward and firm them. They made sure the material would be available by checking what was needed and rescheduling it to be delivered earlier. They checked the summary capacity plan and made sure the adjusted required capacity would be reasonably level in the periods prior to the planned shutdown of the burners. Of course, the capacity requirements during the two weeks of the shutdown were now zero and were reflected as such on the capacity report. With that accomplished, all that had to be done was for Dan to execute the plan.

When Dan saw how the capacity planning system helped him resolve this apparent dilemma, he was ready to begin in earnest to maintain the information required to support it. He now realized he could use these new tools to manage his department better. He even pledged to use the technique for reserving capacity that he had summarily rejected earlier.

RESPONSIBILITIES

Capacity management is not merely a computer exercise. It's true that in most environments capacity planning cannot be accomplished without a computer, but neither can it be done without good people who understand what it's all about and how to deal with the information produced by the computer. Also, capacity management cannot be performed by one isolated group. It takes teamwork and commitment.

The first consideration in analyzing a capacity requirements report is to ask the supervisor if he can meet the capacity plan. If the supervisor can, there's nothing further to do. If he can't, alternatives must be found. Can capacity be increased? Can alternate work centers be used? An option may be to subcontract that operation. The last option to be considered is to reschedule some of the workload. This does not mean all jobs are rescheduled, but only those selected jobs that will impact least on the master schedule. This is not handled automatically through the computer, but rather the production supervisor, capacity planner, and material planner select the jobs to be rescheduled, using the detailed capacity report from CRP and the material plans from MRP. The key to success is for the supervisors and the capacity planners to work together, bringing both their expertise and knowledge of their jobs to bear. No matter how helpful a computer can be, it cannot solve problems that require human judgment. It can supply information, but people need to make the decisions based on that information.

If the area supervisor and capacity planner can't get the capacity required, it's the capacity planner's responsibility to notify the material planner. The capacity planner and the material planner must then work together to try and reschedule the components. If they can't, it's the material planner's responsibility to notify the master scheduler of the capacity constraint and the inability to reschedule the components to satisfy the master schedule requirements. A customer reschedule may be required, which should involve the Sales Department. If the problem is of such magnitude that the Production Plan can't be supported, top management is going to have to review the Production Plan. Obviously, middle-management people will also be involved in this process every step of the way. Fortunately, if the entire capacity planning process is followed, the need to change the Master Production Schedule is very infrequent, and changing the Production Plan is almost unheard of.

A capacity planning meeting should be held every week to review the capacity plans and to begin any corrective actions that may be required. This meeting should include the production supervisors and capacity planners. Attendance by the material planners may also be helpful in some situations. A common mistake made by some companies is to focus attention only on the near term. It is important to review the entire planning horizon at least monthly and recognize potential problems in advance. This will give people plenty of time to resolve any constraint.

Brian was pleased with the job they had done implementing capacity planning. It provided him with the ability to see the capacity required to meet the latest Production Plan, Master Production Schedule, and Material Requirements Plans by work center and time period for a full year. With this future vision, he no longer had to check work-order boxes to know he needed more capacity. Nor did he have to wait until the work in a work center dried up to know he needed less capacity. Brian had the information he needed to take corrective action, to balance the planned capacity with the required capacity. He knew that capacity planning required accountability, and he saw to it that he stepped up to his responsibility—the planned capacity. The capacity planner was also required to meet his responsibility—the required capacity. If a major change took place that would alter his capacity requirements, Brian could always have the capacity planner run the capacity plan in the middle of the week. It didn't take Brian long to realize that with the right tools and the right management, it is indeed possible to get the right job done on time and still be very productive.

Although Brian felt good about what they had accomplished with capacity planning, he was concerned about a couple of work centers where the ability to flex capacity was limited. He knew he needed to schedule those work centers differently. Brian will learn how to handle this situation in Chapter 6.

Chapter Five

Controlling the Flow of Work

Brian could see that things were getting better at Hayes. With dispatch lists communicating valid priorities and Capacity Requirements Planning (CRP) letting him know what his capacity needs were going to be, the shop had never run better. That didn't mean that things were great, but they were definitely improved. Brian could actually afford the luxury of finishing a morning cup of coffee in his office before hitting the floor. It was a small sign, but there was a time when it would have been impossible for him to have even considered it.

However, the luxury of a morning cup of coffee did not a well-run shop make. There were still problems that needed to be addressed. Brian's coworkers, Dan and Mickey, had to agree that some of this "new stuff" had made their lives easier. Dan was starting to come around, fully embracing the use of the dispatch list and Capacity Requirements Planning. In fact, he now swore by it. Of course, Dan tended to swear about everything. The one thing that Dan did resist was when Ralph, the Production Manager, tried to get him to use the Input/Output (I/O) report.

The Input/Output report was a part of the software that Hayes had purchased. Brian had started using the report at the same time he started using Capacity Requirements Planning. This report monitors the total amount of work that moves into a particular work center and how much output is produced by that work center. The report is comprised of information regarding planned and actual input, planned and actual output, and planned and actual queue levels. All the data are expressed in standard hours. The focus of this report is on the performance of the work center against the capacity plan week by week. It also provides a convenient means of monitoring the actual queue against the plan.

The ideal situation would be to have a smooth workflow into a work center and a similarly steady output. However, things are rarely ideal. In the typical job shop or "batch" environment, rather than continually moving a few pieces at a time, work usually moves from work center to work center in larger batches because of lot sizing. Breakdowns and delays in the feeding work centers often interrupt the input process. Similar delays and interruptions in the producing work center makes the output anything but smooth.

Production areas usually establish queues in their work centers as a buffer against such interruptions and variances. Some supervisors believe that having lots of work in queue will enable them to increase the productivity of their work center. The assumption is, at this point, that it is expected and, in fact, desirable to have some queue in the work center. (The reduction of queues and the impact on Input/Output control will be discussed later in this chapter.)

A common misunderstanding regarding Input/Output control is that the output should always be kept equal to the input. Although the intent is to keep the incoming and outgoing work in sync, there are circumstances where they will not be equal. Normal day-to-day fluctuations mean that sometimes the input is higher than the output and sometimes it is lower. Of course, we do not expect such fluctuations to be very big. There are other circumstances that call for the input to be different from the output by design. For instance, if the work center has gotten behind schedule, and the queue has built up, it needs to be brought back in line with the objective level. Or if the queue level has fallen below an acceptable level, it needs to be brought back up. In either case, the only way to bring about an adjustment in queue level is to make the input different from the output, either more or less as the case may be. The objective of Input/Output control is to keep actual input, output, and queue equal to their respective planned levels. This is the essence of control. It is when we deviate from the plan that we get into trouble.

The Input/Output report contains the information to support this control (see Figure 5.1). The report should display the recent-past performance against the previous plan. The latest 4-week period is recommended. The report should also display the planned input, output, and queue levels for the short-term future. Some companies

FIGURE 5.1 Input/Output Control Report

| WORK CENTER NO: 24 | DATE: 9/03 |
| DESCRIPTION: LATHES | DEPARTMENT: M |

WEEK	8/06	8/13	8/20	8/27	9/03	9/10	9/17	9/24

INPUT

	8/06	8/13	8/20	8/27	9/03	9/10	9/17	9/24
PLANNED IN	128	118	116	126	130	144	140	150
ACTUAL IN	108	98	124	142				
CUM. DEV.	-20	-40	-32	-16				

OUTPUT

	8/06	8/13	8/20	8/27	9/03	9/10	9/17	9/24
PLANNED OUT	120	120	120	120	132	132	132	180
ACTUAL OUT	110	120	100	90				
CUM. DEV.	-10	-10	-30	-60				

QUEUE

	8/06	8/13	8/20	8/27	9/03	9/10	9/17	9/24
PLANNED Q	50	48	44	50	48	60	68	38
ACTUAL Q	40	18	42	94				
DEV.	-10	-30	-2	44				

TOLERANCE: ± 25 HOURS   **DESIRED Q: 50 HOURS**

prefer to show only a couple of weeks each way, while others want as much as 12 weeks. The right amount varies by work center, but it must give enough visibility to indicate a trend without becoming overburdened with data.

Planned input is the input into a work center that is required to meet the production schedule (which is derived from the master schedule) and maintain the planned queue within a predetermined tolerance. The data for the planned input comes directly from the capacity plan and is the same as the required capacity for the work center as found in the capacity plan (see Figure 5.2).

The rationale is that if the work center is to be able to meet the capacity plan, work must be fed to each work center in accordance with its scheduled output (planned capacity) unless an adjustment in the queue level is desired. If the actual queue is lower than necessary to support efficient work-center operation, the input would have to be temporarily increased beyond the scheduled output or the scheduled output decreased to build the queue to its desired level. Conversely, if we want to reduce the queue, the input would be decreased or the output increased. If no adjustment of input is necessary to increase or decrease the queue, the required capacity numbers from the capacity report can be loaded directly into the Input/Output report. Some people prefer to smooth the planned input by averaging the data from the capacity planning report over a four- to eight-week period. A note of caution is in order here. This is not acceptable in companies where the philosophies of Lean Manufacturing/Just-In-Time are bringing about significant reduction in queues (see Chapter 9).

As the queues get smaller, so does the cushion for meeting the schedule. If the supervisor is going to meet the schedule, he is going to have to produce what the schedule calls for every week or every day. Averaging capacity requirements might actually shift some load to a following week, a result which is totally unacceptable from a scheduling perspective. As a company moves closer to the ultimate goal of zero queues, daily capacities must be planned and monitored. (For further reference, please refer to the capacity bucketing rules in Chapter 4.)

Actual input is the work that has physically been received by the work center. It is equal to the pieces moved multiplied by the standard hours per piece for the operations to be performed. The actual input is then compared with the planned input. The cumulative de-

FIGURE 5.2 Summary Capacity Plan

DATE: 8/06	NO. MACH.: 5	HOURS/SHIFT: 8
WORK CENTER: 24	NO. OPER.: 2	SHIFTS/DAY: 1
DESCRIPTION: LATHES	MACH./OPER.: 2	DAYS/WEEK: 5
DEMO. CAP'Y.: 120	MAX. CAP'Y.: 336	LOAD FACTOR: 75%

MACHINE CAPACITY

WEEK	REQ'D CAP'Y. (HRS.)	PLAN CAP'Y. (HRS.)	LOAD VS. CAPACITY (%) 50 100 150
8/06	128	150	XXXXXXX
8/13	118	150	XXXXXX
8/20	116	150	XXXXX
8/27	126	150	XXXXXXX
9/03	130	150	XXXXXXX
9/10	144	150	XXXXXXXX
9/17	140	150	XXXXXXXX
9/24	150	150	XXXXXXXXX
10/01	166	150	XXXXXXXXXXX
10/08	160	150	XXXXXXXXXX

LABOR CAPACITY

REQ'D CAP'Y. (HRS.)	PLAN CAP'Y. (HRS.)	LOAD VS. CAPACITY (%) 50 100 150
64	60	XXXXXXXXXX
59	60	XXXXXXXXX
58	60	XXXXXXXX
63	60	XXXXXXXXX
65	60	XXXXXXXXX
72	60	XXXXXXXXXXXX
70	60	XXXXXXXXXXX
75	90	XXXXXXX
83	90	XXXXXXXX
80	90	XXXXXXXX

7/28 →

viation (CUM. DEV.) line on the I/O report monitors the variance between what was planned and what actually arrived in the work center. Since the actual will seldom be exactly equal to the plan because of normal fluctuations in work flow, a tolerance should be established to trigger any corrective action that is necessary to maintain the planned input. The input line measures the performance of the feeding work centers. In the case of a late job release or a material shortage, the input line measures the performance of another department, not this one. It is the capacity planner's responsibility to determine the cause and initiate corrective action.

There is no single right answer as to what the tolerance should be. Some companies use a portion of a day's worth of work, such as 75 percent. Others use a percentage of the planned queue level. The way to establish tolerance is to get the supervisor and capacity planner together and work it out. A number will need to be negotiated that is mutually acceptable. The number may also change over time as circumstances change.

The second part of the Input/Output report is also divided into planned and actual data. The planned output is what the supervisor has agreed to produce in order to meet the capacity plan and maintain the planned queue within the previously agreed upon tolerance (see Figure 5.1). Again, this tolerance is used to trigger any necessary corrective action. The planned output should be equal to the planned capacity from CRP. Short-term adjustments in output may be required to change the actual queue or to accommodate week-to-week fluctuations. When this is the case, the planned output on the capacity requirements report should be altered to reflect what the expected output is going to be.

The actual output is the work that has actually been completed by the work center. In capacity terms, the actual output is the demonstrated capacity. It is calculated by multiplying the pieces completed by the standard hours per piece. Again, it is measured against the established tolerances of the planned output. Monitoring output in this manner is a measurement of the work center's performance against the previous commitment by the production supervisor during the capacity planning meeting.

The third section of the report monitors the queue level. The planned queue is the result of the planned input and planned output. It is computed by taking the beginning actual queue and adding the planned input, then subtracting the planned output period by period. The actual queue is calculated in similar fashion by starting with the beginning actual queue, adding the actual input, and subtracting the actual output period by period.

Figure 5.1 shows how this report was implemented at Hayes. During the week of 8/6, José, the work-center supervisor and Tony, the capacity planner, got together to review the CRP and Input/Output reports. Since this was the first time they had run the reports, there was no past history displayed. The planned-input data on the I/O report came directly from the machine-required-capacity column of the Summary Capacity Plan. The planned-output line came from José after looking at the planned capacity from the labor side of the Summary Capacity Plan, which told him the amount of hours the machine would have operators present. He then multiplied that by two (because one operator was running two machines) to give him the total standard machine hours work center 24 was expected to produce. The resulting 120 hours was José's commitment. The Input/Output report was simply a reflection of the summary capacity plan.

Next they reviewed the queue levels.

Work center 24's planned queue was two days (see Figure 3.5 in Chapter 3). Since the planned output is approximately 25 hours per day, the desired queue was 50 hours (see "desired Q" in lower-right corner of Figure 5.1). The actual beginning queue from the previous Friday was 42 hours.

José and Tony understood that normal everyday occurrences would cause variations in the actual input and output. They agreed that there was no cause for concern unless the cumulative deviation from the plan exceeded plus or minus 25 hours. By doing so, they set their tolerance at plus or minus 25 hours.

They computed the planned queue across the eight-week horizon and compared it against the desired queue. They found that the queue would end up way out of tolerance if they didn't make a correction in the first weeks of September. José agreed to work one shift on each Saturday for the weeks of 9/3, 9/10, and 9/17. This raised the output to 132 standard hours for each of those weeks. Since this adjustment would bring the queue back in tolerance, they approved the plan.

The following week, 8/13, Tony and José again sat down to review the Input/Output report. The planned input for the week of 8/6 was 128 standard hours. The actual input was 108 standard hours, which produced a cumulative deviation of minus 20. Since this was within tolerance, no action was necessary. The actual output of 110 for 8/6 was only 10 hours short of the plan, so no corrective action was required on the output side either. The next week, 8/13, however, the planned input was for 118 standard hours, but only 98 actually arrived. This pushed the cumulative deviation to minus 40 standard hours, exceeding the tolerance. This triggered action by Tony. José added emphasis by saying that, although he didn't run out of work, he was worried about the future because the actual queue was now only 18 hours.

By examining the previous operation's Input/Output reports, Tony found out that the saws had not met their planned output. When Tony spoke with Dan's supervisor in the saw department, he learned that the reason that the input fell below the tolerance was a quality problem with the raw material. He called the material planner. She told him that Purchasing was having some new material shipped in right away. Dan had already instructed the saw department to work overtime when the material came in and to get it to the lathes as soon as possible.

The next week when they reviewed the Input/Output report the actual input to the lathes for week 8/20 was 124 hours versus a plan of 116. This was a result of the action taken by Tony, Dan, and Purchasing. Eight of the delinquent 40 hours were made up. It was still below tolerance, however, and Tony told José he would stay on top of things until the input got back within tolerance.

Tony, meanwhile, produced 100 hours in week of 8/20, 20 hours below plan and 30 hours cumulative deviation. José and Tony didn't get too excited about it, even though it was outside of the tolerance. They thought that as long as the actual queue for that week—42 hours—was within tolerance, they had things under control. In the week of 8/27, true to his word, Tony had kept on top of the input problem and the actual input was 142 hours, bringing it back within tolerance. Things were different for José. One of José's operators was out sick for two days, and he didn't have anyone to fill in. By the end of the week, he was 30 hours short of his plan for the week and minus 60 hours cumulative deviation. The actual queue was a whopping 94 hours. Tony had been doing a good job getting the input within tolerance. Now José was going to have to pull out all the stops to get his output caught up.

José had also become painfully aware that the dispatch list was showing the same problem. He was falling way behind schedule. When he was running about 25 hours behind on the output report, the dispatch list was showing some of that, but the downstream work centers were making up the difference by not allowing the work to sit in queue. With this large amount of past-due work, they were unable to make up the time. It was then up to Tony and José to figure out when the work would actually be completed, so they could communicate that to the material planner.

José suddenly recognized the importance of keeping his output close to the plan, regardless of what the input did. He knew he had to do his part and rely on others to do theirs. He was also thankful that he had this new report. It showed him exactly what his status was and gave him some good data to help him plan his corrective action. He also knew that the report had been a big help to Tony in his endeavors to get the incoming work on schedule.

Now, why would Dan have any objections to using a report like this? When Ralph asked him why, he replied, "Because it's garbage, that's why. These reports," Dan said, pointing down at the pile of sheets before him, "are reporting movement of material that never arrives. What good is that to me?"

Ralph pointed out to Dan that the shop movement transactions that fed the Input/Output report were also used to update his dispatch list and capacity requirements plans. If the data on the Input/Output report were unreliable, so was the dispatch list. If Dan had really been using his dispatch list properly, he would have seen that there was work indicated as being in the work centers that wasn't really there, and he should have questioned it. As it would turn out, the source of the problem was in Dan's own department. It was his people's move transactions that had created the inaccurate reports. It was later brought to Dan's attention that an inspection operation was missing from several of the routings. When the previous operation was reported as completed, the software system indicated that the work had been moved to Dan's work centers as indicated on the routing. The material handlers had in fact moved the jobs to inspection as was necessary. So when the Input/Output report said the work was in Dan's department, it was really in inspection. Had Dan's supervisors used the Input/Output reports properly, they could have immediately tracked down the problem and eliminated it. It was also clear that these work centers were not using the dispatch list as they should have. Had they been using it correctly, the problems would have been seen, because the status column on the reports would have been incorrect. Instead, Dan ignored it, and tried to pawn it off as a Production Control problem.

When this was pointed out to Dan, he threw up his arms. Not known for his even temper, he blurted out what would surface as the real reason behind his dislike of the Input/Output report. "You know, there's another thing about that report. It's like I've got a bunch of spies hanging around my department." Suddenly, it dawned on Ralph what the problem was: Dan didn't like being held accountable for the work he had committed to produce, so he reverted back to the old behavior of shifting the blame onto Production Control and discrediting the report.

Manufacturing Resource Planning, when operated properly, clearly identifies the problems and people who are accountable for them. The Input/Output report makes people accountable for what they say they will do. It also provides a valuable control on the process. Brian had heard from Hal at Good Health Vitamins about an episode that had taken place in his factory. Like Hayes, Hal's factory had just gone through the process of implementing Manufacturing Resource Planning (MRP) and they were generating dispatch lists and capacity reports. One day, Hal got a call from the packaging department supervisor about a problem that had surfaced.

The supervisor was using the capacity plan to plan her people levels, but she had to work overtime to get the work out. "Something isn't right," she said. She showed Hal the I/O report, pointing out that a lot more work was coming into the work center than was planned. The incoming work was also more than what was required according to the capacity plan.

Upon further investigation, they found that because there was a relatively short lead-time process involved in packaging, the master scheduler was taking emergency orders from customers within the same week that the product had to be shipped. The material planner was just loading the orders into the system on top of what was already scheduled. The capacity plan, which was run only once a week, never showed the additional work, because it was in and out so fast.

The supervisor, however, saw the orders on the dispatch list. Consequently, to get everything done, she ended up working Saturdays on an ongoing basis. The good news was that everything was getting done. The bad news was that the supervisor had to work her crew every Saturday but didn't have the information in time to plan for it in advance.

The Input/Output report helped them to quickly identify the problem. They realized they had two options. They could say "no" to the customers, which was not something they particularly wanted to do. Their second choice was to anticipate that customers would order inside of lead-time and plan for it in the master schedule. This would increase the required capacity via Capacity Requirements Planning and allow the supervisor to plan to have the additional capacity available. This is the reserved capacity issue discussed in Chapter 4. The risk was that the supervisor would have people with nothing to do if the orders did not come in.

The message here is that with an Input/Output report, a supervisor can be held accountable for meeting the committed output that was agreed upon via capacity planning. It gives the supervisor the ability to monitor performance against the plan. If what was supposed to arrive in the work center is either greater or less than what was expected, the capacity planner is accountable for initiating corrective action.

Unfortunately for Brian and his colleagues at Hayes, this was a lesson they had to learn the hard way. The problem arose shortly after they replaced the three old burners. As mentioned in Chapter 4, Hayes was going to need two weeks to finish the job of installing the new burner. And, without a great deal of trouble, Dan, Joan, and Brian, together with the material and capacity planners, had worked out a plan to cover their future capacity requirements for the weeks that the burners would be out of service.

Everything went according to plan. When it came time to shut down the old burners, Dan and his crew had met their schedule. Maintenance had asked for two days to tear out the old burners, three days to install the new one, and a five-day learning curve to bring the new one up to full production. It all started smoothly. In fact, they started using the new burner earlier than they had anticipated.

Then, problems started to surface. The machine wasn't coming up to the expected output level because of problems with the Numerically Controlled (N/C) programming. Two weeks after it was installed, the cumulative actual output was below the agreed-upon level and outside the tolerance. Three weeks later it was further outside the tolerance. Roy, the Materials Manager, scheduled a meeting in Ralph's office. Dan was there, as was Joan. The discussion centered on the I/O report, which showed the low output and a large queue. Joan was the first to speak. "Roy, we're going to have to subcontract this work until they figure out how to get the programming right, or we're going to be in real trouble."

"I don't want to subcontract," Roy said. "The cost difference will be too much, and since the subcontractor won't use our material, it's going to cause our inventories to rise. If that happens, Pete will have us strung up. Dan, you and Elliot have to get out there and get that blasted burner working."

Everyone agreed not to subcontract the work. Roy, Pete, and Joan felt good about the plan of action, but Dan and Elliot were concerned because they weren't sure that they could fix the problem.

The following week, Ralph, Dan, and Pete descended upon Roy's office. Joan happened to see them going in and could tell by the red color of both Pete and Ralph's bald heads that they weren't happy campers. Dan was surprisingly laid back.

"Gentlemen," Roy said, the calm before the storm, "what seems to be the problem?"

Ralph, with his customary brashness, said, "There's no work for the welders. You haven't released any work orders for them and now we're going to have to send people home."

Pete stepped forward, trying his best to maintain his calm, only to be betrayed by his beet-red head. "Why aren't you releasing the work orders?" Roy, of course, had no idea, but suggested they go check it out with Carl, the planner. As they went by Joan's office, she decided to tag along and see what all the ruckus was about.

As they arrived at Carl's desk, Roy asked, "Carl, are you not releasing work orders to the welding shop?" Roy was afraid of the answer to follow.

"That's right."

"Why, Carl?" Roy was feeling the back of his neck begin to burn from the trio of fire-breathing dragons behind him.

"Well, I'm supposed to review each work order to see if the components are in inventory before I release it, and if the components aren't there, I shouldn't release the work orders, right?"

Roy nodded. "That's right, isn't it, Dan?"

"Absolutely!" came Dan's reply. "I don't want you sending me jobs without all the parts." Dan's voice echoed off the walls of the room, and the other material planners in the room cringed.

Joan stepped in. "Why aren't there any components, Carl?"

Carl pulled up an order on his computer screen. "Well, this first job is missing part numbers 136469, 192423, and 182630, and this job is missing part number 173268, and this job is missing. . . ."

"Hold it. Hold it. Where are those parts?" Joan asked.

Carl switched to the open order status screen and looked up part number 136469. "It's at the burner," Carl said, showing Joan the location. Then, looking up all the other numbers, he summarized, "They're all at the burner."

Pete just about went through the ceiling. He immediately called Ralph, Dan, and Elliot into his office. The meeting was not quiet.

When they exited Pete's office, Ralph was immediately on the phone to get a technician flown in from the manufacturer to show Hayes's numerical-control programmers how to correct the problem.

Joan, Dan, and the production supervisors had been monitoring activity with the Input/Output reports, and they had seen this problem developing. The reports showed that the output from the burner was lagging behind the plan, and there was a steady buildup of queue in the work center. At the same time, the report for the welding work center showed that the input was below plan and their queue was approaching a dangerously low level. Seeing the evidence of a problem and taking action to fix it are two different things. By observing these trends, they should have been able to do something before the situation reached the critical stage. Since they hadn't initiated the corrective action in a timely manner, they ended up sending the whole shift of welders home on Thursday and Friday. Then they had to call them back on Saturday and Sunday because the technician had easily solved the problem and had the burner running at near full capacity in a matter of hours. The moral of this situation is that you can't just plan and measure, you must also take the appropriate action.

ESTABLISHING QUEUES

One important factor in the proper use of the Input/Output report is in establishing realistic queue levels. The queue level is the total amount of work, expressed in standard hours, that is physically in the work center, waiting to be worked on at any given time. Although there may be some pieces running on the machine, most software leaves these pieces in queue until they are reported completed. The other jobs that have not been started are also in queue.

Since queues have a significant impact on throughput time in the work center and the work-in-process inventory levels, the queue levels should be as small as possible, and a plan should be in place to continuously reduce them. This raises a couple of questions. How much queue is appropriate? Which work centers should have queue and which shouldn't? The reality is it's going to be difficult to come to a complete agreement on these questions.

Invariably, production people want a lot of queue. It gives them flexibility. It also relieves the Mother Hubbard's cupboard syndrome. No supervisor wants to go to the cupboard and find the cupboard bare. Queue acts as a cushion just in case something goes wrong.

On the other hand, the smaller the queue in the work centers, the faster the throughput and the lower the work-in-process inventory. Short throughput time gives the company the flexibility to respond quickly to customer demands. The practice of having large work-in-process inventories in the hopes of maintaining maximum flexibility is outdated: The most flexible companies are those that can produce products in extremely short lead times. There is really no standard answer to where and how much queue a work center or department needs. It varies from work center to work center and from plant environment to plant environment. But it should be repeated that the ultimate goal is to get queues down as low as possible. This topic will be discussed further in Chapter 9.

To settle the issue, it must be understood why there are queues in the first place. The purpose of queue is to uncouple operations from one another, so that the work centers aren't negatively impacted by variations in the rate of incoming work. In determining how much queue is desirable, several things must be considered. Capacity is like time; it can't be stored. If it's not used, it's lost. If a machine typically has a full load, it is not desirable for it to run out of work. So in order to prevent interruptions of production due to delays in incoming work, there should be queue in front of it. Common practice is to have queues in front of bottleneck equipment to avoid shutting it down.

Another area that typically has queues is equipment that has little or no rescheduling capability. If there are constraints on the ability to offload work to alternate work centers—including outside subcontracting—queues are put in place to avoid losing capacity. Equipment, however, isn't the only consideration. If high labor skills are involved, there is a good chance a capacity constraint exists. Operations such as these would be candidates for queue.

Those are some of the considerations for establishing queues. But who decides how much queue? The people involved in this decision are the production supervisors, capacity planners, and material planners. Production is involved because of the objectives that they must meet on the shop floor, including productivity and schedule attainment. The material planners have to have input because of the impact that queue has on lead time and work-in-process inventories. Each of these parties has their own objectives regarding the amount of desirable queue. The capacity planner's role is to view the issue from both sides and to draw consensus on what is best for the company as a whole.

When Brian, Dan, and Joan sat down to establish the desired queue levels with their supervisors and planners, Brian and his production partners had a lot of good reasons why they wanted more queue. They all felt it improved their productivity. Dan was particularly adamant about having queue because it helped avoid delays when suppliers or feeding work centers didn't deliver on time. He also wanted queue because of potential tooling delays and material shortages. They all believed that queues were motivational for the labor staff, offering a sense of job security. Queue protected them against the loss of capacity that resulted from machine breakdowns upstream and against part shortages. It gave them the flexibility to combine setups, thus reducing changeover time. It offered a buffer against variation in the workflow. There seemed to be no end to the list.

What they didn't want to accept was that queues are a cover-up for the real problems that face production. An argument in favor of queue says, "I believe the input will be interrupted, so instead of fixing the problem, I'll have some extra work here just in case." For each and every one of the reasons this group offered for needing queues, there was a solution to the problem that would eliminate the need for queue. This is not to imply that these alternative approaches are easier to accomplish than adding more queue, but they will be more productive and better for the company in the long run.

It would be helpful to take a closer look at the reasons that the Hayes staff gave for needing queue and some alternate approaches.

1. Queues equal job security.

The effect that a light workload has on productivity is that things just slow down. One way to handle this is to routinely share the information on the dispatch lists and capacity plans with the work force. If they understand it, they will know how much work is ahead of them without needing to see it there in queue. Of course, they must develop confidence in the information and that the work will really be there as scheduled.

2. Queue is valuable to fall back on when suppliers or feeding work centers don't deliver on time.

Wouldn't solving the problems that cause these delays be a better solution? If the feeding work centers use capacity plans, dispatch lists, and I/O reports effectively, and if they solve their quality and machine breakdown problems, their on-time completion to schedule is going to improve dramatically. The technique of Supplier Scheduling has also proven helpful in getting suppliers to deliver on time. When the feeding work centers and suppliers deliver on time, the need for the queue "buffer" is diminished.

3. Queue protects against delays from tooling availability problems.

Using better planning and scheduling techniques for the tooling can avoid these delays. Many companies put tooling on their bills of material and routings, thus enabling them to schedule tooling availability in concert with the shop orders on which they will be used (see Chapter 8).

4. Queues protect against upstream equipment breakdown.

Implementing good preventive maintenance programs in all work centers can minimize interruption of incoming workflow because of breakdowns in equipment upstream.

5. Queues offer protection from parts shortages.

Our old nemesis, parts shortages. One of the primary goals of Manufacturing Resource Planning is the elimination of parts shortages because of better scheduling and planning. If we are able to do a good job with Material Requirements Planning, Capacity Requirements Planning, Input/Output, and the rest of the tools, we won't experience the parts shortages.

6. Queues allow for combining setups.

Practically every production supervisor in the world tries to save setup time by combining jobs with similar setups. But rather than just accept setup times as they are and juggle the schedule around, it is better to reduce the setup times so they are not a problem. There are techniques that can radically reduce setup times. One such technique is the Single Minute Exchange of Die (SMED)[1] approach. Such reductions eliminate the need to resequence work to combine setups. Grouping parts in the schedule with similar setups will reduce the need for queue. The planners/capacity planners should do this, but it is a cumbersome process whenever multiple operations are involved.

7. Queues allow time for maintenance to be performed in the feeding work centers without interrupting production downstream.

Maintenance operations can be scheduled using the Material Requirements Planning system to schedule the work in the same manner as a production part. That work will also be loaded into the capacity planning system where it can be analyzed and rescheduled if necessary because of a capacity constraint. The dispatch list will reflect the preventive maintenance work, as in any other job. In fact, instead of Brian trying to push maintenance work into the future because it always seems to be scheduled in an overload period, Brian would now be insisting that Maintenance do the work in the scheduled period because the capacity has been reserved (see Chapter 4).

The point is that rather than accepting the need for queue, it is entirely possible to eliminate it. The money saved from the lower work-in-process inventories can be used to solve the problems that create the need for queue.

ADVANTAGES OF QUEUE REDUCTION

The reality is that there are far more significant advantages to reducing queues than there are to sustaining them!

One of the greatest advantages in reducing queues is the reduction in lead times. When the need for queue in a work center is reduced, the planned queue for the work center should be reduced in the database. When that happens, the back-scheduling logic will reschedule the operation start and due dates out into the future by the amount of time that the queue was reduced. If we look at the two examples in Figure 5.3, we can see that by reducing the queue at operation 10 by four days, the start date for operation 5 changes from M-day 90 to M-day 94. By also reducing the queue at operation 5 by four days, the order release date will be moved from M-day 82 to M-day 90. The impact is that no work will be released for eight M-days. If the work center were eight days behind schedule, reducing the queue by eight days would stop the release of work for eight days allowing the work center to get back on schedule. Caution needs to be exercised here to be sure that any queue that is removed is really excess and that everyone realizes the cushion has been removed and the dates are realistic and have to be met. Reducing queue also reduces work-in-process inventory and factory-space requirements, because there is less material out on the floor. We can reduce the rework quantity resulting from defective upstream operations since there is less defective material in the pipeline. And we reduce damage to work-in-process because there is less inventory sitting around the shop floor to be bumped into, knocked over, rusted, or spoiled. We also need less material handling and storage equipment.

In spite of all these advantages, it is still difficult for production supervisors and material planners to find agreement on establishing

FIGURE 5.3 Impact of Queue Reduction on Lead Time

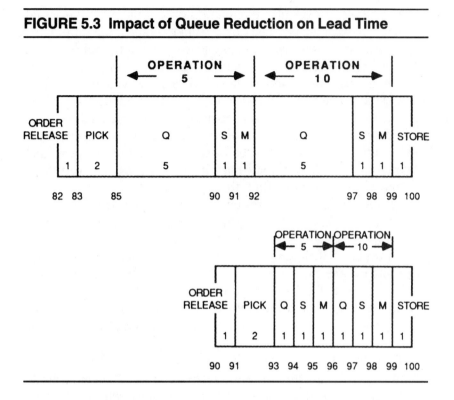

planned queues. And typically, there is no concentrated effort to reduce queues.

The goal is to get the actual queue as small as possible, without losing capacity or productivity or missing schedule. A queue-reduction program starts by collecting information. We need to know what the current actual queue is. How much material is actually out on the floor? That information can be obtained from the Input/Output report or from the dispatch list. We also must know what the current planned queue is. This is the figure that has been loaded into the computer by the capacity planners that we used in the back-scheduling exercise. We also need to generate a list of problems that people believe are the reasons that queues are necessary.

For Brian, this meant talking to each of his supervisors and asking, "Why do you need this much queue here?" and recording the answers.

The next step of the queue reduction process is to get the actual queue in line with the planned queue. If in looking at the Input/Output report, we see that the planned queue is 70, but the actual queue is 100, we know there's 30 hours more work in the work center than there should be. This excess workload will also be evident on the dispatch list and will likely be past-due work. That queue needs to be worked off unless an immediate reduction in the planned queue is reasonable. If it is, simply reducing the planned queue is all that is required. If not, the queue must be worked off. That means overtime, subcontracting, using alternate machines—anything and everything the supervisor can do to reduce the workload.

Once the actual queue is brought down to the planned queue level, the production supervisor and planner should review the list of reasons for queue and prioritize them. We suggest working on the problems in order of their simplicity when trying to solve them. Don't tackle the toughest one first. It is often possible to get as much reduction in queue from solving a lot of little problems as it is from solving one big one, and it usually won't take as long. It is important to show some quick benefits from the process to build enthusiasm and commitment to the process.

Brian's department decided that since a preventive maintenance program was already underway at Hayes, they would focus their attention on that issue in each work center. A short while later, José came into his office. "We've got the preventive maintenance program set up on the 2ACs and I'm willing to part with one day of queue on the Hobbs."

"Good work. Just think of eliminating that queue as an old friend who's moved away," Brian said, with his tongue planted in his cheek.

"Right, like quitting smoking," José said, "only without the weight gain."

Brian called Joan and asked her to have the planners remove a day of planned queue from the database for the Hobbs. This has to be done carefully. When a day of planned queue is removed, it means that the lead time has also been reduced by a day. Therefore, all the orders that are supposed to go through that work center will be rescheduled. The software, utilizing its backward-scheduling logic, will reschedule the orders to be released one day later than before.

Oliver Wight, known for his ability to explain complex concepts in simplified terms, compared work flowing through a work center to water flowing through a funnel. Using Ollie's analogy, the release of work has been continuous, like water running out of a valve (see Figure 5.4). The work flows into the work center where it is stored in queue, like water in the funnel, until it is worked on and moved out of the work center. Now, for one day, we are shutting off that valve for all orders that are routed to that work center. That won't create a problem if we have more than one day of queue in the work center. At the end of the day, the work center will have produced one day's worth of output, while receiving no input. This reduces the actual queue by one day. Then, the input of work is resumed, which allows the work center to maintain the actual queue at the lower level.

The key to resolving and avoiding these queue problems is communication between all participants. We need to recognize that when we change the planned queue time for a particular work center in the database, all jobs yet to go through that work center will be rescheduled. When we change the planned queue time, the backward-

---

FIGURE 5.4 Valve and Funnel Concept of Queue Reduction

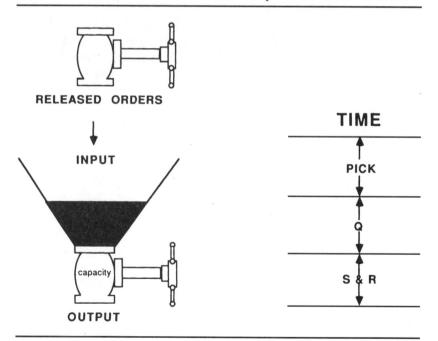

RELEASED ORDERS

INPUT

TIME

PICK

Q

S & R

capacity

OUTPUT

---

scheduling program will recalculate the operation dates. The calculated lead time should be compared to the lead time on the item master file in MRP and should cause the MRP lead time to be adjusted by the amount of queue reduced. Then, when we rerun Material Requirements Planning, the order start dates are recalculated, in turn causing the order due dates for lower-level parts to be adjusted. This cascading effect causes further adjustments to the operation dates. In a really successful company, it is essential to reduce queue levels. This must be done with care. Making large reductions in queue without solving the problems first can result in a delay in the incoming work to the work centers and this can cause the work center to run out of work.

After all the heat he took for delays and excess work-in-process in the welding shop, Dan told Joan to have the welding planner just go in and take three days of planned queue time out of the weld area. Joan figured Dan knew what he was doing, so she did it. After the schedules were rerun, Brian didn't get any new work for the milling machines for three days.

"Joan," Brian said, "we have a problem out here. My milling machines haven't received a thing to work on in three days."

Joan went to the terminal and looked up the schedule of work to be released. She explained to Brian that numerous jobs had been scheduled to be released earlier, but they had been rescheduled for a later release because she had reduced the planned queue time in the weld area.

"Why did you do that?" Brian asked.

"I just did what Dan told me to do," Joan replied. "I assumed you two had talked this out and understood the impact."

At that moment Dan passed by.

"Hey, Dan, come here a minute." Brian called to him, "Can you explain to me why you didn't talk to me when you were planning on making a large change to your queue? Didn't you understand that you couldn't just remove queue without talking to everyone concerned? It not only affected the burning machines, but a lot of my machines also." Brian was the victim of a breakdown in communication. The real reason there was no communication was that Dan didn't understand the impact that changing queue levels would have on the other work centers. Education was the solution to the problem. People need to understand the "what" and "why" of an action before jumping into action.

Input/Output control allows companies to reduce queues in a controlled fashion. The report displays what the queue levels are currently and what they were intended to be. It also predicts what the future queue levels will be. The plans can then be changed by either increasing or decreasing the input or output to bring the queue in line with the desired queue levels.

It has been shown how the I/O report is used to monitor input, output, and queues by work center and time period. Corrective action is initiated when the variance between the actual and the plan exceeds the preestablished tolerance. When used in conjunction with capacity planning, the work levels can be kept under control.

An integral part of this monitoring process is to make queue reduction a conscious effort in each work center. As queues are reduced, they become much more easily managed, making their control easier as well.

Effective use of Input/Output control requires good teamwork. The capacity planner is responsible for monitoring the input plan and verifying the integrity of the input data; the production supervisor is accountable for creating the output plan and the integrity of the output data. In the weekly capacity planning meeting, they review the Input/Output report at the same time as the CRP report. Working the two together is critical to successful capacity management.

Step-by-step, the planning process led Brian and his colleagues into a better quality of factory life. Step-by-proven step, they found planning becoming less of a burden and more of a tool with which they could fine-tune their ability to deliver to their customers needs, while operating more efficiently. Step-by-step, they gained the necessary knowledge and applied it, making everyone's job, from the bottom to the top, easier and more productive.

Chapter Six

Scheduling to Capacity Constraints

Brian was feeling good about the job they were doing with capacity planning and Input/Output control. The capacity planning reports gave the shop supervisors a clear picture of what workloads lay ahead, and the Input/Output reports told them how well they were doing against the capacity plan. It hadn't been easy to instill the disciplines to assure that the information was correct, and it had been equally difficult to get people to respond early to future problems as they appeared on the capacity reports. Brian was feeling very satisfied with the progress they had made.

Then one day Brian got a call from Dan.

"Brian, I know I gave you a hard time on this new scheduling and capacity planning stuff. I may have been a little slow in coming around, but I have to admit, it's making a difference. I also know that we wouldn't have done it without your persistence."

Brian was amazed. He wasn't used to hearing compliments from Dan. He couldn't think of anything to say, so he waited for Dan to continue.

"However, . . ." Dan said.

"Oh, oh," thought Brian. "Here it comes. He was just softening me up."

Dan went on. ". . . I've got a problem in Heat Treat. I'm starting to have difficulty meeting the schedule. I've never had any problem before, but the workload has gradually increased to the point where it's chewed up all of my reserved capacity. I've been watching this coming on the capacity planning report. Some weeks are a little over-loaded, some weeks a little under. I figured the overloads and under-loads would about balance themselves out. Trouble is, I can't get the work done during the overloaded weeks, and little by little, I've been falling behind. We're running three shifts, seven days a week. I'm just about at my maximum capacity. In fact, I have been for a few weeks now. I don't have any capacity left."

Brian recalled that this issue had come up during this morning's dispatching meeting in the shop. He was starting to have difficulty meeting his own schedules because of jobs coming out of Heat Treat late.

Dan continued, "I'm trying to run to the dispatching rules that we agreed on. You know, when behind schedule, run to the due dates on the dispatch list. The problem is that running in that sequence forces me to change the furnace temperature and sometimes the atmo-sphere between almost every job. It takes a lot of time to change the temperature and get it stabilized, and I lose a lot of productive time. If I could run the jobs that require the same temperature back-to-back, I'd get a lot more throughput. You seem pretty up-to-date on all this scheduling stuff, so I thought I'd call you to see if you had any ideas."

"Can't you send some of the work to an outside heat treating fa-cility?" Brian asked.

"Sure," Dan responded. "That's what I've been doing. But the cost is half again what it costs us to do it internally. It also adds four to five days to our processing time. The worst thing, however, is that their quality isn't up to our standards. I have to reject a lot of their work."

Hayes had only one heat treat furnace, and Brian knew it was un-reasonable to suggest a second furnace to solve the problem. That equipment was very expensive, and it wasn't in the budget. Brian also knew that it would take months to get a new furnace in place even if they could get it approved.

"I don't want to seem too negative, Brian, but I'm not sure this scheduling method we're using works in situations like this where the capacity is fixed. I just don't have any flexibility."

"Let me give this some thought," replied Brian. "I'll get back to you."

Brian headed for Joan's office. Maybe she had some ideas on how to handle the Heat Treat problem.

"I've been reading about all kinds of new scheduling techniques, including some that schedule operations within some finite capacity constraints such as Dan has in Heat Treat," Joan responded when Brian explained the situation. "Technology is changing too fast for me to keep up. In fact, Roy and I are heading to an Oliver Wight seminar on scheduling next week to try and get up to date on what's going on. Why don't you go with us?"

After Joan explained further about some of the things she had been reading about new developments in scheduling software, Brian agreed that it would be good for him to tag along.

Brian caught up with Ralph as he was headed to the cafeteria for a cup of coffee. He told Ralph about the call from Dan and the conversation with Joan.

"You know, Ralph, Heat Treat has become a bottleneck for us. If we don't do something to nip this scheduling problem in the bud, we could lose everything we've gained. I'd really like to go to this seminar with Joan to see if there is anything that would help. The seminar is next Thursday and Friday, and I would need to travel on Wednesday."

"Are you crazy?" Ralph sneered. "I can't have you out of the shop for three days, especially at the end of the week. We're just starting to make some real headway around here. Who's going to keep it all together out in your area if you're gone?"

Brian assured Ralph that with the new planning and scheduling tools that they had in place, the next two weeks were well under control barring some emergency. He also told Ralph that his supervisors were well equipped to handle any emergency that came up and that his absence would not cause any problems. Brian was mildly surprised when Ralph, after giving it a little more thought, grunted, "Well, all right. Go ahead."

Brian hurried back to his office to make his travel arrangements. He called Dan to tell him what was going on and that he would talk to him after he got back from the seminar.

On the flight to the seminar, Brian was leafing through some of the materials that Joan had given him on new scheduling techniques. He turned to Joan in the seat next to him. "What do think about all this finite scheduling stuff? The last seminar that we went to cautioned us about using finite scheduling because it automatically rescheduled the jobs if the work center was overloaded."

"From what I've been able to learn, the advancements in technology have overcome that problem," Joan replied. "Earlier finite scheduling software leveled the load across the entire planning horizon. That meant that you wouldn't ever be aware of any need to increase your capacity because the software would just reschedule the load to fit within the capacity constraint. That would put the Master Production Schedule at risk. Modern software gives you the ability to limit the automatic rescheduling of overloads. Although it seems that each software package has its own ideas about how to do that, it appears that most of them provide an opportunity to put in your own scheduling rules, generate a recommended schedule based on those rules, and give the planner the option of overriding the recommended schedule. You now know everything that I know about the subject. That's one of the reasons that I wanted to attend this seminar. I want to find out more about it."

As he was settling into his seat at start of the seminar, Brian scanned the list of attendees that was among the materials placed in front of him. Just as he had at the earlier seminar, he noticed the variety of products and manufacturing environments represented by the attendees. Remembering the value of the contacts that he had made from the other seminar, Brian carefully tucked the list away in his briefcase for safe keeping. He made a mental note to talk to as many of the people as he could while he was there to see if any of them had any experiences they were willing to share.

The seminar leader began to speak. "The primary goal of plant scheduling is to support the Master Production Schedule—and consequently customer demands—while making optimal utilization of constrained resources. It is important that the scheduling system provide predictable, stable work schedules."

"So far, so good," thought Brian. The scheduling system at Hayes was doing a pretty good job on this latter point, but maybe there was more they could do regarding their resource utilization, particularly in cases like Heat Treat.

The speaker continued. "Production schedules are generated using one of two techniques: infinite capacity scheduling and finite capacity scheduling. Within each of these approaches are the variations of forward scheduling and backward scheduling."

Brian made a note as a reminder that the scheduling method they were using at Hayes was an infinite capacity scheduling technique utilizing backward scheduling (see Chapter 3).

"Infinite capacity scheduling works well when the capacities are flexible and can be expanded or contracted or when resources can be reallocated as needed," continued the speaker. "This is particularly the case with labor-intensive work centers or when overtime or alternate processing is a readily available option. Infinite capacity scheduling is based upon the notion that it is possible to adjust the available resources to match the workload.

"Finite capacity scheduling is generally appropriate for use in capital-intensive environments where it takes longer and is generally more costly to change the capacity of the resources available to do the work or where alternative processing is not an option. In this situation, it is necessary to adjust the workload to match the available resources. One of the most important uses of finite scheduling is to assist the factory in getting maximum utilization out of a bottleneck or capacity-constrained work center.

"Since most work in manufacturing is planned based on the due date, backward scheduling is typically used with either technique, although forward scheduling is used to some extent with finite capacity scheduling, as we will see later.

"The use of finite capacity scheduling—we use the acronym FCS—has increased dramatically in recent years to where it is quite the norm in some industries."

"Oh, boy," thought Brian. "Just what we need. More acronyms."

"It's only fair to warn you," the speaker went on, "that this rise in popularity has led to the development of many different software packages. Even though they may all be labeled as finite capacity scheduling systems, not all FCS software is created equal. They do not all have the same capabilities nor all of the features that we will talk about over the next two days. And some may even have features that we don't include in our materials here. While there may be significant differences in how each package performs its scheduling calculations, however, the basic underlying concepts, principles, and practices are similar. Those basics will be the focus of this seminar. We do not intend to get into the pros and cons of a particular software package.

"It is highly unlikely that any particular finite scheduling software package will meet all the scheduling needs of all of your companies. Each company needs to sort out its own needs and make sure that the software meets them."

The speaker stepped to the flip chart and began to sketch a graphic representation of a schedule. "The scheduling approach used by most finite scheduling software is to start with the order with the earliest operation start date and schedule it with no queue time. This start date is derived by running a backward-scheduling calculation from the scheduled order completion date using the production routing to determine the operations to be scheduled and the setup and run times for each operation."

"Hmmm," thought Brian. "Just like we do with our system."

The speaker then went on to explain the rest of the scheduling process. The setup of the next job in line would be scheduled to start on that machine immediately after the first job finishes. The third job would then be scheduled after the completion of the first and second jobs. This would continue for each succeeding job on the work list until the total workload equals the predetermined capacity constraint of the work center. "The question is how to determine which job is next in line," he said. "That's the key to finite scheduling, and that's what we'll talk about next."

RULES-BASED APPROACH

Finite scheduling systems use a rules-based approach that defines how the next job is selected for a specific resource. Most finite scheduling packages have a standard set of rules that are typically available and can be specified by machine by the user. Some of the software has relatively simple single-criteria rules such as earliest due date, shortest processing time, shortest setup time, or highest dollar value.

Published articles have claimed that the manufacturing cycle time can be significantly improved by deploying more sophisticated rules (than single-criteria rules) that take into account the Theory of Constraints[1]. The Theory of Constraints (TOC) is built around the notion that just as a chain is only as strong as its weakest link, the shop floor throughput is constrained by a few bottleneck work centers, and the manufacturing schedule should be driven by these constraining work centers. The resolution of the constrained situation involves both scheduling within the limits of the constraint and consideration of the removal of the constraint. (See Chapter 9.)

Leading FCS software provides planners the option of developing custom, multi-criteria rules that are tailored to a factory's unique constraint situations. Conceptually, multi-criteria rules are a series of tasks, decision points, and choices that the software logic uses to branch among different scheduling algorithms using "if/then" logic (if this is the case, then do this). For example, the planners might choose earliest due date as the first rule. Then they could look for jobs that minimize changeover time. Depending upon the precise situation at the time and the particular company environment, planners might use rules that give priority to urgent jobs, tooling availability, setup time, material type or availability, or preventive maintenance requirements. Rules that consider overlapping operations, parallel operations, variations in queue, and move times are used. Although employee work schedules in manufacturing tend to be relatively static, as flextime becomes more widespread, the scheduling process must deal with planned time off, unscheduled time off, and skills availability.

SCHEDULING BEYOND CONSTRAINED CAPACITY

Once the total scheduled workload has reached the capacity constraint and there is more work to be scheduled, additional scheduling rules come into play. The simplest, of course, is to merely schedule that job to a time period where the capacity is available, either earlier or later. If the operation is scheduled later, then the remaining operations on that job must also be rescheduled using forward-scheduling methods. If the operation is scheduled to an earlier date, then its preceding operations must be rescheduled using the backward-scheduling technique. If the remainder of the schedule cannot be compressed sufficiently to meet the original start or completion dates, then a new scheduled order start date or completion date must be generated.

A more complex approach is to employ scheduling rules that look upstream and downstream and resequence jobs to optimize the total schedule. This may require several iterations of the schedule by the software, including rescheduling those jobs that have already been scheduled. Modern computers can process millions of calculations per second, so it is not unreasonable to expect it to be done easily.

The use of the computer to aid the scheduling process allows us to take into account a variety of important factors that impact scheduling. Although some software is limited to the extent to which it addresses the interaction of these other factors, other packages provide almost unlimited flexibility in rules development. Carried to the extreme, rules could be developed such that virtually any scheduling decision can be represented using these rules.

"One thing you should know," the speaker said. "Finite scheduling is far more complex than infinite capacity scheduling because it tries to simulate all the conditions that could happen on the shop floor and incorporate them into the scheduling process. Each additional factor that is considered increases the software design complexity, makes the human interface more complex, and can significantly increase the computer processing time. As computer power keeps increasing and becomes more inexpensive, we can expect significant increases in the complexity of these scheduling tools.

"A word of caution: avoid using those functions or features of the software that you don't need just because they are there. It may result in increased run time and, more importantly, makes it more difficult for the user to understand. When in doubt, err to the side of simplicity."

During the first break, Brian grabbed a doughnut and a cup of coffee and made his way through the crowd to a young man named Tom who had been sitting just in front of him. Brian introduced himself and learned that Tom was the Master Scheduler for Supreme Enterprises, a company that made several different consumer products, including detergents, cleansers, aerosols, and other chemical products. Tom told Brian that he had only recently started working for Supreme Enterprises, having moved from a company that made automotive parts.

Brian was curious about the differences in scheduling between the fabrication and assembly environment and the high-volume process industry.

"I'm pretty familiar with how we did things at my old company," Tom told Brian. "We had an MRP II package that used infinite-capacity-based scheduling techniques." But at "Super Soap"—as Tom said they referred to themselves—they were using finite capacity scheduling. Tom said that his presence at this seminar was part of his company's education program to bring new employees up to speed on finite scheduling techniques as quickly as possible. When he got back to the plant, he was scheduled to begin a hands-on training program to learn their system.

"So," Tom said to Brian, "I'm afraid I can't tell you much about how we do it. But my boss is very charged up about our scheduling system, and I'm sure he would be more than happy to talk to you about it. Why don't you give him a call and see if you can set up a visit to our plant?"

Bingo! Touchdown on the first possession! The seminar was not even two hours old and Brian had his first lead on a user visit.

Tom gave Brian the name and phone number of his boss, Joe Crowe, the Production Manager at Supreme.

Back from break, the speaker picked right up. Brian followed the presentation in his notebook, highlighting the pertinent points and scribbling notes.

In a material-driven environment, the scheduling focus is on meeting demands, and due dates are the controlling variable. In a capacity-driven environment, the scheduling focus is the utilization of resources, and resource capacities are the controlling variables.

"In any company," said the speaker, "situations are likely to be encountered where a constrained resource will force an adjustment to the component schedule that mandates a change to the master schedule. Typically, in a material-driven environment, every effort is made to avoid this situation and to preserve the master schedule due dates. While it may be undesirable to change the master schedule, we must admit that it does happen. The reality that we face is that the when the original master schedule due dates cannot be met because of the capacity constraint, then a new schedule must be worked out. This is not really any different whether you are using finite capacity scheduling or infinite capacity scheduling. When an overloaded resource cannot be adjusted to fit the work in, the schedule—potentially including the Master Production Schedule—must be adjusted.

The difference lies in how much computer support is used in making the change. In the infinite capacity environment, the planner adjusts the schedule based on the information from Rough-Cut Capacity Planning or Capacity Requirements Planning and the production people. In this case, the Master Production Schedule essentially becomes a finite capacity schedule, having been adjusted to the capacity constraint. In finite scheduling, the software makes the changes based on the scheduling rules."

The question becomes not one of *can* the computer do it, but of *should* it? Even though a computer can perform any process that can be programmed, planners, schedulers, and shop supervisors are not likely to respect the results if they don't understand the process. This is what the late Oliver Wight referred to as the "principle of transparency": if it isn't transparent to the user, the user won't believe it.

"Therefore," said the speaker, "it is critical that your people understand the concepts and principles of your scheduling system."

Tom turned around to look at Brian. He gave him a knowing look that said "That's why I'm here."

SIMULATION

Good finite capacity scheduling systems have simulation capability. The software provides a simulation module that is capable of running through different scenarios of scheduling rules without changing the active plant schedules. This module should use the constraints and decision rules from the active factory scheduling system.

After the work order schedule has been has been determined by MRP, the FCS system simulates the effect of the plan with all the constraints and decision rules to verify its feasibility. The sequence of the orders at each work station is determined by FCS based on the scheduling rules.

The FCS software will run through the various forward/backward scheduling iterations within the constraints of the capacity of the work center until it has a best-fit schedule. This best-fit plan is displayed for the planner's review and approval before being loaded to the active schedule for the factory. If the software cannot schedule the jobs to meet the planned need dates and fit within the capacity constraint, it must send the planner a message to that effect along with the best-fit plan. The planner then must make adjustments if the demand is not being adequately met. In this sense, finite scheduling is a "predictor" of pending problems, and it is up to the planner to address the situation. The key to success in scheduling manufacturing is having people make the final decisions, not 'he computer.

The simulation horizon should be variable so the user can ask for assistance in solving a specific future problem. The FCS simulation should be used to address shop operation scheduling problems. Simulations where multiple components, subassemblies, and assemblies are involved are better done by the Material Requirements Planning process.

REAL-TIME RESCHEDULING

When executing the schedule, some performance variance to schedule is expected to happen. In the infinite capacity scheduling approach, this variance can typically be absorbed in the queue and move times or by flexing the capacity. Since capacity cannot be flexed in a capacity-constrained environment, finite capacity scheduling must schedule operations much more tightly.

Brian asked the seminar leader, "What happens when a job does not arrive in the work center on schedule, or the setup takes a little longer than planned, or the scheduled run time is exceeded due to problems?"

"Finite capacity scheduling systems typically will rerun the scheduling algorithms to create a new schedule," the speaker replied. "Some software performs these reschedules in real time as input is received from the shop floor. Depending upon the scheduling rules, this rescheduling could alter the sequencing of the jobs that are in the work center in real time. There is concern on the part of some people that this makes the schedule very unstable. It is constantly changing. As I said at the beginning, it is important that the scheduling system provide stable work schedules. Frequent rescheduling may be a symptom that all is not well with either the planning system or the execution of the plans. The issues mentioned above infer a lack of execution, but they could also be caused by inaccurate data. If frequent rescheduling persists, it is best to determine the cause and correct it and not just tolerate the symptom.

"The biggest concern, however, when operating in the real time mode is that we have delegated the responsibility to change the schedule to the computer with no human intervention. Success in this environment is dependent upon the frequency of rescheduling, the degree to which schedules are changed, and the ability of the people to understand and cope with the changes."

ACCURACY OF INFORMATION

The "garbage in results in garbage out" adage has never been more applicable than with FCS systems. The precision of the FCS approach uses a tremendous amount of detailed information. The quality and timing of the input information will be reflected in the quality of the schedules. Therefore, production models must be extremely accurate. The 95 percent routing accuracy threshold commonplace with MRP II systems should be raised in order to support finite capacity scheduling.

In the infinite capacity environment, variances to standards are compensated for by the use of demonstrated capacity and load factors as discussed in Chapter 4. Both of these factors have much less significance in the finite capacity scheduling environment. More emphasis is placed on the precision and accuracy of standards. Demonstrated capacity is often tracked by part number rather than by resource.

Many FCS systems require the precision of the operation time standards to be in one-minute increments or less. If the actual operation run times for each job are not repeatable within that sort of range, or if they vary from the standards by more than that, then it is difficult to produce a reliable, stable schedule.

OUTPUT

Most FCS software produces Gantt charts, business graphics, and statistical reports to assist planners in analyzing and presenting the results. The graphical output is particularly useful for people who are not thoroughly familiar with the processing logic of the system.

A typical output from FCS is displayed in Figure 6.1. This particular report is for a two-week period in daily increments. If appropriate (for example, each resource processes several jobs each day), the output can be displayed in hourly increments for each day. Each job is typically represented by a different graphic pattern, a different shade of gray, or a different color for easy identification. Note in this example that preventive maintenance periods are scheduled on each machine. In environments where work orders are not used, the product or part number is displayed on the schedule instead of the work order number.

When they returned from the seminar, Roy, Joan, and Brian met with Ralph in his office to decide where they should go from here. They told Ralph that two things were clear to them. First, the power of finite scheduling is unquestionable. Today's computer technology makes it possible for software to simulate numerous situations on the shop floor and aid in making decisions to improve productivity and throughput. Second, there are many approaches to scheduling in a constrained capacity environment, and each software supplier seemed to have some unique ideas.

After listening to their report, Ralph said, "Let's not rush into anything. It's clear to me that we need to know a lot more than we do before we make a decision on this. Brian, when we were starting out to fix our scheduling and capacity planning processes, you and Joan got a lot of benefit from talking with and visiting other companies. See if you can find a company or two that has implemented finite scheduling successfully and then pay them a visit. You know, it may be technically feasible to do all this with the computer, but let's look at the practical side of it. I think it would be best if we talked to someone who has actually done it, and. . . ."

"Actually," Brian broke in, "I'm way ahead of you. I picked up a couple of leads at the seminar, and I've already contacted one company who is willing to have us visit their plant."

"Good." Ralph responded. "Why don't you and Joan go talk to them? In the mean time, Roy, I want you to work with Information Systems (IS) to pull together all the information you can get on the various finite scheduling software packages. This doesn't sound like something that we can modify our current software to do, but maybe there is a "plug-and-play" package that is compatible with what we have."

FIGURE 6.1 Finite Capacity Scheduling: Work Center Schedule

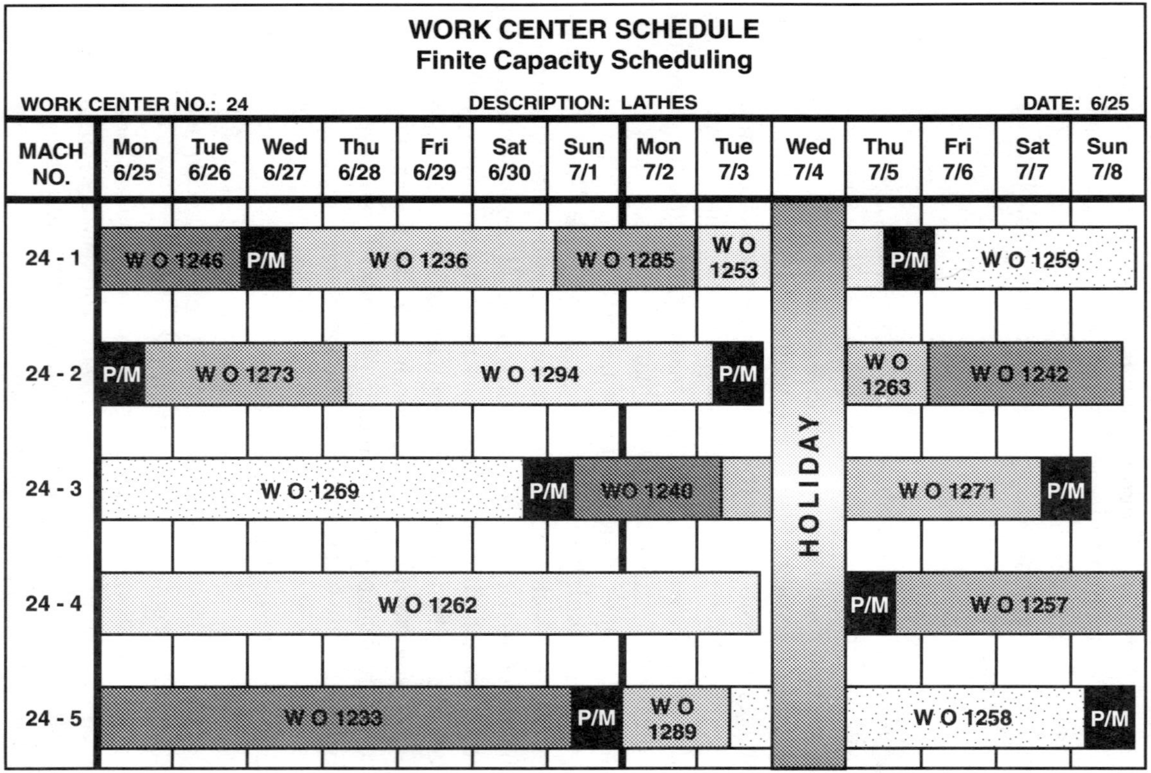

The next week, Brian and Joan went to Supreme Enterprises. Joe Crowe met them in the lobby. "Welcome to Super Soap," he chortled. "I believe you know Tom already," he said, as the Master Scheduler joined them and they all shook hands.

As they made their way out to the factory, Joe told them, "We are a high volume, make-to-stock company. Most of our processes involve very expensive capital equipment. We work three shifts, seven days a week. Our business is so competitive that we can't afford to send any work outside. The costs and lead time would kill us."

Brian smiled. "Sounds just like our Heat Treat situation—except for the make-to-stock part."

"We are very excited about what we have accomplished with finite scheduling. Before we put this system in, it would take us up to twelve hours to develop the master schedule, what with all the trial fits and gyrations we had to go through. Now it can be done in less than an hour. Our software takes the requested master schedule and schedules it around our constraining resources, which are the aerosol packaging line and one of our chemical processing tanks.

"On the aerosol line, the changeover time between different products is quite long because of the cleanup required. The changeover of can sizes can also be quite lengthy as well. So we schedule all the runs of a particular product and can size back-to-back, regardless of the label or final package size. Of course, this means that we have to schedule the bulk product production to coincide with the aerosol line schedule, and we have to coordinate the labeling station and the boxer and palletizer with the line schedule. Then, of course, wouldn't you know, we run smack into the capacity limits of that one chemical processing tank.

"Of course, we're no different than any other manufacturing company. We could put together the best schedule in the world, and it probably wouldn't last five minutes. Things are constantly changing around here. Line breakdowns, process problems, and things like that. So one of the big benefits we get from our software is the speed with which it reschedules the factory. We are able to feed a whole host of variables into the scheduling system and then select the schedule we like best.

"Oh, man," Joe sighed, "there I go again. I just get so charged up I can't shut up. Tell me a little about your operation."

"Well," Brian said, "as you know, we make tractors for both the agricultural industry and homeowners. I'm not sure how that relates to soap and cleansers, but I've learned not to be too narrow-minded about things like that.

"First of all, we're able to flex the capacity of just about all of our work centers," Brian continued. "Until recently, a constrained-capacity resource has not been our problem. Our capacity planning system loads the work into daily buckets just like your FCS system does. And we use the backward-scheduling logic that is common to most of the software packages, finite or infinite. However, we don't try to have the software do anything more than back-schedule from the order due date from MRP. Our scheduling software doesn't consider all the variations and permutations possible on the shop floor. Just simple, straightforward, backward scheduling. We believe that the shop supervisors can—and should—sort out which job should be run next. This has worked well for us in most cases. What we use is pretty simple logic, but it makes some assumptions that are not always true, like fixed queue sizes and setup times and, of course, infinite capacity. My take on it is that our infinite capacity scheduling approach is fundamentally about the same as your finite scheduling approach. The difference is in how we handle an overload condition."

"I'm not so sure that it is all that simple, Brian," Joe piped. "Let's take for example the assumption you mentioned about queue time. The logic of your system assumes that the queue level for a specific work center would always be relatively the same. But in reality, the queue varies day by day based on the amount and type of work moving to and through the work center on that day. Finite capacity scheduling systems consider the actual jobs scheduled through the work center and calculate the amount of queue that will be in front of the work center when a specific job arrives. Therefore, a job scheduled via finite capacity scheduling may be scheduled to start sooner or later than it would if scheduled with a fixed queue, depending on whether the actual queue was less than or greater than the fixed queue data. In either case, finite scheduling would more accurately simulate what would be expected to happen on the factory floor.

"The second assumption that you mentioned—that the setup time will always be the same for a particular part number—is similarly flawed. There are numerous reasons why the setup time will vary, the most predominate of which is that the prior job running has a similar setup. If that is the case, then the amount of time allocated for setup could be significantly different. Finite capacity scheduling systems can recognize this situation and adjust the schedules accordingly. To predict the setup time more accurately, FCS systems use data from the database—typically group or sequence codes—to identify those parts that have similar setups and also note the degree of similarity. They can then schedule them to run in a sequence that minimizes changeovers. This is the feature that we use to schedule the aerosol line."

Joan was concerned about the apparent complexity of FCS and the detail required to generate realistic schedules. "Finite capacity scheduling requires a tremendous amount of information. Not just in the routings, but the scheduling rules as well. Isn't it difficult to create and maintain this much detail and precision and keep it accurate?" she asked.

Joe had a ready response. "When you have capacity flexibility, and can absorb schedule variations in your move and queue times, you don't have to be as concerned about very precise queues, moves, and setup and run times. However, when you don't have the luxury of flexible capacity, you are forced to be more precise in your data. Sure, it's more difficult, but it's the price you have to pay to get better schedules. Besides, you should be trying to control those queue and move times and reduce them anyway if you are going to be competitive in a global market. The pressure for more accurate scheduling is becoming greater all the time."

Joan followed up on her point. "Finite scheduling is more precise in its scheduling logic than is infinite capacity scheduling, and therefore the schedules and capacity requirements are more precise also. However, because the finite scheduling process is much more complex, and the computer has to crunch a lot more data, aren't the computer run times much longer, and doesn't it require a significant increase in computer power?"

"I am aware that some companies have reported long run times with FCS, but that has not been a problem for us, and we're running on the same computer we had nine years ago," Joe answered. "Now, I understand that we don't have a large number of end items, and even fewer components and subassemblies to schedule, so we probably have it a little easier than you might. Of course, you have to have the processing capability. If you can't complete the scheduling runs in time for the factory to use the information, you would be just wasting time and money. We are able to process our rescheduling in less than an hour, even with a major upheaval in the schedule. In many cases, it takes just a few minutes."

Joan walked over to watch a molding machine that was spewing out plastic caps. She turned back to Joe. "I understand that there are occasions when the computer isn't able to come up with a schedule that is practical, or at least preferable. Once the finite scheduling system has produced a plan or schedule predicting undesirable results, such as rescheduling an order out, isn't it difficult for planners to determine what changes must be made to improve the plan, because they don't understand how the computer came up with its plan?"

"Let me add to that thought," said Brian. "We've got some folks who aren't all that comfortable with computers. They'd rather do without them. I'm concerned with the rescheduling aspect of FCS. I don't want to have the computer rescheduling operations and orders without some involvement of our people. It takes the decision making totally out of the hands of the supervisors. How do you hold people accountable for the schedules? Don't they just blame things on the computer?"

Joe looked first at Brian and then at Joan, trying to figure out which question to answer first. After a moment's thought, he said, "Both of your questions deal with related issues: understanding and accountability. The interesting thing is that you can't have one without the other. People will accept accountability if they have the understanding. And they will go out of the way to build an understanding if they know they will be held accountable. We put a great deal of stock in giving our people the best opportunity we can to get them to understand the scheduling system. That's why Tom here was at the seminar with you. We want him to have a solid understanding of the basics before we immerse him in the details of our system.

"On a similar note," Joe went on, "it becomes obvious when someone doesn't have a good handle on the process. Perhaps they need additional training, or maybe they aren't cut out for that particular job. It is management's responsibility to step up to these issues and correct them."

Joan had another question. "How do you cope with the fact that the schedule changes by the software may alter the completion date of the order which in turn may impact on the master schedule due dates?"

"We have not found those changes to be very big—maybe a few days at most," responded Joe. "Since we are a make-to-stock company, we can absorb those fluctuations in inventory. We may dip below the safety stock level from time to time, but isn't that what safety stock is for—to protect against problems with schedule execution?"

Brian introduced a new thought. "We need to have visibility of the real future capacity requirements so that we can do something about future increases in business. I wouldn't object to finite scheduling the short term as long as we are able to see the actual future capacity required in order for a work center to support the needs of the master schedule."

"That can be done," replied Joe. "Our FCS software provides the option of infinite loading to display that information so that you can see the actual capacity required to support the schedule as it is presented. You can then specify the horizon over which you want to finite schedule within the constrained capacity. Besides, we use Resource Planning (see Chapter 7) to predict our long-range capacity requirements. This process does not consider the capacity constraints."

Joe shifted topics. "You know there are a few special situations that we have to deal with that you should be aware of. I don't know if they are issues for you, but let's talk about them. Some of our operations experience significant losses during processing. To properly schedule the operation times, our FCS system uses yield data on each operation instead of only at the part number level. As each operation is scheduled, the quantity of parts is reduced by the yield shown for that operation and the run time calculated based on that lower quantity."

"We have that situation in our shop, too," Brian said. "Our software doesn't handle it too well now, but our IS Department told me that it wouldn't be too difficult to fix it."

Joe continued, "Another consideration is that in order to effectively do finite scheduling, each resource needs to have its own scheduling calendar. In addition to including allowances for holidays and weekends, scheduling calendars for finite capacity scheduling need to provide for shift differences, planned down-time, or other factors that affect the availability of the resource."

Joan jumped in with another question. "What about raw materials and component parts needed for the manufacturing process? They are potential constraints to the process. Do you consider material availability in your scheduling algorithms?"

"We tried to do that, but we decided that it was too complex for the benefit obtained. Besides, our MRP system provides a capability for checking material availability before an order is released, and the planner has the option of releasing the order or not. We think it is better to have that decision made by the planners rather than add that level of complexity to the scheduling system. This should be an issue only with jobs that get released inside the normal material or component lead time. If the planners are doing their job well with MRP, it is reasonable to assume that the material will be available for jobs that are planned outside the lead time."

"One final caution," said Joe, as they headed for the cafeteria for coffee. "Unplanned activities wreak havoc in a finite scheduling environment. We don't have any problems in that regard as far as product schedules go. All of our production is planned through the master schedule and then fit into the factory schedule via FCS. Nobody can get a job into the factory without going through the master scheduler. However, we learned the hard way that preventative maintenance and equipment overhaul should be scheduled rather than be treated as an unplanned activity. It needs to be a part of the planning and scheduling system."

Brian was elated to report that this was one situation that Hayes had under control. "We've got that covered. We create routings for maintenance work and put work orders into MRP. Our scheduling system then schedules it appropriately and puts it on the dispatch list like any other job."

"That's just what we had to do," replied Joe. "Beyond that, you still have to be prepared to deal with unplanned events. Any scheduling system is built on the premise that all of the scheduled events will happen as planned. Unfortunately, unforeseen events do occur. Although you may keep them to a minimum, they will occur. That's where the dynamic update feature of finite scheduling is a plus. Our software lets us update the FCS model in a dynamic and timely fashion."

During the rest of the tour, Brian and Joan had the opportunity to talk to some of the production supervisors and planners. They spent some time at Tom's desk going over his master scheduling process. He pulled up the schedule for the aerosol line. It was very similar to the sample from the seminar. It was in color so that it was easy to differentiate the different jobs. It had the projected inventory displayed on the bottom of the screen so that the he could see the effect of the schedule changes. Tom showed them how he could "drag-and-drop" jobs around on the screen to adjust the inventory if it was necessary to do so.

The work-center schedules were also available on-line. Joe pointed out that they could get hard copy printouts, but if the schedules changed during the shift, they would need to print out new ones, so they only printed them by exception for meetings or the like. The supervisors all had terminals at their desks, and there were several others throughout the shop.

Brian was impressed with how well everyone understood and liked the scheduling system. Several people said that even though they didn't totally understand the details of all of the manipulations the computer went through to produce the schedule, they all knew what the scheduling rules were that were used by the software. They had participated in establishing the rules. They were very confident that the schedules generated by the computer were valid schedules, and they readily accepted the accountability for their execution.

As they were headed for the lobby to leave, Joe added one final thought. "The biggest hurdle with FCS is preventing people from thinking that it is a magic cure-all. Management shouldn't perceive finite scheduling as a solution to bad data or bad disciplines. You still have to have valid plans driving the FCS system and long-range capacity planning to know when you should expand facilities or buy more equipment."

Joan and Roy thanked Joe for his help and headed for their car.

The day after the visit to Supreme Enterprises, Ralph called Brian, Joan, Roy, Dan, and Mickey into his office. "Well," he drawled, "tell us about the trip."

Joan summarized what they had learned from their visit. "Those folks at Supreme really have their act together. They seem to have made finite scheduling work quite well for them. But, before we jump to any conclusions about changing our scheduling system, we've got a lot more work to do."

"Well, let's review what we are doing now in comparison to the finite capacity scheduling approach," Ralph began. He had clearly done his homework before the meeting and summarized the situation for the group.

"We've learned that the purpose of capacity management is to identify and solve capacity issues before they become problems. We use the infinite loading technique as part of our Capacity Requirements Planning process to identify potential capacity constraints and resolve them before they hurt us. And I must say, we've been doing a pretty good job at it." Brian smiled to himself as Ralph continued. "If we need more capacity than is expected to be available, we've only got two choices: either we get more capacity or we reduce the requirements. And you all know how reluctant we are to say no to a customer. Where we have the flexibility to increase capacity, it seems to me that our infinite-loading-based approach is perfectly fine. On the other hand, in situations where we cannot increase the capacity, it seems that the finite capacity scheduling approach would be helpful. According to what I've been reading, it might even help us utilize our equipment better, reduce lead time, and improve our costs."

Picking up on Ralph's lead, Roy jumped right in. "Capacity Requirement Planning has been very effective in most of our work centers. We've scheduled overtime, changed the shift schedule, and added people based on what we saw in our CRP reports. We've been watching the situation in Heat Treat closely and sending the overload to an outside shop. But their quality and delivery has been unreliable, and it has put us in a bind. We're likely to face more of these situations as our business grows and we don't have the luxury of extra capacity. Things are going to get more competitive in the marketplace, and we have to continue to drive our costs down. This finite scheduling technique sounds like just the ticket."

Ralph sat up a little straighter in his chair. "Now let's not get ahead of ourselves. This could be a pretty big undertaking, what with all the education and training we would have to do. And I'm not sure we have to do finite scheduling across the whole shop. Can we do it on just a few work centers like Heat Treat?"

Roy looked at Brian and Joan before speaking. "That's one of the things we'll have to ask the software suppliers. From the information that I've gathered so far, there is a wide range of software features and functionality available on the market. We'll have to be very careful how we approach this."

"It sounds like this could take a while," declared Dan. "What about my problem in Heat Treat. I need to do something right away. I can't get blood from a stone."

Brian said that he had a couple of ideas that might help. "First off, we could increase the queue time in front of Heat Treat. That would get the jobs moved to Heat Treat earlier and give Dan's people time to sequence them properly. Of course, that would extend the lead time through the factory. We'd rather not do that, but we have to do something to alleviate the problem.

"The second thing I thought about is based on something we learned at the seminar and we saw in action at Supreme Enterprises that just might help us out here. Finite capacity scheduling systems use a code to identify those parts that have similar setups. The software then uses a "same-setup" rule to schedule those jobs sequentially. I think we can use that notion in our scheduling of Heat Treat. We can put a code on the routing for each part that has to be heat treated so that we can identify those that require the same combination of temperature and atmosphere. We can then modify our dispatch list to print that code. Then, Dan, you or your supervisor can look ahead at what's scheduled for Heat Treat and schedule all of those with the same code back-to-back. You would have to maintain close communications with Joan's planners and the shop schedulers so that the jobs you pick to run early can be rescheduled as necessary."

"Interestingly enough," quipped Dan, "that's more or less what we were doing before we got behind schedule. Of course, we don't have the code on the dispatch list, so we have to spend time figuring out which jobs to run together. It sure would be a lot easier with that code on the dispatch list."

Joan nodded in agreement. "Of course, this may be only a temporary thing until we figure out what we're going to do about new software. I'll talk to Laura Sanderford in IS about modifying the dispatch list. Since it only involves putting an additional data field on the routing and the dispatch list, I don't think that it would be too large a programming job. I can get on it first thing Monday morning."

"Okay! Here's what I want you to do," said Ralph as he stepped to the white board on the wall and picked up a marker. He wrote:

1. Queues and dispatch codes

"First, as a stop gap measure until we figure out if and how to take advantage of finite scheduling, go ahead with the queue time increase and dispatch codes." Then he wrote:

2. Software

"Finish up your investigation of the software, Roy. Find out if finite scheduling can be used on some of our operations while continuing to do what we do now with the rest. Then, based on what you find out about that, come up with a short list of software packages that seem to be best suited for our environment and we'll look further into each of them. Get some preliminary cost estimates. Brian, you and Joan put together a proposal for education and training." He wrote the third item on the board:

3. Education and training

and followed it with a fourth:

4. Proposal

"Then the three of you put together a cost proposal for putting it all in place. Give me a proposal for each of two approaches: (1) a plant-wide implementation of finite scheduling and (2) finite scheduling limited to a few selected work centers, if that turns out to be feasible. If this is something we decide we want to do, we'll put it in the budget for next year. I'll put these four items on the agenda for my weekly staff meeting until we reach a decision on this matter of finite scheduling."

It was late as they left the meeting. Brian and Joan chatted about how it had had gone. They were impressed with the way Ralph had handled it. He was beginning to show a noticeable change in his behavior. In the past, he would have likely made a snap judgement and either told them to go ahead immediately with finite scheduling, or more likely rejected the whole idea—since he had never been much of a computer fan—and told Dan to just "do the best you can." They knew that they needed to learn a lot more than they knew at that moment, and Ralph had shown a willingness to take the time necessary to do so.

It appeared for once that they were going to make an intelligent decision based on facts and information, rather than on emotion. "Maybe all this effort is beginning to pay off in more ways than just our planning and control systems. I'm beginning to see some real changes around here," Brian said to Joan as he headed out the door for the weekend.

Chapter Seven

Applying Rough-Cut Capacity Planning

Several weeks later, Brian had just returned from a four-day weekend, an anniversary present he'd promised his wife. Four days off—Friday through Monday! Brian was somewhat surprised that Ralph had approved his request, particularly after his initial reluctance regarding the earlier APICS conference. Things definitely must be getting better at the plant.

Brian had barely eased himself back into his chair with the smell of the fresh mountain air still lingering in his memory when he saw Tony's note expressing concern over the gear shaver attached to the new capacity planning report. He thumbed through it quickly. Everything had been running smoothly. His capacity planning reports had effectively been allowing him the visibility to successfully plan ahead. Why else would Ralph have given him those days off?

But when he came to the gear shaver, he couldn't believe his eyes. The workload for the gear shaver that showed up on the plan for October and November was well above anything they had ever done before. It would be impossible to turn out that much work, even if he worked his people all the overtime he could. Brian also knew that the work couldn't be subcontracted. That bubble of work hadn't been on the report last week.

Brian turned on his computer terminal. Working back through the information that was creating the overload, he found out that the

Master Production Schedule had been changed over the weekend. Knowing that any change to the master schedule during that time frame had to have Ralph's approval, he immediately called Ralph to find out what had happened.

Sure enough, Ralph had changed the Production Plan mix from small tractors to medium tractors to satisfy a shift in demands from Iowa Tractor, one of Hayes's best customers, and had instructed the master scheduler to make the corresponding changes to the master schedule.

"Why did you make those changes without considering whether or not we had the capacity to do it?" Brian asked as politely as he could. "I thought we had gotten away from just shoving stuff into the master schedule without running through the material and capacity planning processes to be sure we could do it."

"You know how Lenny gets when he has a hot customer," Ralph said, referring to the Vice President of Sales and Marketing. "And Pete insisted on an answer right then. There wasn't time to run through all those processes. They agreed to move out the forecast for small tractors to make room for the additional medium tractors. Since there were the same number of total tractors in the schedule, I figured that we would have the capacity to handle it."

What Ralph didn't realize was that the medium tractors had gears that required a shaving operation, but the small tractors did not, and the gear-shaver work center was already scheduled at its maximum capacity. When he changed the product mix, he was not aware of the additional load that it would put on the gear shavers. After making the change to the Production Plan and the Master Production Schedule, those changes were processed on down through Material Requirements Planning into Capacity Requirements Planning, where, for the first time, the impact was visible.

After Brian showed him the capacity requirements report, Ralph shrugged his shoulders and said, "Sure, now I can see the impact, but when you're in a meeting with all that pressure on you, who's got the time to go through all that? We needed to give Lenny an answer right away."

Knowing the news they brought was not good, Ralph and Brian went back to Lenny and Pete and told them they couldn't meet the new plan. Pete's immediate reaction was to tell Ralph that they had made a commitment to the customer and that he and Brian would have to "do the best you can."

Ralph reminded them of an earlier situation when one of Brian's supervisors had gotten the dispatch list for one of his work centers and immediately saw that the work center was overloaded. Remembering similar occasions when management had told him to "do the best he could," the supervisor arbitrarily decided to work on a small-tractor part as opposed to a medium-tractor part. At the same time, one of Dan's supervisors looked at the dispatch list for one of his work centers, which was also overloaded, and, "doing the best he could," decided to work on a part for a medium tractor instead of a small one. As a result of their actions, the Assembly Department ended up with some of the parts for both the medium and small tractors, but not all of the parts required for either tractor. The result was that neither tractor shipped on time.

Ralph asked Pete and Lenny if they wanted the production supervisor to decide which parts to work on at the shavers and thus decide which customers would get their tractors. Of course, Pete and Lenny did not want that to happen. Brian explained that when an overload situation exists, it makes sense to address the issue up front and adjust the master schedule, so that at least some product will be assured to ship on time.

Both Pete and Lenny knew, in spite of what they wished could happen, that when Ralph said he couldn't do something, it meant he really couldn't do it. They also figured it was better to call their customer now than to wait until later. Reluctantly, Lenny went through the ordeal of apologizing to one of their best customers for having promised something they couldn't deliver. The customer was not pleased with the news, but thanked Lenny for calling now instead of waiting until the orders went past due.

Brian realized that if the Hayes senior management team had known the impact of their decision prior to making the commitment to the customer, they could have avoided making this embarrassing and potentially costly mistake and having to redo the plans. He had to come up with a way to enable them to quickly evaluate the impact of such decisions on capacity before the commitment was made. Ralph needed the ability to make a quick assessment of the capacity requirements, regardless of what Pete and Lenny threw at him.

Brian knew he had to come up with something quickly. Suddenly, he remembered a discussion about Rough-Cut Capacity Planning during the seminar that he had attended. He recalled that someone from the ball-bearing company had mentioned that they had been using this approach. He found the seminar attendance list and the telephone number for Marty Bloch, the Plant Superintendent from Beartone Manufacturing. He picked up the phone and called Marty.

Marty explained to Brian how they used the process of Rough-Cut Capacity Planning to estimate their capacity requirements before they committed to any changes in their overall plans. First, they would run a set of rough capacity calculations against the Production Plan. If the resultant capacity requirements were considered feasible, they would approve the Production Plan. Once the Production Plan was set, they would make the necessary adjustments to the Master Production Schedule (MPS) and run a second set of rough capacity calculations against the proposed MPS. Again, if the resultant capacity requirements were feasible, they would approve the MPS and initiate the detailed material planning and scheduling processes.

Marty reminded Brian that the speaker at the seminar had defined the first process (i.e., at the Production Plan level) as "Resource Planning" and that the term "Rough-Cut Capacity Planning" was generally used to describe the capacity estimating process used with the Master Production Schedule. He noted that in some circles, however, the term Rough-Cut Capacity Planning is used to describe both processes.

According to Marty, Beartone used Resource Planning whenever they wanted to make high level or long range changes, such as changes to the business plan. They also used Resource Planning in conjunction with their Sales and Operations Planning process. The Sales and Operations Planning process permitted senior management to establish an overall game plan for the company, which was then used as a framework for the master scheduler. They used Resource Planning to test their plans for reasonableness before releasing them to the master scheduler. As Marty explained it, "The idea is not to determine detailed capacity requirements at this stage, but to get a rough-cut sense of the plant's capabilities. We're simply asking, 'Are we in the ball park?'" He went on to explain that by following this procedure before decisions are made regarding the

Production Plan, senior management can get a good idea of whether or not they can accomplish what they want to. If the plan that senior management wants to execute is not valid, they need to examine the alternatives and make adjustments accordingly. Resource Planning allows them to do this, and to address critical decisions promptly. It gives them the opportunity to see the impact of future plans and to initiate capacity changes well before they become crises.

Marty explained that the next level of capacity planning, Rough-Cut Capacity Planning, was to test the validity of the Master Production Schedule from the perspective of capacity requirements prior to committing to the changes and running Material Requirements Planning (MRP) and Capacity Requirements Planning (CRP). This allowed the master scheduler the opportunity to initiate action early in the process to make midrange capacity adjustments or to avoid making commitments beyond the company's capabilities. "If we know ahead of time that there is a problem, we can avoid wasting a lot of computer resources to run MRP and CRP before the capacity constraint has been resolved. Perhaps of even greater importance, is that once MRP is run, everyone starts trying to execute the new plan that has been generated. Then if only one resource, whether it be an internal or external one, can't accomplish the required work, the plan has to be changed and people will have to undo what they have just started. It is better to know that the MPS is at least feasible before doing all of that. A little effort up front with Rough-Cut Capacity Planning can alleviate a lot of nervousness in Material Requirements Planning, as well as the frustrations felt by the users trying to execute a schedule that is changing so fast that they can't keep pace."

Brian asked Marty if he felt that it was necessary to do the rough capacity calculations at both the Production Plan level and again at the MPS level. "Why not just do the Resource Planning and then let the detailed Capacity Requirements Planning process handle the rest?" he queried.

"Well," replied Marty, "the Resource Planning process assumes that all members of a product family consume the same amount of resources. But our product variability is quite significant in regard to the amount of capacity required for each end item. This means that the mix of product in the MPS could cause the capacity requirements to vary considerably even though the total units in the MPS are within the Production Plan guidelines." Marty thought a moment before continuing. "But I suppose in some companies it may not be necessary to do both if the effect of product mix changes is not significant."

Brian told Marty about the problem that they had at Hayes when Ralph changed the Production Plan. "Sounds like Resource Planning is what we need to do."

"If I were you, I'd get it in place right away," Marty agreed. "And then once you have Resource Planning working, I'd get Rough-Cut Capacity Planning implemented. The two processes are similar enough that it shouldn't take long to set up Rough-Cut Capacity Planning."

As Brian started to thank Marty for his time and say goodbye, Marty interrupted him. "One more thing, Brian. We initially used these processes only when the plans were increasing like the situation you had with Ralph. We have since learned that management needs to concern themselves not only with situations that require the company to increase its capacity, but also with decreasing capacity. When the workload is decreasing, it means the company won't be fully utilizing its equipment or people. It could mean that we would have to reduce our workforce. Of course, another alternative would be to keep the people and build inventory, or take in some subcontract work. These are decisions that senior management should make, and the Resource Planning process helps them do so."

After hanging up the phone, Brian pulled his seminar notes out of the bookcase behind his desk. He read from his notes that the first step in implementing the Resource Planning process is to identify the key resources. Since the process is to be used to get a quick, rough estimate of the impact of high-level decisions on capacity, there is no need to look at every work center. Brian's notes defined these key resources as the critical resources that are involved in the manufacturing process—those that are most likely to be a constraint. The seminar speaker had explained that potential candidates for Resource Planning are bottleneck work centers and work centers that can't be offloaded, such as unique processes or a unique piece of equipment. Other candidates are work centers with long lead times to change capacity, such as a work center with a highly skilled labor content. Work centers with a scrap/yield problem or low utilization/high downtime should also be considered, as should critical suppliers. If a company is an engineer-to-order manufacturer, design engineering should be another important candidate for consideration as a key resource. Other resources to consider are quality control, purchasing, floor space, and tooling.

Brian realized that Hayes needed to identify the resources that were most likely to constrain their process. He knew that the best people to decide what resources to include in this process were the managers of the resources themselves because they were likely to know the constraints better than anyone else would. He sent a memo to Ralph, the Production Manager; Joan, the Production Control Manager; Elliot, the Manufacturing Engineering Manager; Carol, the Quality Control Manager; Harold Bloom, the Purchasing Manager; and Dan and Mickey, asking them all to meet with him the next day to discuss the process.

As the meeting started, Brian reported on his phone conversation with Marty Bloch at Beartone Manufacturing. He briefly explained what the Resource Planning process was all about and said that it would give senior management some key information to help them develop the Production Plan for the future while minimizing the risk of overloading the factory.

Ralph leaned forward in his chair and gave Brian a hard stare. "That matter we had recently regarding the shaver overload. That's what this is all about, isn't it?"

Brian swallowed hard. A confrontation with Ralph in front of this whole group was the last thing he wanted. "Well, as a matter of fact, that incident did prompt my investigation. It seems to me that if we can come up with something that could have avoided that mess we got into, we should do it."

Ralph settled back in his seat. "Well, Miller, if you have an idea that will keep me out of that kind of hot seat, I'm all ears."

Brian then suggested that they limit the list of key resources to the 10 most critical. He reasoned that if they exceeded that number, the Resource Planning process would become too cumbersome and time consuming and senior management probably wouldn't pay attention to them all. When Ralph and Joan voiced concern that there were likely to be more than 10 work centers that could impact on their ability to meet senior management's desires, Brian explained that the Rough-Cut Capacity Planning (see later in this chapter) and the Capacity Requirements Planning (see Chapter 4) processes would provide them additional opportunities to address these other work centers. The focus of Resource Planning needed to be high level.

In devising their list, Brian, Joan, and Elliot came to an agreement that the most critical resources in Brian's area were the shaver, the NC lathes, the NC mills, and the broach.

Resource Planning is done by product family, using the same families that are used for the Sales and Operations Planning process. The Hayes Tractor Company has three product families: large, medium, and small tractors.

The primary information that Hayes needed to compile was a resource profile, sometimes referred to as a bill-of-resources or a load profile. This is the tool used to determine what the resource requirements are going to be. The resource profile is an estimate of the capacity required in each key resource to produce a single finished unit (end item or finished good) in each of the product families (see Figure 7.1).

The capacity requirements numbers can be obtained either directly from the existing database or from estimates. If the bill-of-material and routing files exist and are reasonably accurate, a computer program can be written that will access the bill of material to extract the manufactured parts for each product. If the data from the bill-of-material and routing files are not available or not reliable, or if the computer support to calculate the numbers is not available,

FIGURE 7.1 Resource Profile for Hayes Tractor Company

KEY RESOURCE		PRODUCT FAMILY		
NO.	DESCRIPTION	SMALL	MED.	LARGE
24	TURNING, NC	.70	1.00	1.40
35	MILLS, NC	.50	.60	.80
40	SHAVER	.00	.60	.80
90	BROACH	.15	.18	.20

the data for the resource profile should be estimated from information gathered from Production and Manufacturing Engineering. It is not difficult to get useful data in this manner. These people are knowledgeable because they work with the information day in and day out. It is not necessary for these numbers to be precise since the data will be used only for rough-cut estimates of capacity requirements.

Brian pulled up the multilevel bill of material for one of the medium tractors. (See Figure 7.2.)

By looking at the routings for those parts, Brian could determine

FIGURE 7.2 Bill of Material for Hayes Tractor Company

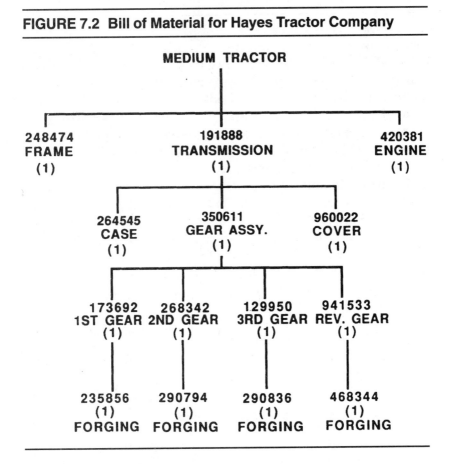

FIGURE 7.3 Resource Profile Data for a Work Center

1ST GEAR TIME = (.13 + (1 ÷ 100)) (1) = .14

2ND GEAR TIME = (.15 + (1 ÷ 100)) (1) = .16

3RD GEAR TIME = (.15 + (1 ÷ 100)) (1) = .16

REV. GEAR TIME = (.13 + (1 ÷ 100)) (1) = .14

TOTAL (Σ of P/N TIMES)   = .60

TIMES PER P/N = (RUN/PIECE + (SU ÷ ORDER QTY.)) X BOM QTY.

---

which of those parts were processed through the critical resources. He could then extract the necessary data for those key work centers.

Brian found that the gears for the medium tractor needed to go through the shaving work center. Looking these parts up on the routing file, he saw that for a three-speed transmission gear set, it took .13 hours to shave the first gear, .15 hours to shave the second and third gears, and .13 hours to shave the reverse gear. If he took the normal lot size and setup time—in this case 100 pieces and one hour respectively—he could amortize the setup time for each gear manufactured. In this case, it was .01 hours (1 hour divided by 100 pieces). By adding together the run time for the gears with the amortized setup time, he had the total time to produce one gear set. Then, he multiplied that by the quantity in the bill of material. In this example, that number is one, because only one of each gear set is used per tractor.

When Brian added the gear numbers together, he found he needed .6 hours of shave time to produce the three-speed gears for a medium tractor (see Figure 7.3). He put the .6 into the resource profile under shaver/medium tractor. He then took the same steps for every key resource and product family. The result for Brian's machine shop looked like Figure 7.1.

RESOURCE PLANNING CALCULATIONS

To calculate the Resource Planning capacity requirements, the Production Plan quantity for each product family is multiplied by the hours in the resource profile corresponding to that key resource/family combination. The capacity required to support the Production Plan for each family is then added together to provide the total capacity that is required for each key resource. This process is then duplicated for each month in the planning horizon.

At Hayes, to produce the NC-turned parts for the 300 small tractors planned for October, Brian multiplied the resource profile hours of .7 hours per tractor in work center 24 (see Figure 7.1) by the planned production quantity of 300 tractors. The result was 210 hours of capacity required (see Figure 7.4). The medium tractor resource profile of 1.0 hours per tractor times the 200 planned tractors equals 200 required hours. The large tractor takes 1.40 hours per tractor. Multiplied by the 20 tractors planned, Brian calculated 28 hours required. He added the 210, 200, and 28 hours together and got the required capacity for the NC lathe of 438 hours. He continued this process through all the key resources for each of the next twelve months. Then, he compared the required capacity with the planned capacity for those work centers for each time period. This told him the capacity status of the critical resources. The final report for the NC lathes looked like Figure 7.5

FIGURE 7.4 Resource Requirements—Original Production Plan (October)

KEY RESOURCE		PRODUCT FAM. & QTY.			REQ'D. CAP'Y.	PLAN CAP'Y.
		SMALL	MEDIUM	LARGE		
NO.	DESCR.	300	200	20		
24	NC TURNING	210	200	28	438	500
35	NC MILLING	150	120	16	286	300
40	SHAVER	0	120	16	136	130
90	BROACH	45	36	4	85	120

FIGURE 7.5 Twelve-Month Resource Plan

RESOURCE: NC TURNING				
Month	Required Capacity	Planned Capacity	Variance	Maximum Capacity
Oct	438	500	+ 62	560
Nov	512	500	- 12	560
Dec	512	500	- 12	560
Jan	512	500	- 12	560
Feb	512	500	- 12	560
Mar	512	500	- 12	560
Apr	624	500	-124	560
May	624	500	-124	560
Jun	624	500	-124	560
Jul	624	500	-124	560
Aug	624	500	-124	560
Sep	624	500	-124	560

If the required capacity is reasonably close to the planned capacity, management can approve the plans and proceed with the development of the Master Production Schedule. However, this does not preclude having to make some adjustments to planned capacities once detailed CRP has been run. Remember that this is only rough-cut.

As a rule of thumb, if the difference between the required and planned capacities is greater than about 15 percent, some corrective action should be taken to balance available capacity with the projected requirements. This break point—15 percent—is somewhat arbitrary. It depends upon the individual work center's ability to flex capacity.

Looking at the plan for NC turning (see Figure 7.5), Brian saw that October is underloaded by just over 12 percent (62 divided by 500). Brian figured that he could use that time to do some maintenance and to do some further education and training of his crew. For November through March, the plan indicated that the work center would be overloaded by 12 hours, or less than 3%. Considering that the plan was only a rough estimate of the required capacity, Brian wasn't concerned about it. However, the increase in the Production Plan starting in April was going to cause problems. Not only were the estimated resource requirements greater than Brian's current plan, they were significantly greater than what Brian considered his maximum capacity. He was going to have to talk to Ralph about that. This Resource Planning approach was giving him a six-month advance warning of a rather serious problem. He hoped that Ralph would appreciate that.

Alternate plans at the Sales and Operations Planning level can be quickly evaluated by looking at the Resource Plan. We can easily see what product families are impacting on which work centers. By altering the capacity in these work centers and/or the Production Plan, we can vary the results of that impact.

There are several ways to get more capacity if necessary. Actions such as overtime, hiring more people, cross training, using alternate work centers, and subcontracting are likely to impact the cost of the product. Increasing capacity to meet the requirements of the Production Plan may require capital investment in equipment or facilities. Another shift may need to be added, requiring additional supervision and training. Major make-or-buy decisions may also be considered.

Similarly, reductions in capacity requirements may increase costs as a result of underutilized equipment or labor. On the down side, potential labor reductions may be identified. Management should be made aware ahead of time of the potential cost impact of these actions.

All of these are senior-level management decisions that must be made. Since the Production Plan belongs to senior management, they should be informed of the consequences of their decisions and actions before they approve the Production Plan. By using Resource Planning, they can look ahead at the future capacity requirements and test the validity of the Production Plan during the Sales and Operations Planning process, thereby improving the chances of being able to meet the plan within reasonable costs.

Brian and his associates had set up their Resource Planning model on a personal computer using spreadsheet software. When they felt that the process was ready to go, they set up a personal computer and connected it to a large-screen television in the conference room and invited the management staff to a demonstration. Brian walked them through the process. By looking at the Resource Plan for the original Production Plan (see Figure 7.4), they agreed that Brian could probably have worked around the tight situation in the gear-shaver work center (136 hours required versus 130 hours planned). However, when they ran a second scenario changing the mix between small and medium tractors (decreasing the small tractors from 300 to 200 and increasing the medium tractors from 200 to 300), they could see that the required capacity would be 196 hours required versus the 130 planned (see Figure 7.6). Brian calculated the maximum capacity for the shavers running 3 shifts, 7 days a week to be 150 hours if they could maintain the current 90 percent load factor, which was unlikely. It was clear that the revised mix in the Production Plan created a major problem.

Ralph, Pete, and Lenny recognized that with this information, they easily could have avoided the hassle they had encountered earlier. They complimented the team for the work that they had done. They agreed that they would use the Resource Planning process as an integral part of their Sales and Operations Planning process from

---

FIGURE 7.6 Resource Requirements—Revised Production Plan (October)

KEY RESOURCE		PRODUCT FAM. & QTY.			REQ'D. CAP'Y.	PLAN CAP'Y.
		SMALL	MEDIUM	LARGE		
NO.	DESCR.	200	300	20		
24	NC TURNING	140	300	28	468	500
35	NC MILLING	100	180	16	296	300
40	SHAVER	0	180	16	196	130
90	BROACH	30	54	4	88	120

now on. They also agreed that they would use it to evaluate any emergency situations like the one with Iowa Tractor.

Once Hayes had the Resource Planning process up and running, Brian called Joan to talk about Rough-Cut Capacity Planning at the master schedule level.

Joan was way ahead of him. "You know, I have already been checking on that. Our software has the capability to do Rough-Cut Capacity Planning. We just never considered using it since we had Capacity Requirements Planning available to us. I have the master schedulers and capacity planners working on it now. We'll be able to have a more detailed look at the capacity requirements than Resource Planning provides, yet be able to check it quickly prior to running MRP and CRP."

ROUGH-CUT CAPACITY PLANNING CALCULATIONS

Whereas Resource Planning uses the Production Plan as input, Rough-Cut Capacity Planning (RCCP) uses the Master Production Schedule (MPS). The purpose is to test the validity of the MPS before firming it up and running the detailed MRP and CRP calculations. The same key resources that were used with Resource Planning should be used.

The differences between Resource Planning and Rough-Cut Capacity Planning are:

1. The resource profiles for RCCP are developed for each master scheduled part number rather than product family (see Figure 7.7). In Hayes' case, part numbers 36492, 32846, and so on represent specific models of the small tractors. Some software packages provide the capability to generate the resource profile for master scheduled items by searching the database for the parts and operations involved and doing the calculations based on the current bills of material and routings.
2. The RCCP resource profile data is multiplied by the master scheduled quantities rather than the Production Plan quantities.
3. Additional resources may be added to the Rough-Cut Capacity Planning process that were not in the Resource Planning process

FIGURE 7.7 Resource Profile for Small Tractors

KEY RESOURCE		ITEM NUMBER					
W / C	DESCR.	36492	32846	25173	31962	26874	21349
24	NC TURNING	0.65	0.75	0.70	0.60	0.70	0.80
35	NC MILLING	0.55	0.60	0.50	0.45	0.40	0.50
40	SHAVER	0	0	0	0	0	0
90	BROACH	0.12	0.18	0.15	0.10	0.20	0.15

if desired. The people doing RCCP (typically the capacity planner and/or the master scheduler) have the time and interest to handle the additional information. To keep the process manageable, the total number of resources planned with RCCP should not exceed approximately 10 percent of the total work centers in the company.

Figures 7.7 and 7.8 are the resource profile and the rough-cut capacity requirements for the members of the small tractor family only. For example, in the case of MPS part number 36492, the resource profile time of 0.65 (see Figure 7.7) would be multiplied by the quan-

FIGURE 7.8 Rough-Cut Capacity Requirements for Small Tractors (October)

KEY RESOURCE		ITEM NO.						
W / C	DESCR.	36492	32846	25173	31962	26874	21349	TOTAL
	QTY. SCHED	50.0	40.0	100.0	20.0	80.0	10.0	300
24	NC TURNING	32.5	30.0	70.0	12.0	56.0	8.0	209
35	NC MILLING	27.5	24.0	50.0	9.0	32.0	5.0	148
40	SHAVER	0.0	0.0	0.0	0.0	0.0	0.0	0
90	BROACH	6.0	7.2	15.0	2.0	16.0	1.5	48

tity for that MPS part number, which is 50 (see Figure 7.8), resulting in 32.5 standard hours of capacity required. This would be repeated for each item and work center to get the total capacity requirements. One would go through the same process separately for the medium- and large-tractor families, and then total all three numbers for each key resource (see Figure 7.9).

Doing Rough-Cut Capacity Planning at this level provides an opportunity to see the impact of product mix changes in the Master Production Schedule. For example, referring to Figure 7.8, if the master scheduled quantities are changed, the changes in the capacity requirements for the key resources can be immediately seen. The total capacity requirements calculated in this manner (see the "REQ'D CAP'Y" column of Figure 7.9) are slightly different from the capacity requirements calculated for the small-tractor family from the Production Plan (see Figure 7.4). That is because the production-plan calculation uses the representative-item approach, whereas the Master Production Schedule calculation uses different resource profile data for each MPS part number. Therefore, a mix shift in the master schedule can cause the required capacity to change.

FIGURE 7.9 Rough-Cut Capacity Requirements—Master Production Schedule Summary (October)

KEY RESOURCE		MPS SUMMARY			REQ'D. CAP'Y.	PLAN CAP'Y.
		SMALL	MEDIUM	LARGE		
NO.	DESCR.	300	200	20		
24	NC TURNING	209	197	29	435	500
35	NC MILLING	148	138	18	304	300
40	SHAVER	0	114	12	126	130
90	BROACH	48	35	6	89	120

Since the Master Production Schedule is in weekly or daily increments, Rough-Cut Capacity Planning can be displayed in weekly buckets if desired rather than the monthly buckets commonly associated with the Resource Planning process.

OPERATIONAL REQUIREMENTS

Varying levels of computer support are used for Resource Planning and Rough-Cut Capacity Planning. Some companies have complete modules as part of their Manufacturing Resource Planning (MRP II) software. Others use standard spreadsheet programs on a personal computer. Still others execute the process manually.

Assuring that the data is available and that Resource Planning and Rough-Cut Capacity Planning are done in a timely manner is the responsibility of the capacity planner. In companies where that position does not exist, that responsibility is usually delegated to either the master scheduler or the material planner.

Even though top management members don't perform the actual Resource Planning calculations, they are responsible for those numbers. They must accept responsibility for the identification of the key resources and the development of the resource profiles. They are also the ones who must take action based on the Resource Planning information when action is required.

Resource Planning should cover a minimum of one year. Some companies go out five years or more. The resource requirements should be expressed in monthly increments for the first year. After that, those periods can be lengthened to a quarterly view if preferred. At the end of each month, that month is dropped, and another month needs to be added to the end of the horizon. The Resource Plan needs to be reviewed every month. Although changes may not be made, reconfirmation is important. Resource Planning can also be used to evaluate any major change scenario at any time.

Rough-Cut Capacity Planning should be run after Resource Planning to be sure no capacity problems arise because of product mix or actual scheduled quantities. If additional key resources are planned in RCCP that were not considered in Resource Planning, this is the opportunity to evaluate the validity of the MPS in regard to those resources. The RCCP horizon should be equal to the master schedule horizon (typically 52 weeks or more). The Rough-Cut Capacity Plan should be expressed in monthly or weekly increments and reviewed at least monthly. In addition, if changes to the master schedule are suggested, a quick Rough-Cut Capacity Planning check can be made at any time to be certain there are no capacity problems before releasing the changes to Material Requirements Planning.

Keep in mind that even though neither Resource Planning nor Rough-Cut Capacity Planning may indicate a problem, that does not mean that a capacity problem will not be subsequently revealed via Capacity Requirements Planning. Neither Resource Planning nor Rough-Cut Capacity Planning provides enough detailed information to assure a viable plan. These techniques only serve as a warning that there is some risk involved in proceeding with the planning process in light of the capacity situation. The decision to approve the plans or to require further analysis is a judgment call by the managers involved in the process.

ADVANTAGES OF RESOURCE PLANNING AND ROUGH-CUT CAPACITY PLANNING

It is important to keep in mind that these processes are a rough estimate of the company's capacity needs. This, as might be expected, has both its advantages and some limitations when compared to calculating detailed Capacity Requirements Planning. Let us first take a look at the advantages.

As we have mentioned, Resource Planning tests the validity of the Production Plan and Rough-Cut Capacity Planning tests the Master Production Schedule. They are done at least once a month or whenever there is a major change to be sure that the Production Plan and Master Production Schedule have been developed within the realm of reason with the planned available capacity. They should cover the full planning horizon for the Production Plan and Master Production Schedule. By doing so, Resource Planning and Rough-Cut Capacity Planning provide an early handle on whether anything has to be done to alter planned capacity or the Production Plan or Master Schedule.

As opposed to Capacity Requirements Planning, Resource Planning and Rough-Cut Capacity Planning do not require the use of a routing for every item being built. These processes can use a resource profile developed from a so-called typical product, one that is representative of the other products in that family. Both Resource Planning and Rough-Cut Capacity Planning are simple processes where precision is not critical. Resource Planning examines only those key resources in the process. Neither process takes long to implement with the proper focus. In many cases, the implementation can be accomplished in less than a week. To do so may require that the number of key resources included be limited to only a few.

Neither Resource Planning nor Rough-Cut Capacity Planning takes much computer time. It allows us to correlate families with key resources, thereby enabling quick assessment of the impact of changes in the plan. For example, in Figure 7.4, we can see that a 10 percent increase in the Production Plan for the small tractors is not a serious problem, since it would not impact on the shavers. The other work centers are well within their capacity capabilities. On the other hand, as we have seen, a 10 percent increase in medium-tractor production causes trouble.

Because Resource Planning and Rough-Cut Capacity Planning require relatively little time, they allow us to pose and evaluate alternative "what-if" questions quickly.

Frequently, at Hayes, the Product Sales Manager would come into the Sales and Operations Planning meeting and inform the group of a new opportunity. One day he said, "We've just broken into a new segment of the market that we didn't anticipate. After talking to these customers, our assessment is that we could get between a 12 to 20 percent gain in business with our medium-tractor family. Should we pursue that?" The figures were immediately put into the Resource Planning model to determine if it was at least feasible to get the resources for the job.

Shortly after implementing Resource Planning at Hayes, Lenny's first words at these monthly meetings were usually "What if?" Since it was relatively simple to run a Resource Planning analysis on any new possibility, the management team could address the situation without requiring a lot of time.

RESOURCE PLANNING AND ROUGH-CUT CAPACITY PLANNING LIMITATIONS

These processes have plenty of things working in their favor, but there are also some limitations to be aware of. First, the Resource

Planning approach assumes that the resource profile chosen to represent the family is typical of all of the products in that family. This, of course, does not address those environments where product variability within a family is significant. In such an environment, Rough-Cut Capacity Planning takes on a greater significance since it deals with individual products.

Resource Planning also assumes that the production lot size is proportional to the Production Plan, and that the company will produce exactly what will be required for that particular month. However, since different lot-sizing rules are often used at the component levels, the actual capacity requirements may differ from the Resource Planning calculations. Resource Planning also assumes that the setup times are distributed proportionally to the Production Plan. In reality, as the Production Plan is either increased or decreased, the allocation of setup times can vary. These shortcomings are also helped out somewhat with Rough-Cut Capacity Planning because the master schedule breaks the Production Plan down into the actual scheduled quantities.

The resource profile also does not typically provide any lead-time offset. It predicts the need for the capacity in the same period in which the product will ship. This, too, is generally not true. We know there's going to be some lead-time offset in the work centers that appear at the beginning of the manufacturing process. This, however, can usually be accommodated in the mechanics of the process by offsetting those capacity requirements appropriately. At first, Brian didn't recognize the impact of the lead-time offset issue. But, once he did, it was relatively easy to resolve it. Typically, all four of Brian's work centers worked on the product a month earlier than the product was due to ship. By offsetting the required capacity one month earlier, Brian was able to give himself a better representation of the timing of the capacity requirements. Mickey's work tended to fall in the month the product would be shipped, but some of Dan's had to be offset as much as two months earlier.

The Resource Planning process ignores component and work-in-process inventory. It assumes we have to make all the parts necessary to build the product. This can be a problem if the company is planning to reduce the inventory levels of the family or if a product or family is being phased out or has become obsolete. By design, it also only considers specific, designated key work centers, not the total process. Conceivably, a potential bottleneck work center could be left off the list. Generally, this is only a temporary problem, since once an additional work center is recognized as a key work center as evidenced by information from Capacity Requirements Planning, it is merely added to the list of key resources.

COMPARING RESOURCE PLANNING, ROUGH-CUT CAPACITY PLANNING, AND CAPACITY REQUIREMENTS PLANNING

A question often asked is, "Do we need to do all three: Resource Planning, Rough-Cut Capacity Planning (RCCP) and Capacity Requirements Planning (CRP)?" In most cases, the answer is yes, except in the flow environment, as we will see in Chapter 9. Each technique has its own purpose, strengths, and weaknesses. Let's compare the three techniques.

The primary difference between Resource Planning, Rough-Cut Capacity Planning, and Capacity Requirements Planning is that their focus is different. Resource Planning is focused on the Production Plan. Rough-Cut Capacity Planning is driven by the Master Production Schedule. Capacity Requirements Planning is concerned with the detailed material plans and shop schedules.

The horizons of the three processes also differ. Because of its limitations mentioned earlier, Resource Planning is a long-term planning process. Since RCCP can use more detailed routing information and is based on specific master scheduled items and quantities, it provides a more precise view of the capacity requirements than does Resource Planning. Consequently, the Rough-Cut Capacity Planning is more useful in the mid-term time frame. Because of the limitations noted above, neither Resource Planning nor RCCP should be applied to the first month or two of the planning horizon. Capacity Requirements Planning does an excellent job of providing very accurate information for the short- to mid-term time frame.

Because it deals with monthly periods, Resource Planning typically is run only monthly. Rough-Cut Capacity Planning can be run either monthly or weekly and display information in either monthly or weekly buckets. Capacity Requirements Planning is always run weekly and displays information in weekly or daily periods.

Different people use the three processes. Resource Planning is a tool primarily for top management; Rough-Cut Capacity Planning is used primarily by the master scheduler and capacity planner. Capacity Requirements Planning is a tool for the capacity planner, middle managers, and first-line supervisors.

Resource Planning and RCCP look at only the designated key resources, whereas CRP considers all resources on the database. Resource Planning and RCCP are run before Material Requirements Planning is run. Capacity Requirements Planning is done after Material Requirements Planning, because it needs input from MRP. With Resource and Rough-Cut Capacity Planning, inventory on hand or on order is not netted out from the capacity requirements calculations. This inventory, however, is netted out in the MRP process before CRP is run. Resource Planning and RCCP typically have no lead-time offset applied to the timing of capacity requirements, whereas lead-time offset is a standard feature of CRP. Also, Resource Planning can be done with very little, if any, computer support. Although Rough-Cut Capacity Planning can be run with only minimal computer support, better results are obtained when it is included as a module of the full MRP II system. On the other hand, CRP requires a complete database, full-function software, and relatively long computer run times.

Resource Planning and RCCP should be periodically compared with CRP to be sure they are reasonably in sync.

So, as is evident, Resource Planning and Rough-Cut Capacity Planning have the advantages of speed, flexibility, and simplicity. Capacity Requirements Planning has the advantages of thoroughness, detail, and accuracy.

Once Resource Planning and Rough-Cut Capacity Planning were properly implemented at Hayes, surprises in the capacity report rarely reached Brian's desk. Through Sales and Operations Planning, management had assumed responsibility for deciding what aggregate levels of product would be built and when. Through Master Production Scheduling, Material Requirements Planning, Capacity Requirements Planning, and the dispatch list, Brian would receive his production schedules. It was then up to him to execute the plan and deliver on time.

With the addition of Resource Planning and RCCP, Brian's confidence that he could consistently deliver on time was boosted immensely.

Chapter Eight

Joining Forces

The variety of capacity and scheduling problems Brian had encountered at Hayes were not necessarily problems that were unique to the production floor. Carol Barrow, Manager of Quality Control, had been watching and listening with great interest to the changes happening at Hayes. She had seen how the production departments had gotten their schedules and capacities under control. Her operation, however, was still out of control and she couldn't figure out why. Finally, she decided to talk to Brian about it. "I'm getting buried out there. I never know what's a priority until Mickey needs it, which means I constantly have to move people around at the last minute. I'm always working overtime. When I go to Pete to try to hire more inspectors, he always puts me off by telling me that things will get better and I probably won't need more inspectors. The problem is things aren't getting better. Now, to my way of thinking, Manufacturing Resource Planning could improve my operations, too. Couldn't I get a capacity plan for QC, like you guys in manufacturing do?"

Brian thought about Carol's request. "What you're asking for is a priority list for inspection and a way to determine how many inspectors you need. . . . You know, I bet we could do that if we put the inspection operations on the routing."

"You mean make inspection a regular operation?" Carol asked. "We've never done that before. I mean we're inspectors, not production," she stammered.

"So what?" Brian shrugged. "The inspectors are a resource, aren't they? We can schedule them just like any other operation."

"You'll have to convince me," replied Carol.

They went to the inspection layout table and picked up a work order. "Look," said Brian, "this part has to come here to be inspected prior to going on to the next operation. We could insert an operation, assign a work-center number, and put in a setup and run time (see Figure 8.1). Do that on all the routings that require the inspection operation, feed it into the computer, and it will give you a dispatch list just like we have for the production operators. Not only that, but you'll also get a capacity plan for the 12-month horizon. That will be the information Pete is looking for to support your request for more inspectors. Ever since I started using the capacity plan, I've always gotten the people I need. Pete knows the predicted hours are accurate. When I've gotten the people I asked for, there has never been a loss of productivity. I have been able to hold overtime at the planned level. I'm also sure that if I asked for a reduction in people, he'd believe it, because we've shown we can accurately predict our needs through this system. We really understand where the numbers come from and we can support them. I used to have the same exact problems you're having, but not anymore."

"Slow down, slow down," Carol said. "I can't use run times. I don't inspect all the parts. We only do a statistical sample. If you put the

FIGURE 8.1 Routing Showing Inspection as an Operation

594706	SUB. ASSY. - FRAME	
PART NUMBER	PART DESCRIPTION	

OPN. NO.	DEPT.	WORK CTR.	OPERATION DESCRIPTION	SETUP	RUN
			RELEASE		
			PICK		
10	FAB	53	WELD, TACK	.5	1.00
20	FAB	57	WELD, FINISH	.1	1.00
30	QA	60	INSPECTION, LAYOUT	2.0	.00
40	MACH	36	MILL, KNEE	1.0	.50
50	MACH	35	BORE	.5	.25
			STORE		

time in to inspect one part and multiply it by the order quantity, it will overstate the lead time and capacity requirements."

"You're right," conceded Brian. He thought a second. "Tell me, Carol, is the sample size typically the same?"

"Well, we use statistical sampling to determine the sample size, but in general the sample size is the same even if the order quantity varies a little."

"Then why don't we just figure out how long it takes to inspect the whole sample and put that into the routing instead of using a run time per piece?"

The process that Brian suggested using here is often called a "block" standard—a block of time to do the complete job. Another term that is used to describe this is the "total elapsed time" for the operation.

When Carol told Brian that their software did not provide the "block standard" or "elapsed time" feature, Brian said "Why can't we just put that information into the setup field on the routing. It amounts to the same thing, a block of time to do the entire job instead of a time per piece."

"You know," Carol said, visualizing how this would come together, "I think that will work, except for one thing. The inspectors aren't going to like having a standard time set on their inspection."

"You're probably right, Carol. I had the same problem with the production people when we asked them to help establish realistic standards. They were constantly asking for them to be loosened."

"How'd you resolve that?"

"We still have some problems," Brian admitted, "but we are working really hard to educate the operators about how the standards are used for capacity planning, scheduling, and calculating the cost of the product. That helped, but it wasn't until we stopped using the standards as a way to pressure them for better performance that we really started to get their cooperation."

"Wait a minute, Brian. You still use your efficiency performance measures. I hear your supervisors talking to the operators about them all the time."

"You're right," Brian said, "but we are trying to use the correct approach with the operators. Instead of demanding that they improve their efficiency, we ask them what can be done to improve it. For example, when an operator says a standard is too tight, the supervisor asks the operator to call him over the next time that job is run so they can review it. They try to improve the process to meet the standard time. If they can't, they'll call the manufacturing engineer to help with the process improvement. If they still can't meet the standard, the manufacturing engineer will change the standard. As soon as we started doing this, productivity went up. But don't let me mislead you, Carol, it didn't work for everyone. We still have a few diehards out there. But, what's really interesting is that they aren't getting any support from their peers or the union. What you'll find is that if you approach the problem properly, your inspectors are going to see this as a real help to them and not a hindrance."

"What about the roving inspectors?" Carol asked.

"I don't know what to do there," replied Brian. "How do you plan their capacity now?"

"Well, I know a roving inspector can cover about 20 production people. I just don't know how many people you'll have on any one shift. You see, I've got to provide coverage on all the shifts regardless of the number of people."

"Well, that's no problem," Brian said. "I'll give you my capacity plans and you can calculate your requirements from that."

"Hey, Brian, that'll be great. I really appreciate this."

Walking back to his office, Brian felt good. He felt that he and Carol had actually accomplished a great deal. They were working together to constructively solve a real problem, and they had done so without any bitterness. Most of Brian and Carol's previous conversations involved arguments over acceptability of parts. Brian had to admit this one was much more satisfying. He realized that Hayes was finally starting to operate like a team. That didn't mean there wasn't more to do, but people had begun working things out together.

Similar problems to Carol's were also cropping up in the area of tooling. It always seemed there were never the right tools available to start a new job. Brian had been running his operations off his dispatch list, and things were getting better. But they still ran into problems, like the time they introduced a new hub onto the medium-sized tractor. The date for introduction had been changed and changed again, and Brian had been able to reschedule the hub's work centers around management's indecision. Finally, the introduction date arrived and production was ready to begin. There was only one problem: the new tooling hadn't arrived.

Brian knew whom to call. "Elliot, we're ready to start the new hub. . . ."

Elliot didn't need to hear more. "The new hub? Is the tooling ready?"

"That's why we're talking, Elliot."

"Is there anyway you can make the old fixture work?" Elliot asked.

"It's just not possible. You know the new hub's larger, and it needs a new fixture." Brian felt some of his old exasperation returning. "Tell me, Elliot, when are we ever going to have the tools done on time, so we can proof run the first production like we're supposed to?"

"What do they expect from me? I mean, how many times have they changed their minds, and now I'm once again the last to hear about it. I'm sorry, Brian. All I can do is react around this place. I'll have to check on the hub tooling, but you can bet if it isn't done, it's because Design Engineering didn't get their design done until well inside of lead time."

"I wish I could help you, Elliot, but I can't get these parts out unless I get my tools from you."

"Look, Brian, I didn't have the slightest idea when these tools were supposed to be ready, especially the way everyone's priorities change around here. I mean, it seems everything is behind. And it's primarily because the design engineers never seem to get the designs finished on time."

The pattern was beginning to seem obvious. The first step to solving this problem was to head up to Design Engineering and figure out what was going on there. They were the ones that caused the delays with the late design releases. This problem stemmed from the fact that the new hub required a fixture for the NC drill, and the drawings for the new design were two weeks late, which meant that the fixture would be late.

Elliot and Brian tracked down the Manager of Design Engineering, Lloyd Adams. When they told him their problem, Lloyd was not very sympathetic. "What do you want from me? We're under the gun to get this new product line out pronto. I'm just trying to get the whole project out. How am I supposed to know which drawing should be done first?"

As Brian and Elliot went through some of Lloyd's method of scheduling, they realized that his schedule was not in sync with production's and consequently had been sending out some designs earlier than they were needed and others later. Lloyd reiterated that he had no clear idea what is needed when, he just sees his workload according to each project. Individual-parts requirements don't come into play. "Hey, Elliot, you know what's happening up here. We're dealing with customer changes on a daily basis. And we're not even talking about Manufacturing's input for improvements in manufacturability. If you mix that together with your production needs or Purchasing wanting specific designs finished early, it makes it impossible to schedule."

There was no way Brian could argue with Lloyd. He knew there had been numerous times when they might not have had the capacity they needed on one of their lathes, so they decided to proof run a new part early. This meant they needed tooling earlier, along with the purchased material and other components. This became a scheduling nightmare. The priorities were constantly changing, as were the capacity requirements on the lathes.

"Believe me, fellows," Lloyd said as calmly as he could, "I know everything that's supposed to get done and we're getting to it as fast as we can."

The only problem for Brian and Elliot was that because of the lead time for manufacturing, some of the designs that were getting done later needed to be done earlier. All Lloyd could do was shrug. "I understand your problem, but the priorities are only being communicated by customer ship date. On the individual parts, I can only do what I think is right."

Later in the day, Elliot stopped by to see Joan. He explained the problems he and Brian were having. Joan reached into a pile of papers in a tray and pulled out an article. "I just finished reading this," she said, tossing it to Elliot. "It's all about how you structure engineering and tooling requirements into the bill of material."

The light had slowly been coming on for Joan. Manufacturing had been using the capacity plan and dispatch list, so why couldn't Tooling and Engineering? The article spoke about how to use Manufacturing Resource Planning software to aid the various support departments. It detailed how Material Requirements Planning could release past-due messages for activities, as well as parts, and how capacity plans and dispatch lists could be provided for these activities, too, reflecting all projects. The simulation capabilities available in the

MRP system could be used for all activities, not just manufactured and purchased parts. The article also explained how changing the master schedule caused all activities for a project to be rescheduled in sync.

As they discussed the methodology, Elliot realized he could put the tooling number right on the bill of material. He could then establish operation numbers on the routing for the various steps in tooling, put that on the MRP system, and he could have accurate dates via the dispatch list and capacity plans for the tool room. Elliot and Joan sat down and structured how it would work on a special design loader they had to produce (see Figure 8.2).

Looking at the proposed bill of material, the loader required a special bucket. They had changed the shape of the bucket, which required a new back and two new sides. The teeth remained the same. In order for Dan's department to weld it properly, some new slots had to be milled on the locator brackets. Elliot and Joan entered the five steps required to accomplish the modification to the fixture into the routing database (see Figure 8.3).

When Joan brought these ideas to Lloyd, as a way for him to get a handle on engineering resources, he was a little reluctant. "That's all well and good for machines and mechanical operations, but I'm dealing with people up here. How do you schedule creativity? How can I expect an accurate time from an engineer about how long a project will take?"

Joan explained to Lloyd how it would work. "We have the bill of material for our product (see Figure 8.2). The bucket assembly back and sides are our new engineered parts. Directly under those parts, we list that the assembly needs a drawing to make those parts, and we give that drawing a part number. Then, we create a routing for the process of making a drawing. It may take a sketch, which requires a specific kind of engineer. So instead of saying we need drills or mills, we say we need an electrical engineer or a mechanical engineer, etc. Then, it should go through a manufacturing review to assess manufacturability. Someone will have to lay out the drawing, and then someone else will have to check that. Having completed those steps, we document the drawing."

"Hang on a minute," interjected Lloyd. "I need the customer specifications in order to start the design. Why can't that be put on there also?"

FIGURE 8.2 Special Product Bill of Material

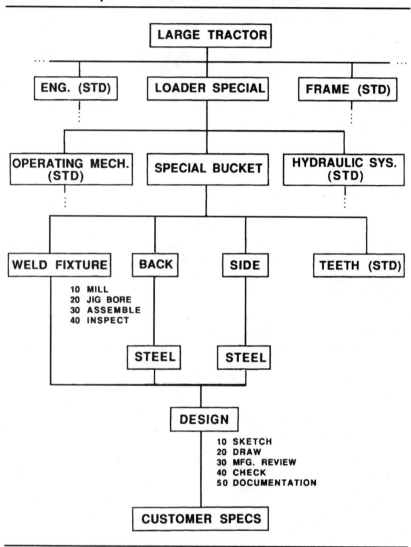

FIGURE 8.3 Tooling Routing

999243	FIXTURE - WELD	
PART NUMBER	PART DESCRIPTION	

OPN. NO.	DEPT.	WORK CTR.	OPERATION DESCRIPTION	SETUP	RUN
10	TOOL	76	DISASSEMBLE	.10	3.00
20	MACH	36	MILL	1.00	.50
30	TOOL	71	JIG BORE	2.00	3.00
40	TOOL	76	ASSEMBLE	.10	6.00
50	QA	63	INSPECTION, TOOL	4.00	0.00

Joan painfully recalled the frequency with which the Sales Department asked for product inside of lead time but never seemed to get the customer specifications in on time. "I don't see why not," she replied. "Getting a customer specification is an activity just like anything else. So why not let the computer schedule it as an integrated part of the whole process?"

"Count me in, then," Lloyd said, "this stuff is beginning to make sense, especially if it can help get my customer specifications on time and meet my schedules." Joan and Lloyd sat down and developed a routing that reflected the design steps required to produce a drawing (see Figure 8.4).

FIGURE 8.4 Engineering Routing

188642	BUCKET	
PART NUMBER	PART DESCRIPTION	

OPN. NO.	DEPT.	WORK CTR.	OPERATION DESCRIPTION	SETUP	RUN
10	ENG	80	SKETCH, MECH.	12.00	0.00
20	ENG	84	DRAW, MECH.	21.00	0.00
30	ENG	86	MFG. REVIEW	3.00	0.00
40	ENG	88	CHECK	4.00	0.00
50	ENG	89	DOCUMENTATION	3.00	0.00

Once the engineering requirements are structured on the bills of material and routings have been created, Manufacturing Resource Planning can be used to plan the engineering resource requirements and schedule the engineering activities.

The planning system was helping to bridge the gaps between areas like Manufacturing, Engineering, Tooling, and Inspection, by linking everyone to the same schedule. It also brought these areas in sync with one another, so they were working together not as separate departments, not as adversaries, but as a cohesive team.

Manufacturing, Tooling, Engineering, Inspection, and Sales began a pilot project. They made the changes to the bills of material and routings they had developed and used the computer to calculate their schedules. The system worked so well for Engineering that within a short time Lloyd was looking for ways to link in his Computer-Aided Design (CAD) systems. Hayes was starting to look and work like a competitive manufacturing company.

What Brian and his colleagues would soon find out, however, was that even though they had begun to plan and execute well, they still needed to maintain their dedication to becoming better. It was easy to become complacent.

Chapter Nine

Continuous Improvement

Brian took his customary seat for Ralph's monthly staff meeting. He was pleasantly surprised when Ralph complimented both Dan and him for what they had achieved with CRP, Input/Output control, and dispatching. Ralph told them, "Things have never run so smoothly out in the shop. Oh, sure, there are still glitches now and then, but they don't happen because everything is out of control out there."

It was true. Brian was continually gaining greater confidence in his ability to control his own area. No longer was he just reacting to what came his way day by day, but now he was actually able to plan several months in advance. He jokingly told Ralph that after operating in the dark for so long, having this much visibility was almost scary.

Ralph, however, was not finished. "Although you guys have done a good job out in the shop," he continued, "very little seems to have been done in Assembly. What's the story there?

Brian responded. "Dan and I have tried to get Mickey to use the dispatch list and the Capacity Requirements Planning reports like the rest of us, but he has been dead set against it."

"Why don't you want to use them?" Ralph asked, as he turned to Mickey.

"Because," Mickey replied, "I have an assembly line, not a job shop. It's a continuous flow process, not like the batch operations they have out in the shop. I don't need a dispatch list to tell me when each operation on the assembly line is due. The master schedule tells

223

me what I need to start on the assembly line, and everything just moves down the line until we ship it out. Nor do I need a capacity requirements report to tell me how much labor I need. Again, the master schedule tells me how many tractors a day I have to produce. I know how many people it takes to assemble them, so when the production schedule changes, I can simply calculate on the back of an envelope how many people I need. I know the maximum number of tractors I can get off the line on each shift, so I also know when I need to schedule overtime or add another shift."

Ralph reminded him, "One thing we've learned through all this, Mickey, is that the function of capacity management is identifying and resolving potential future capacity constraints before they become a problem. You do have capacity constraints, don't you?"

"Well, sure" Mickey said. "Remember when you changed the plan to call for more medium tractors and fewer small ones? I had to move a bunch of people from the small line to the medium line to meet the new schedule. Of course, it wasn't just that simple. I had to do some additional training, which cut into my productivity for a while. And we needed some additional assembly fixtures."

"You still need to be able to anticipate such situations," Ralph said. "You could be right that you don't need as much detail as Brian and Dan do to manage your capacity. But the question is, what's the best way for you to do it? Should you use the formal system we have, or is your manual approach good enough? I want you all to give some thought to that and report back to me with a recommendation."

Ralph continued, "Next topic. Even though things are better than they used to be, we need to get a lot better if we're going to remain competitive in this market. We've lost a lot of small tractor business to overseas manufacturers. There is still plenty of room for improvement around here."

Brian picked up on Ralph's lead. "You're absolutely right. Lately it seems like I'm wasting a lot of resources. For instance, I'm working overtime on the drills because we are behind schedule according to the dispatch list. We're pumping out the parts, but all we do is push them on ahead to the milling machines where they sit, because that whole work center is shut down for some maintenance on the central coolant system. It seems a little silly to be spending all that overtime when the parts don't go anywhere."

"I'm glad you brought up the subject of waste," Ralph said. "I think there's a lot of waste around here. For one thing, we have too much inventory around to suit me. We just seem to cover up our problems with inventory instead of solving them. We're going to have to change that. Now that we've gotten our shortages down and our on-time delivery performance up, we need to refocus our priorities. We need to reduce our lead times, improve our quality, and reduce our costs. I've just read an article about Lean Manufacturing that talks about eliminating waste in a manufacturing company. It sounds like something we should look into. And, by chance, I just happen to have this flyer about a seminar on the subject. We need to learn more about it. Looking back on the benefits we got from sending you to the last two seminars, I think you ought to go to this one, too. I want all of you to sign up for it."

That night, Brian ran into Hal from the Good Health Vitamin Company at the Ram's Horn Inn, a local restaurant. Brian's wife was out of town visiting her mother, and Brian figured a meal out was better than eating his own cooking. After exchanging greetings and briefly bringing each other up to date on their respective companies, Brian told Hal about the conversation at Ralph's staff meeting.

"Let's have some dinner and talk more about this," Hal suggested.

"You know, Brian," Hal said, as they settled into a booth, "we're trying to keep up on some of these new things ourselves. We've just begun some preliminary education on Just-in-Time (JIT) Manufacturing. It's an approach to reducing waste in manufacturing. We think we can reduce our lead times significantly with JIT. It seems to me to definitely be the right direction. You should look into it."

"Oh, great, you and Ralph," Brian said a little sarcastically, as he checked out the menu. "Hal, the last time you gave me advice, it meant we had to educate the whole company in new methods and processes. We've been through an incredible learning curve, and I'm amazed that we've accomplished what we have. Now I've got both you and Ralph talking about more changes. I don't think I could take it again."

"Well, unless you guys at Hayes have some sort of lock on your marketplace, you'd better realize that the learning isn't about to stop. Remember Alice in Wonderland? It takes all the running you can do just to stay in the same place. If you want to stay ahead of the competition, you're going to have to plan on continuous education to keep up with new developments. I'm telling you, Brian, I think this

Just-in-Time approach goes hand in glove with what you've just completed."

"Well, I'm confused. Just-in-Time and Lean Manufacturing are both being touted as a way to reduce waste. Which is better?" Brian asked.

"As I said, we've just started a JIT program at our company. I've also been reading about Lean Manufacturing," Hal said. "Even though the purists try to explain that there is a difference, it appears to me that they are quite similar. Lean seems to be an extension of JIT."

Brian then told Hal about Mickey's resistance to CRP and Ralph's challenge to do something about it. "What do you think, Hal?"

"Mickey's right, you know," said Hal, taking Brian by surprise. "If he doesn't need a detailed planning and scheduling system, don't force it."

"But he's still got problems. He needs most of the information that's on the dispatch list and capacity reports. He can just use what he needs and ignore the rest. It's just paper."

"The only problem with that logic, Brian, is that it's a lot of work to maintain the system if he really doesn't need it. And that seems wasteful—wasting paper and wasting time. Maybe Mickey could easily get by planning his capacity manually on a simple PC-based spreadsheet. Sure he needs an accurate schedule, but it sounds like the master schedule provides that. What we've learned so far in our education sessions is that some environments can get along just fine without computer-generated schedules. We haven't gotten far enough yet to know all the details, but we've seen enough to know that there is an opportunity here. I really think you should go to this Lean Manufacturing seminar. I might even send some of our people."

Two weeks later, Brian, Dan, Mickey, Joan, Elliot, and Carol Barrow went to the seminar.

The speaker began by telling the audience, "Let's start by clearing up some confusion. The subject of this seminar is Lean Manufacturing. Some of you are familiar with Just-in-Time Manufacturing, known as JIT. Some people feel that there are differences between the two processes, while others believe that Lean is a logical extension of the concepts and principles of JIT. It is primarily a debate of terminology. I'm not going to spend any time debating the differences between concepts. Both of these approaches are designed to continuously improve our ability to economically respond to change through the constant elimination of constraints to the process. Lean Manufacturing has its roots in JIT. I am going to proceed on the notion that JIT and Lean are inseparable. Our focus today will be on eliminating waste in manufacturing and some of the techniques to assist in waste elimination."

The speaker continued, "As we try to increase the velocity of the flow of work, problems are revealed that impact on quality, delivery, or cost. These problems are typically caused by the presence of constraints that appear in the form of waste. In this context, waste is defined as any activity that does not add value to the products. It's the use of resources in excess of the theoretical minimum required, whether it is people, equipment, time, space, or energy. Waste can be in the form of excess inventory, setup times, inspection, material movement, transactions, or rejects. Things that can stop production such as faulty material or missing material, tooling, or specifications cause wasteful activities. Any activity that is not actively involved in a process that adds value is waste.

"Lean Manufacturing is a methodology that drives change in the company. It is built on the philosophy of continuous improvement and the elimination of waste, the cornerstones of Just-in-Time Manufacturing. While our focus today will be on the production departments, the principles, concepts, and practices of Lean apply equally well to the order entry, engineering, accounting, and all other functions in the company.

"To work effectively, Lean requires valid plans. I see from your registration forms that most of you are using Manufacturing Resource Planning (MRP II) as a planning and scheduling methodology. You already know that MRP II is a time-proven superior methodology for providing those valid plans. But let me point out to you that improper or ineffective use of these planning tools can contribute to waste."

The speaker pointed out that as you move to Lean Manufacturing, things are definitely going to change on the shop floor. Lean is characterized by small lot sizes, short setup times, and small, often zero, queues, all of which lead to short lead times. "There have been statements made by others that MRP II does not work well in this environment, but that is not true," he said. "MRP II works perfectly fine with small lot sizes, short setup times, and small, often zero, queues. The Lean process starts where you are today and works its way toward these characteristics a little at a time. So don't throw your MRP II system away."

Brian suddenly felt a lot better. He glanced at Joan, sitting to his left, and saw her nodding in agreement. At least all the work they had done at Hayes wasn't going to go for naught.

By the end of the day, Brian and his associates from Hayes knew a lot more about Lean Manufacturing—and JIT—than they had hoped for.

Another cornerstone of Just-in-Time Manufacturing—and an integral part of Lean Manufacturing—is a technique used to authorize the movement or the making of more product. This technique is called *kanban* (rhymes with bon-bon) and is used in place of a dispatch list. Loosely translated from its Japanese origin, kanban means visual signal. Kanban signals to a work center to replace inventory—raw material, parts, or assemblies—when it is consumed by a downstream work center or a customer. Kanban is a manual method that replaces the need for work orders and dispatch lists between operations that are linked by a kanban. It is often referred to as a "pull" system since it pulls product through the manufacturing process on a replenishment basis.

The kanban technique is similar to the process once used by the milkman delivering milk door-to-door. If you needed milk, you put the empty bottles on the porch and the milkman replaced them with full bottles.

Kanban works the same way. The kanban is the signal to replace what has been used. If the kanban authorization is present, you start production. If it is not, you don't. The kanbans themselves can come in many different forms including empty shelf spaces, squares taped on the floor, cards, and returnable containers like milk bottles.

Kanban differs from operation scheduling and finite scheduling in that it authorizes a work center to perform its operation only when the next downstream work center has used a predetermined amount of material. In the operation/finite-scheduling approaches, work is performed as long as it is available to the work center—that is, in queue—and is authorized on the dispatch list. When coupled with the many other Lean Manufacturing practices, the kanban approach results in lower inventories and smoother production flow.

One fact about kanban is often overlooked. Although it is a very powerful control technique, it is not a planning technique. The kanban technique can communicate to the shop floor what to make, when to make it, and how much to make—but only for the present time frame. Kanban cannot predict what materials or how much will be needed in future time periods, nor can it predict what future capacities will be required. A planning process is necessary to predict material and capacity requirements in the mid to long term. Some companies have a simple enough product that they can schedule material and capacity either manually or, as is more often done, on a simple spreadsheet. Others in a more complex environment use MRP II to fulfill that need. More and more companies are learning how to let MRP II do the mid- to long-term planning and let kanban do the shop scheduling.

Kanban has certain advantages over the operational-scheduling/dispatch-list approach. It is simple, provides visual indications of requirements and controls over material movements, and readily exposes problems in production operations and quality. It creates an awareness of problems in production operations and quality. It creates a sense of urgency to resolve problems and encourages reduction in inventory and lead time, thereby increasing the velocity through the process.

Kanban by itself will improve results, but the real benefits from implementing Lean Manufacturing comes from the employment of a concept of continually striving to "economically manufacture one less at a time."[1] By reducing lot sizes, queues, safety stocks, or setup times one less at a time, problems are revealed that impede the acceleration of the workflow. This is a process of continuously identifying and removing constraints one by one—whether they be inventory, quality, production, or administrative procedures—and continually improving the manufacturing process. One of the essential ingredients of the process is the participation of the direct labor work force. They have excellent ideas for improving their operations, the processes, and the product itself.

One overriding aspect that companies should be aware of with kanban is that it requires significant changes in the traditional shop-management philosophy. The success of kanban is based on the principle of fixing problems as they occur rather than working around them. This can result in line stoppages that are contrary to traditional management thinking. The long-term effect of such practice is problem elimination and productivity improvements. However, if management hasn't made the commitment to alter their thinking and habits and to take an aggressive approach to fixing the problems, kanbans aren't going to help. On one level, this is one of its greatest advantages. However, to some companies that have yet to get their planning systems and data under control, they may not be ready to make such changes.

Brian decided the best way to get a handle on these new techniques was to take a firsthand look. He asked the seminar speaker if he could recommend a company using Lean Manufacturing that he could visit. The speaker was more than happy to provide Brian with the names of several companies and people to contact. One of the companies that the speaker strongly recommended was Mercury Electronics, a company that he had worked with personally. Mercury built computer printers, and their Lean process had been on-line for nearly a year.

"Mercury is a good example of the issue of different terminology," the speaker said. "When I first did a special seminar for them, I was quickly advised that their initiative was called Just-In-Time. Their senior vice president had come from a company that had implemented JIT several years earlier when it was the popular term, so that's the term they use. It took me a little while to adjust but it wasn't that hard.

"I have tell you," Brian confessed, "I'm not too sure how making computer printers resembles making tractors. . . ."

"Trust me on this one, Brian," the speaker assured him. "You're about to enter a new world."

The day of the Mercury tour arrived, and Rob Erickson, the Production Manager of Mercury Electronics, greeted Brian, accompanied by Elliot, Dan, Mickey, and Joan, in the lobby. Rob took them to a conference room where he gave them a brief overview of their Lean implementation. Then they moved out into the plant. Mercury had arranged their shop layout so that production moved as a continuous flow, a single part at a time, throughout the shop. Everywhere they went, there were manufacturing cells—groups of operations linked together to produce a high-velocity flow of production. The whole place was a lot like Mickey's assembly area, with work moving through cells and down production lines. Rob pointed out that this layout had helped them practically eliminate queues, and that the product throughput time had been shortened from weeks into hours.

In one cell, Brian watched them change over a circuit-board assembly line to accommodate a different-size board. The complete setup was accomplished in less than ten minutes. Brian was amazed by the efficiency of the process, and he wondered about the planning that had obviously gone into it. Rob also showed them a dedicated line that Mercury had established on their most popular circuit board. It was never changed over, even if it was idle at times.

They saw the kanban technique in live action. The printer assembly people pulled completed circuit boards from small boxes resembling pigeonholes. Whenever a board was removed from one of its boxes, it authorized another board exactly like it to be replaced by the circuit-board assembly area.

In all areas, the components and subassemblies were pulled directly from the production floor as they were needed. The assembly line had been linked with the packaging cell and the shipping dock. Finished printers were built and shipped in one day. There were no component or finished-goods stockrooms.

Since there were no stockrooms, Brian asked Rob where they stored their purchased materials.

"We keep them right on the production line. Our suppliers replenish the stock using the kanban approach. The suppliers deliver our high-usage items daily. Lower volume items are replenished less frequently. We have reduced our purchased material inventories significantly, and we have cut our material handling costs to practically nothing.

Controlling production at Mercury Electronics was done completely with kanbans. The schedule was given daily to the Assembly department. It told them what models to build that day. When the subassemblies and component parts were pulled by Assembly to build the printer, the empty kanbans signaled the production areas to build replacements.

Brian commented to Rob, "This process seems to be okay when you build a few standard models all the time, but we build a lot of special tractors and spare parts."

Rob told Brian that in addition to their standard models, they often build products from a choice of options, and that they also got occasional orders for customized printers. Rob said that they do not schedule the option or special subassemblies with kanban, but instead they insert a special "order" into the production flow. He showed him the schedule for that day, and it had two specials on it. The bills of material for the special configurations were attached to the schedule, so that when the assembly line got to those items they knew what parts to use. Then, when the Assembly Department pulled the components and built the subassemblies as needed, that would initiate the kanban process throughout the rest of production to replace the parts used on the special printer. If special parts were required, or if they got an order for some spares, a production authorization card (kanban) was sent out to the production area that builds them. They took advantage of the forward-looking capability of MRP to do their planning of future material requirements and used kanban as the release mechanism to actually produce the parts or receive them from the supplier.

"But how do you plan your capacities?" Brian asked. Rob showed him his capacity planning report (see Figure 9.1). It looked very similar to the rough-cut capacity plan that Brian had at Hayes. Rob said that his current plant staffing level in each cell was geared to produce eighty printers per day. The required capacity on the capacity plan was for eighty printers per day for the next eight weeks. This number came directly from the Master Production Schedule. Rob said that his required capacity was directly proportional to the total volume of printers scheduled, since each printer consumed about the same amount of labor resources. He pointed out that several weeks ago the report signaled him that the master schedule had been increased and he would have to start building one hundred printers per day in April, so he had sent requisitions to personnel for additional manpower starting April first. The current capacity plan (see Figure 9.1) now showed him that the increase in the master schedule had been pulled up one week, so he was going to have to call personnel and have those hiring dates moved in.

FIGURE 9.1 Capacity Plan for Printer Assembly at Mercury Electronics

WORK CENTER: P1			DATE: 2/04
DESCRIPTION: PRINTER ASSEMBLY			

	DEMO.		MAX.
NO. OPERATORS:	1 0		12
SHIFTS:	1		2
HRS./SHIFT:	8		10
RATE/DAY	8 0		192

WEEK	REQ. CAP'Y. PRINTERS/DAY	PLAN. CAP'Y. PRINTERS/DAY	DEVIATION
2/04	8 0	8 0	0
2/01	8 0	8 0	0
2/18	8 0	8 0	0
2/25	8 0	8 0	0
3/03	8 0	8 0	0
3/10	8 0	8 0	0
3/17	8 0	8 0	0
3/24	8 0	8 0	0
3/31	1 0 0	8 0	-2 0
4/07	1 0 0	1 0 0	0

After they completed the tour, Rob said to the group from Hayes, "Let me make it clear that there is a great deal more to Just-In-Time Manufacturing than kanban. We've done a lot of things, such as standardizing our product designs, rearranging our shop layouts, eliminating inspection by focusing on the concept of quality at the source, reducing setups, and cross-training workers. We've changed our whole outlook and attitudes about how to run this place. The kanban technique is a very important part, but it is only the most visible aspect of the process."

Brian was more than impressed with Rob's operations. Still, it seemed to Brian that building printers was easy to adapt to this kind of flow manufacturing. Hayes made tractors. Rob emphasized that though the applications might differ, the concepts that drove the process were the same.

Back at Hayes, the group discussed what they had learned in the seminar and had seen on the tour of Mercury Electronics. They talked about the concepts of Lean Manufacturing, especially the problem-solving attitude and the one-less-at-a-time process.

Brian could see now that in Mickey's case, a detailed capacity requirements planning process would be wasteful. The transactions needed to maintain it would also be wasteful. Mickey did agree that there would be value in a capacity report similar to what was being used at Mercury Electronics, which would give him visibility several months out in the future so that he could anticipate and plan better.

Recognizing that the objective of Lean Manufacturing is continuous improvement, and that his major scheduling problems were behind him, Brian admitted that he, too, could begin to look for ways to simplify and streamline to continually improve his operations.

Elliot said that in order for them to be able to reduce lot sizes, they needed to reduce the setup times. He offered to look into the technique of SMED (Single Minute Exchange of Die) that they had heard so much about.

Brian and Dan agreed that kanban would help them to decrease the shop floor transactions.

"Now you're talking," Mickey said. "That's one of my big objections to what you guys are doing on the shop floor. Too many transactions."

Brian reminded them that they had already reduced queues significantly with the queue reduction program, but they could undoubtedly make them even smaller. "There's plenty of fat left in the process, even though we've cut our queues by 40 percent. At the seminar, the speaker pointed to companies that had been able to reduce their work-in-process inventory up to 95 percent after improvements had been realized."

"Don't forget," Elliot reminded them all, "we need to encourage and facilitate progressive thinking by all of the people in the company if we're going to pull this off. I'm sure they've got plenty of ideas that will help. We've just never given them the chance before."

Back in the office, Brian thought over all he had learned. As he recalled the operations at Mercury, he thought about what Rob had said about the application of the concepts. He began thinking where he might begin using kanban at Hayes. He knew that he had more work to do to get the Hayes staff to understand and buy into the one-less-at-a-time concept, but he figured that if he could start a pilot operation using kanban, he could get enough improvements quickly to get everyone's attention. Then, it would be easier to sell the other ideas.

The hubs, which fed directly into Mickey's assembly line, were a perfect candidate. Mickey was constantly complaining that the lead times were too long. "I can't understand the problem," he'd say to Brian. "Every tractor that goes down the line takes two front hubs and two rear hubs. We make three different tractors. That's a total of six different hubs. Is this too difficult to get right?"

Brian got together with Elliot and his first- and second-shift supervisors. They explained what they had learned about Lean Manufacturing and began discussing the possibility of starting a pilot project in the hubs area. They reviewed the existing routings to determine which operations were required (see Figure 9.2).

Their first step was to set up a manufacturing cell to make hubs. They calculated that producing the quantity of hubs they would need per month would require two NC lathes and one NC drill. The first step would be to relocate the machines close together to create a flow from one machine to the next. They figured that the two lathes would have to run at 80 percent capacity, but the drill would be idle about 40 percent of the time. Elliot expressed concerned about machine utilization. Brian pointed out that if they could meet the production

---

FIGURE 9.2 Routing for Front-Wheel Hubs Using Separate Operations

---

163726	HUB, FRONT WHEEL			
PART NUMBER	PART DESCRIPTION			

OPN. NO.	DEPT.	WORK CTR.	OPERATION DESCRIPTION	SETUP	RUN
			RELEASE PICK		
10	FAB	16	SAW BLANK	0.5	.10
20	MACH	24	TURN	3.0	.20
30	MACH	22	DRILL	2.0	.10
40	MACH	19	TAP	1.0	.20
			STORE		

requirements for hubs with only 80 percent utilization of the lathes and 60 percent utilization of the drill, why should they run them at 100 percent? That would be wasteful since it just created inventory. That was enough justification for Elliot.

They agreed to combine the three machines into one work center and use the kanban technique to schedule the parts through the cell and into Assembly. They would also eliminate the need to put the hubs into stock by linking the hub cell directly into Mickey's assembly operations via kanbans.

"If we're going to do this," Brian said to Elliot and José, as they walked around the shop floor, "we'll have to change the routings to reflect the changes in the manufacturing process, the work center assignments, and the setup and run times."

"But if we're not going to use a dispatch list," José added, "why can't we just eliminate the routings for the hubs altogether?"

Brian reminded José that they needed to calculate future capacity requirements for the saw, which was a separate operation, and for the hub cell. "We'll still need the routings, although they will be simpler. You see, unlike Mercury Electronics, where every model uses similar amounts of capacity, the capacity required to make our large hubs is significantly more than that required to make small and medium hubs. And since the mix in the master schedule is never constant, I think we still need to use CRP to tell us what our future capacity requirements will be. Besides, we're going to continue to use the dispatch list to schedule the saws, at least for now."

It didn't take them long to realize that the constraint on their capacity was the slowest operation in the cell, namely, the second turning operation. If the slowest machine had sufficient capacity, the other machines would also. They set the run time for the cell by timing how fast the parts came out of the last machine. This, or course, was the run time of the slowest machine, because it was the one that paced the cell. The setup time was drastically reduced because only hubs were now being run in the cell and the variation from one setup to another was very small. In addition, instead of having one operator set up all three machines, a second operator was added during the setup. The net result was only a fifteen minute setup time. The routing could now be used to tell Brian how many hours of operation were required by the hub cell as a unit in order to meet the master schedule (see Figure 9.3).

FIGURE 9.3 Routing for Front-Wheel Hubs Using Manufacturing Cell

163726	HUB, FRONT WHEEL	
PART NUMBER	**PART DESCRIPTION**	

OPN. NO.	DEPT.	WORK CTR.	OPERATION DESCRIPTION	SETUP	RUN
10 20	FAB MACH	16 C1	RELEASE PICK SAW BLANK HUB CELL TURN DRILL TAP STORE	.50 .25	.10 .20

Brian, Joan, and Tony put together an educational program and began teaching the supervisors and operators the concepts and techniques of Lean Manufacturing. At first, there was some resistance. But when the operators started seeing their ideas immediately incorporated into the process, they all began to offer more suggestions. This was the manifestation of the employee involvement concept that Brian had heard about in the seminar. The results were incredible. After only a few weeks of operation, setup times and lot sizes were being reduced significantly. The assembly schedule was sent to Mickey every day (see Figure 9.4), and kanban had replaced the dispatch list as the priority tool for the hub cell.

Now, every time Mickey pulled a set of hubs from the hub cell's outbound area, he would send a kanban card back to the hub cell. This action authorized Brian and his crew to replace what was taken. Brian and his crew were not authorized to make another hub until Mickey had taken a set from the kanban queue. Mickey's usage authorized the production of the next hub. The kanban cards were sent back to assembly with the hubs when they were finished.

Brian now got a single CRP report for the hub cell instead of individual reports for turning and drilling. The master schedule was set for 26 tractors per day. This meant that the hub cell needed to produce 104 hubs per day. But since the mix of hubs would very accord-

FIGURE 9.4 Assembly Schedule for Small Tractors

WORK CENTER : A1		DATE : 3/10
DESCRIPTION: SMALL TRACTORS		

DATE	PART NUMBER	PLAN. QTY.
3/10	21349	1
3/10	26874	4
3/10	36492	2
3/10	32846	2
3/10	25173	5
3/10	31962	1
	TOTAL	15
3/11	21349	1
3/11	26874	5
3/11	36492	3
3/11	32846	1
3/11	25173	4
3/11	31962	1
	TOTAL	15
3/12	21349	1
3/12	26874	4
3/12	36492	2
3/12	32846	2
3/12	25173	5
3/12	31962	1
	TOTAL	15

ing to the mix in the master schedule and since the large hubs required more time that the small ones, the hours of required operation of the hub cell would vary week to week. Brian could see from the report how his requirements would vary over time. Since the report covered a full 12-month horizon, he could also see if he would have to increase or decrease the capacity of the cell and by how much and when (see Figure 9.5). He continued to manage the capacity in the cell in the same manner he managed prior to establishing the cell.

FIGURE 9.5 Summary Capacity Plan for Hub Cell

DATE: 3/10   NO. MACH.: 1   HOURS/SHIFT: 8
WORK CENTER: C1   NO. OPER.: 3   SHIFTS/DAY: 3
DESCRIPTION: HUB CELL   MACH./OPER.: 1   DAYS/WEEK: 5
DEMO. CAP'Y.: 110   MAX. CAP'Y.: 130   LOAD FACTOR: 90%

MACHINE CAPACITY

WEEK	REQ'D. CAP'Y. (HRS.)	PLAN CAP'Y. (HRS.)	LOAD VS. CAPACITY (%)
3/10	116	108	XXXXXXXXXXX
3/17	103	108	XXXXXXXXXX
3/24	106	108	XXXXXXXXXX
3/31	123	108	XXXXXXXXXXXX
4/07	111	108	XXXXXXXXXXX
4/14	101	108	XXXXXXXXXX
4/21	128	108	XXXXXXXXXXXXX
4/28	110	108	XXXXXXXXXX
5/05	109	108	XXXXXXXXXX
5/12	122	108	XXXXXXXXXXXX

LABOR CAPACITY

WEEK	REQ'D. CAP'Y. (HRS.)	PLAN CAP'Y. (HRS.)	LOAD VS. CAPACITY (%)
3/10	116	108	XXXXXXXXXXX
3/17	103	108	XXXXXXXXXX
3/24	106	108	XXXXXXXXXX
3/31	123	108	XXXXXXXXXXXX
4/07	111	108	XXXXXXXXXXX
4/14	101	108	XXXXXXXXXX
4/21	128	108	XXXXXXXXXXXXX
4/28	110	108	XXXXXXXXXX
5/05	109	108	XXXXXXXXXX
5/12	122	108	XXXXXXXXXXXX

It was during one of the regularly scheduled meetings that Brian and Elliot had begun with the supervisors that José first raised the question about the Input/Output report. "If all of these things are getting simpler," he suggested "do we still need the I/O report?"

"That's a good question," Brian said, not at all sure of what the answer was. "The I/O report is made up of input, output, and queue."

"Well," said José, "queue is no problem. Kanban controls that since we can't start any more through the cell than we need to replenish what Assembly uses." Everyone agreed.

Then Elliot added," But I'm not so sure about output. If you have too much output, what happens then?"

"You can't have," José said. "Kanban keeps that from happening, too."

"Okay," Elliot said, "but what about *not enough* output?"

José and Brian smiled at each other. "I don't think we have to worry about that. Mickey would be over here in a flash," José said with a laugh, "because we'd have his line shut down in no time"

"Okay, so much for queue and output, what about input?" Elliot asked.

They realized that if there wasn't enough input, there wouldn't be enough work in the work center and the cell would shut down. That would certainly call attention to the problem. They didn't need a report to tell them that.

Brian then asked, "What happens, though, when there's work coming to the cell, but it's not the work that we have open kanbans for?"

Elliot was quick to respond. "I can see the possibility of that happening, but it can't be a very big problem unless MRP is setting the wrong priorities for the saw work center. We don't want to cover that up with inventory. We'd want to fix the problem with the MRP system." Once again, they all agreed.

"Then, it's just a matter of being able to see how much queue we have for the hub cell," Brian said.

José responded. "When we moved the machines closer together to create the hub cell, there was a lot of space left over. We could use that as the inbound queue area for the hub cell. We would be able to see all the work that way."

"Now, you're cooking," said Brian. "That will give us the visual controls we need so we'll no longer need the I/O report. It'll also let us see clearly what the queue level is and how we are going about reducing it."

After they started the pilot, one of the critical moments that tested their resolve came when the Assembly Department had to shut down the assembly lines because of a shortage on a purchased part that was used on every tractor. Since they were not starting any more tractors, they were not pulling any more hubs from Brian's hub cell and sending back kanban cards, so the hub cell also shut down. And wouldn't you know it? Just at that time, Ralph came walking through the shop and saw the hub cell at a standstill.

He immediately found Brian and screamed at him. "What in the blazes is going on down there? I thought Lean Manufacturing was supposed to reduce waste. What I see is valuable capacity going down the drain. Why isn't that cell running?"

Brian explained that as long as the assembly line was down, there was no need to make more hubs, since they weren't needed right away. As soon as the line started up again, the cell would be back in full production.

"But, in the meantime," shouted Ralph, "you've got people standing around drawing pictures on a flip chart! We're paying them to work, you know, not to goof off."

Brian said, "They're not goofing off. They are discussing an idea one of the operators had to reduce the run time on the second turning operation. If they can do it, it will increase the output of the cell because that's the slowest operation. I think that will prove more valuable to the company than pumping out hubs that are only going to sit in inventory. Remember, we started this whole process in the first place to make the company more productive over the long pull. We can't just look at the short term. You've got to give it a chance."

"Well, all right, Miller. I see your point. I just don't like seeing idle equipment. I understand we have to change our way of thinking around here. I just have to get used to it, I guess."

"That's something I wanted to talk to you about," Brian said. "If we keep making the kind of progress on reducing the run and setup times, we are going to have a lot more extra capacity. How about taking in work from the other plants to utilize that capacity?"

"And take a chance on missing our schedule because of them? No way."

"Come on, Ralph," Brian said, "we have our capacities under control. If we keep making these improvements, we're going to have to start reducing our work force. That's going to start sending the wrong message to the operators, and they'll quit making the improvements."

Ralph nodded. "Yes, I can see what you mean. Maybe we should take on some outside work."

"I just happen to have a proposal in my office that Elliot and I put together," Brian said, smiling. "For your approval, of course."

Ralph laughed. "I'm going to learn to quit agreeing with you until I've had a chance to figure out how you're setting me up."

All the other work centers at Hayes were still running detailed Capacity Requirements Planning and operation scheduling, while the hub cell ran kanban. By changing the manufacturing environment in the hub cell, the scheduling and capacity management process was greatly simplified, yet still provided the same information as before. Both systems were driven by the Master Production Schedule, and Material Requirements Panning was used to order all raw material, although Harold Bloom in Purchasing had begun a kanban pilot with one of their hardware suppliers. The hubs moved directly into the assembly line in a flow, while the rest of the parts, which operated in a traditional batch environment, moved into final assembly through the stockroom.

The success of the hub pilot got everyone throughout the plant excited about Lean Manufacturing and, in particular, the cell approach. Brian and his colleagues discovered that the philosophy and process of Lean caught on like wildfire. It motivated people to begin looking at how they could simplify their process and procedures. There were some areas where the cell approach was straightforward. The hub cell was one. In other areas, it was hard for Brian to envision making the flow process applicable. That didn't mean Brian stopped trying to apply it, because sometimes the solution didn't just pop out. It also didn't mean that many of the other Lean concepts weren't applicable as well. Brian had learned that Lean was more than kanbans and creating cells. It was reducing and avoiding setups, Total Quality Control, a new look at measuring performance, and new problem solving techniques. Where did it stop? He realized that it never did.

The basic concept of Lean Manufacturing—the continual and relentless elimination of waste—was firmly fixed in Brian's mind. In fact, it was starting to become an obsession. "Why hadn't we done it sooner?" he asked. It all made such perfect sense.

Earlier, he had mistakenly thought that Just-in-Time and Lean Manufacturing meant zero inventories and lead times of one day. At the time, those notions were so completely foreign to him that he quickly dismissed Lean as not applicable to Hayes. Therefore, he simply never took the time to learn more about it. Why? He then remembered the good old days of chasing parts, battling verbally with everyone, and constantly defending himself from all quarters. It was a time of never having what was needed and never knowing what was coming next. It was like a perpetual walk in the dark. Things had had to get better before Brian would ever have had the time to consider something like Lean.

The key was having the time to work on improving the process. He had to have a valid—accurate and feasible—schedule in order to break away from the constant expediting and give him the control he needed so he could attend to process improvement.

The Mercury Electronics tour had really opened everyone's eyes and provided the Hayes team with the initiative to make some real progress. Brian started to wonder if there was more to be learned. The more he thought about it, the more he wanted to visit another user of Lean Manufacturing. He dug out the list of companies that he had gotten from the seminar leader and ran his finger down the list. He spotted McNally Machine Tool and thought they would be an interesting contrast to Mercury Electronics. He picked up the phone and called Buster Jones, the contact name on the list. Buster was very cordial, and two weeks later, Buster was able to arrange for Brian to join a tour of their plant that had been set up for one of their customers. Brian was excited because McNally had a machine shop and a sheet metal fabrication shop, so some of their operations would be similar to Hayes.

The McNally Machine Tool tour started off with an overview of the Lean Manufacturing project. The project manager explained that the initiative was driven by the Senior Vice President of their division. Their charter was to implement product cells, reduce lead times, and cut the cost of production.

Brian, in his usual manner, couldn't resist asking the question of why they had elected to call their initiative Lean instead of Just-In-Time. The project manager explained that Just-In-Time was just a small portion of Lean, and that if Brian wanted to take the time, he would explain in detail the differences. Brian quickly realized that he had found one of the zealots the seminar speaker had talked about and declined.

The project manager went on to explain that they had consultants from an outside firm on site helping them with the changes. That really sounded like a good idea to Brian because it meant that there would be additional resources to help with the implementation.

After the briefing in the conference room, the group headed out to the factory. As they approached the Fabrication Shop, Buster explained to Brian that they had installed an MRP II system a few years ago, but that they had never really got it working well. Brian told Buster that he could understand that, since that was the situation when he first took over his job at Hayes.

McNally had identified six different product groups and had arranged all of the machines necessary to support the manufacturing of those individual products into product cells. However, the parts still moved from one machine to the next in batches. They had not accomplished the single-part flow like Brian had done in his hub cell. They had accomplished a reduction in travel time and had gained some improvement in quality, but there had been no reduction in the move and queue times between operations, nor were there any provisions for overlapping or parallel setups or runs. This meant that they hadn't gotten the reduction in lead time that Brian did when he created the hub cell. When Brian asked him about it, the tour guide said that they planned to address that in the future.

Brian could see that they were having problems meeting schedules. Hot tags were visible on several jobs, and there was a constant stream of people moving around looking for parts. Brian asked the tour guide how they set priorities in the shop. He responded that everything moved on a first-in/first-out basis. Then Brian asked how they planned capacity. The guide said that they planned capacity based on a rate basis and that it was not really an issue. Brian could see that things were not moving first-in/first-out; he recognized expeditors when he saw them. It also appeared to him that capacity was indeed an issue at some of the machines since there was quite a lot of work backed up there.

Brian and Buster stayed toward the back of the group, carrying on a side conversation between themselves. Brian felt Buster was giving him the straight story and had hands-on shop knowledge. While the tour guide droned on about how well the process was working, Brian asked Buster if he could talk to the supervisor of the area. Buster looked around and spotted the supervisor talking with his area manager. Buster led Brian over to where they were talking and introduced him to the pair. Brian asked them how the shop was doing from a scheduling standpoint. He then got an earful.

They explained that they previously had routings with individual work centers prior to creating the cell, and that they used their MRP II system to schedule the operations. The manager told Brian that when the Lean Manufacturing initiative was launched, they had discarded their shop floor scheduling system because they had been advised that anything that was on the computer was not lean. The manager and the supervisor both agreed that creating the cells was a good idea, but they hadn't realized how much they had depended on the data that the MRP II system had provided. They readily admitted that the data had some accuracy problems, but even in spite of that, they felt that they had been better off before than they were now. They had just begun to make some progress with their performance when the turnabout to Lean Manufacturing came. Now they felt out of control with no expectation that they could get back into control.

Brian asked them about creating single-piece flow cells to get the lead-time reduction. They said that they had talked about doing single-piece flow cells, but the higher-ups didn't want to take the time to do the proper design. Management wanted action now. In addition, nobody in the company nor any of the consultants had come from an environment where shop floor systems worked well, and therefore they were all convinced that it couldn't work. The supervisor and manager felt they were not in a good position to argue the point even though they recognized the importance of good schedules in attaining on-time delivery.

Brian asked about capacity planning. They explained that the MRP II system had provided that information in the past, but they had eliminated the CRP system and installed a capacity planning process based on rates. In some areas of the factory, the rate-based capacity planning process worked fine. In the case of this particular cell, however, they were having trouble because the work wasn't coming to them at a steady rate and the run times varied considerably, depending on which specific parts they were running. The new capacity planning system did not adequately account for the fluctuations in orders, mix changes, engineering changes, or problem parts. Even with less than accurate setup and run times, they felt that the CRP system had given them much better visibility.

Brian got an idea. "Why don't you come visit us at Hayes. It might give you some ammunition to use to get back some of the information that you would like to have to manage your area. Then you can work on single-part flows instead of chasing parts."

They thought that would be a good idea and thanked Brian for the offer.

Brian and Buster caught up with the tour group. Brian saw some areas that were running very smoothly, and had clearly made positive strides with Lean Manufacturing. Other areas he saw were similar to the Fabrication Shop, and were struggling with scheduling and capacity issues.

On the drive home, Brian started thinking about some of the things he had learned on his trips, from the seminars he attended, and from his own experiences. There seemed to be a lot of catch words out there: JIT, Lean, kanban, and numerous others that he couldn't even remember. It was all very confusing. What he decided to do was to get agreement from the other managers at Hayes that they use the term "lean" because it was short and did a good job of describing what was trying to be accomplished.

Brian wondered why the JIT/Lean process was working so well at Mercury Electronics and was struggling at McNally Machine Tool. Why was McNally so convinced that they had to back away from computerized planning and scheduling tools when they were working so well at Hayes? Was it because the products were different? Or the manufacturing processes? Brian didn't think so. Fundamentally, things were quite similar in all of these plants. The only real difference was the people.

"That's it!" Brian shouted, as he slammed his palm down on the steering wheel and almost drove through a stop sign. "It's the people!"

Using MRP II-based shop scheduling and capacity planning isn't any different from any other system or process. Bad data, bad schedules, biased people, misguided decisions and/or poor discipline will destroy any system. Brian nodded to himself. No system will provide good information to manage with if you don't put the right processes and accurate data in place.

If people don't understand the concepts and principles of the various systems and techniques, they are likely to either go down some wrong paths or resist the changes altogether. By understanding each process thoroughly and its relationship to and impact upon other processes, people will be able to compare new ideas with the current processes in place on the shop floor to see if a new approach would, in fact, provide an improvement. Understanding the processes and techniques is what is important, not the buzzwords and acronyms.

It is important to align the current planning system with the manufacturing process. If you are operating in a batch environment, you need to recognize it and use the planning system effectively to help manage the business. As you leaned out the processes, then you could eliminate those pieces of the planning system that were not necessary. Brian could see how critical it was to get the manufacturing processes and the planning processes in alignment, or else you could end up wasting a lot of time and effort using the computer to help you when it wasn't needed or, like McNally Machine Tool, not having the tools to run the business with.

Reflecting on it all, Brian realized that Hayes had to continue to build the disciplines and controls before they could make much headway with the continuous improvement process. Both were essential. To get control, they had to have the planning provided by Manufacturing Resource Planning processes. And he knew that in order to properly compete globally, the company needed to adopt the philosophies of continuous improvement and elimination of waste. The Lean Manufacturing process was the way to do that. He knew that integrating Lean Manufacturing with MRP II would give Hayes the best of both worlds.

Chapter Ten

Moving Ahead

How time flies! Almost two years have passed since Brian started his job in the machine shop at Hayes. During that period, the pride of accomplishment had settled in throughout the company. From the shop floor to Purchasing, from Engineering to Sales, and throughout the wood-paneled offices of top management, everyone realized that the hard and dedicated work to improve Hayes's processes had paid off in making their lives less stressful and more productive. The company was enjoying its best year of business ever. Sales volume was up, on-time deliveries were routinely made, and profits of this division were among the best in the entire corporation.

Brian was called up to Pete's office. When he arrived, Ralph was there also.

"Brian," Pete said, "the changes we have made at this division have not gone unnoticed by Hayes's corporate offices back East. There are a lot of changes being made throughout the company because of our success. I am being promoted to Vice President of the Georgia plant to replace Dave Jennings, who is retiring."

Brian enthusiastically offered his congratulations to Pete.

Pete went on to explain that Ralph was being promoted to General Manager here, taking his place, and that Roy was going to the Georgia plant to replace their current Materials Manager. Dan would take over Ralph's job as Production Manager, and Joan would move from Manager of Production Control to the Materials Manager position.

Brian waited for the other shoe to drop. What was in store for him?

Pete continued. "Corporate management has decided to launch a process improvement initiative across the entire corporation. In addition to being thrilled with what we have done here, they have been exposed to something called Agile Manufacturing. I'll tell you more about that in a minute. Our plant here has led the way in process improvements with what we have done with MRP II and Lean Manufacturing. Some of our plants don't even have MRP yet. Others have MRP II installed, but are in the same place we were a couple of years ago and aren't doing much with plant scheduling or capacity management. The Toledo plant has been fiddling around with Just-in-Time for a while but doesn't have much to show for it.

"The corporate process improvement initiative will encompass all of these things plus the Agile Manufacturing concepts. We need someone to lead that initiative and coordinate all of these fragmented projects we have going on. We want someone who knows what it's like to live in a crisis management environment and has successfully made the transition to minimize expediting through proper planning. We also need someone who has the ability to look forward and implement new ideas. You have really impressed us with your abilities in both cases. So I would really like you to take that job. It will be a big promotion and Hayes will be able to use your skill sets better."

Brian was floored by the offer. He didn't know what to what to say, especially since he didn't know what this Agile Manufacturing stuff was all about.

Sensing Brian's dilemma, Pete spoke again. "Let me explain a little about Agile Manufacturing. I've only become aware of it recently myself, so I'm not going to try to give you the whole picture. I've got something for you that will help in that regard." Pete held up a book and then laid it back on his desk.

"The brain trusts of the U.S. manufacturing industry are predicting that the advent of global competition coupled with the technology explosion means that customers in the future will be able to buy a far wider range of product options and specials, get delivery in a matter of days, and do it all for the same or lower price. Neither Hayes nor any other manufacturing company could accomplish that in the environment that exists today. There will have to be a revolution in technology throughout industry. That revolution will include equipment that has such quick changeovers that all products can be made in a single-part flow process. Information systems will be linked not only inside the company, but to customers and suppliers as well. People throughout the organization will require extremely high skill sets. That environment is defined as "Agile Manufacturing." According to one published authority,[1] in an Agile Manufacturing environment, custom products will be made as fast and as cheaply as mass-produced products. Our parent corporation wants to be part of that environment.

"As you are aware, Brian, overseas competition has hit the plant in Georgia hard. It's much like the Japanese impact on the U.S. auto industry. Overseas competition has not affected this plant too much yet, but it's only a matter of time before it does. We need to stay one step ahead and do everything we can meet that challenge."

Brian conceded that maybe that could happen in some industries, but he thought that it would be a real stretch for Hayes. He thought about how tough it had been to make the changes that they had made so far, and this sounded like a giant leap from where they were. Pete had become known throughout the plant for his constant pushing for improvements. Brian was not particularly surprised that he was right in the middle of this one.

Pete handed Brian the book from his desk. "Here is some material on Agile Manufacturing. It will do a better job of defining what Agile Manufacturing is. Take the rest of the day to go home and look this over. Let me know tomorrow if you are interested," Pete said smiling.

On his way home, Brian reflected back on his Chevy convertible. It was running great for an old car. But it sure didn't have some of the options available on the new cars, nor was it as reliable. It requires more maintenance than the new models. His new car goes 5,000 miles between oil changes, 60,000 miles on a set of spark plugs, and doesn't even have a carburetor to rebuild or points to change like the old Chevy does. If General Motors tried to sell a car like his convertible today, nobody would buy it. That's called progress.

Reflecting on the differences between his old Chevy and today's modern vehicles, Brian realized that Pete was right about trying to continuously improve the business, whether through designing new products or improving the business practices. Brian knew from talking with Rob Ericson from Mercury Electronics that the electronics industry is even worse: If you don't stay up with technology in that industry, you can go belly up in just a couple of years. Brian was really starting to appreciate Pete's enthusiasm to keep the company on a path of steady improvement.

Nobody was home when Brian got there, so he flopped into his favorite chair and cracked open the book that Pete had handed him. It was titled *21st Century Manufacturing Enterprise Strategy—An Industry-Led View*, volume 1.[2]

Brian started to skim through the book. Two passages from the book made a particular impression on Brian. He read:

> Entrepreneurial initiative and technical creativity have been hallmarks of American industry for over 150 years. Software development is one of the technologies in which America holds a commanding world leadership position.

> The US is a world leader in information science. It also possesses a diverse supplier base that constitutes a major resource for cooperative ventures in an agile manufacturing environment. Linking these two could create a significant competitive advantage for U.S. industry.

Brian read on.

Agility is accomplished by integrating technology and people into a coordinated reactive process. Highly flexible production machines are necessary if the agile vision is to be accomplished. The required technology to build the machines is either already here or is foreseeable and it is only a matter of time before they are functional.

Machines are only one piece of the equation, however. Another major piece of an agile enterprise is totally integrating the entire organization. Information must flow seamlessly among manufacturing, engineering, marketing, purchasing, finance, inventory, sales, and research departments. Not only must that information flow seamlessly, but it must also provide the information to produce the right product at the right time. In order to produce the product on time, capacity planning must be done on highly sophisticated, expensive equipment. But even more diffcult, all the resources must be managed significantly better because with such short lead time, any resource constraint can stop the product from getting to the customer on time. In addition, the process of having extra resource around "just in case" simply will not be acceptable if we are to meet our cost objectives.

Brian read how the authors envisioned that potential customers could design their own custom product configurations using graphic-intensive software either through their own home computers or at satellite studios located at popular shopping sites. The software would generate an accurate image of the product as well as display the purchase. Brian knew that the technology was available because he had seen it demonstrated at an APICS meeting. It had been referred to as the electronic catalog.

The vision of future technology went on. If the customer wished to proceed with the order, the tentative product configuration would be transmitted to the nearest dealer or manufacturer. The order could be confirmed on-line, and, if so desired, paid for via electronic funds transfer.

What he was reading was really starting to feel good to Brian. Basically, that is what he did with his shop floor system. He had taken advantage of the available technology. It wasn't done by a bunch of technocrats, but rather by the people on the shop floor. No, it hadn't been easy, but the results were incredible. Thinking about the vision created by the authors of the book, he began to recognize that what he had accomplished was small in comparison to what could be achieved.

Four scenarios were presented in the book to highlight selected features of advanced manufacturing after its transformation from the mass production system to an agile, customer-preference-driven, system. The one that caught his attention was the scenario involving the fictitious U.S. Motors (USM) since there were at least some similarities between the automotive industry and the Hayes environment.

The USM scenario proposed that it would be possible to deliver a vehicle within three working days of receiving an order for it. This was to be accomplished with a large range of options on the car. The commitment to three-day delivery served as the driving force behind organizing a manufacturing system at USM that enabled it to address almost any market challenge.

To expect to do all of this with approximately the same price tag had Brian totally enthralled. He could easily see that this would give

USM a competitive advantage, not only because of the delivery time, but also by eliminating inventory and its associated costs.

The key technical factor behind Agile Manufacturing was matching the design of the vehicles to the capabilities of the machines that built them. Product and manufacturing processes and design are done concurrently. The computer made it possible to simulate total vehicle design as well as the process of its manufacture. The result of this integration of production machinery and the design database was that the approved design, whether of modified components or of entire vehicles, could at once be put into the production and customer order entry programs.

When Brian finished reading *21st Century Manufacturing Enterprise Strategy* he started thinking about applying these concepts to Hayes Tractor.

Perhaps they could rearrange the equipment to make custom cabs on the fly. In today's environment, some parts are made in Brian's and Dan's shops and some are made at the supplier. They are then stocked and picked as kits. By taking what they had done with manufacturing cells and Lean Manufacturing one step further, they could move some of Brian's and Dan's machines closer to Final Assembly and make all the components that they now purchased except the molding and the glass. The moldings were standard parts for Hayes, and they could probably get the glass supplier to cut what they needed each day. Bingo! Instant cabs. Customer calls the day before and they can put a cab on a tractor.

Brian thought further. Engines and drive trains were the most expensive option problems. Hayes buys the engines and builds their own transmissions. The current design has the transmission cases machined differently for each engine that they fit on. With four different transmissions and three different engine options for each tractor size it resulted in twelve different part numbers for the transmission cases on each size tractor. With five different size tractors, this made 60 different transmission cases that they built.

The cases had to go through several manufacturing steps. Therefore, the Planning Department has to forecast the cases in advance to reduce the lead time to the customer. Trying to think "agile," Brian concluded that with a new five-axis machining center equipped with loading pallets that could be loaded while the machine is running, he could machine whatever case that they wanted that day. Maybe they could put the machine right in the transmission assembly area. It took less than two hours to assemble and test the transmission. This would enable the customer to make changes on the transmission/engine combination the day before the tractor went on the assembly line. It would also reduce the inventory significantly.

As Brian's mind raced forward, he could see many other issues that they would have to work on, such as reducing setup times, eliminating queue time, shortening lead times on the long-lead-time items, and putting together a cross-functional team for quick design of specials. They had already made significant progress in most of theses areas, but Brian was not willing to think that they couldn't do more. After all, the philosophy of continuous improvement and "one-less-at-a-time" had not been forgotten.

As Brian thought about it, this could be easier than he had initially thought. The MRP system already allowed the master schedulers to hold the release of the option combinations until the last minute. If the bill of material was restructured, the master schedulers could automatically send the request for the transmission case to the five-axis machine via the dispatch list when they configured the tractor. In fact, with a recent upgrade to the software, it could be done on-line in real time.

Brian realized that looking at the process from an agile viewpoint meant a whole different look at order entry, master scheduling, material planning, capacity planning, buying, design engineering, manufacturing engineering, and more. Agile means people will have to be working in close-knit teams and have an in-depth knowledge of the systems, as well as the product. Commitments had to be made quickly with all functions committing to making a quality product in a very short time. He felt the current software was able to accomplish his initial ideas, but it wouldn't be long before they would have to look at upgrading their systems. Jobs would have to change also. Fewer, highly educated and trained people would be working closely together to accomplish making customer specific products with almost no lead time.

The technology is available for them to become agile; the only question was, could he get the people to change?

Brian called Pete first thing the next morning and asked if he could come up to talk with him about his offer of the day before. Ralph was in Pete's office when Brian got there. Pete motioned for Brian to come on in.

"I read that book you gave me," Brian said. "I think I'm interested." Brian then went through all of his ideas with Pete and Ralph.

Pete looked at Ralph. "This is the kind of thinking I want on our team. I knew he was the right choice."

Then Pete turned to Brian. "We want to launch this effort in the Georgia plant. It will mean you'll be moving to Georgia. I'd like you there as soon as possible. Discuss it with your wife and let me know by next week."

The day before Pete and Roy were to head off to Georgia, Pete gathered all of the employees together in the company cafeteria. There were a few things he wanted to make sure they understood. A stage had been erected, and refreshments were being served. You could see the change that had taken place at Hayes not only in the faces of the employees, but even on the walls of the cafeteria. There were numerous displays that recognized and praised the results of the employees' hard work. A banner was draped across the front wall that indicated the change in company mind-set. It said simply "The Hayes Team: Committed to Being the Best." Today, everyone in that cafeteria believed it.

Pete moved confidently to the microphone. "I must admit having this gathering is a bit selfish on my part," he said. "I wanted a chance to talk to you all one last time in order to properly acknowledge what we have accomplished in the last year. First of all, Team Hayes has not missed a single customer commitment in the last six months!" Pete began the applause himself, which soon echoed loudly throughout the room. "Productivity has increased by 23 percent and is still going up. We have installed some new computer systems in the past two years that have also played an integral part in our success. They are, however, only tools to aid us. It is the people using these tools that have made us a success, and that is every person in this room." Another round of applause briefly stopped Pete. "Thanks to Lean Manufacturing, Total Quality Control, and Manufacturing Resource Planning as the key elements in our Total Quality Management plan, we have also been able to reduce our lead time to the customer by 35 percent and our quality costs by over 65 percent.

That is not only significant, it's downright amazing!" A ripple of applause again drifted across the room.

"What does this all mean? It means our profits are up 20 percent. It means that we have attracted the business of four major new customers along with work from other plants for a total of more than a 28 percent increase in business. It means being more competitive and creating more jobs here at Hayes. It means that instead of the corporate offices phasing out this tired old facility, they're planning the construction of a new facility, right here, to take its place!" This announcement was met with thunderous applause. "This couldn't have happened without you. This could never have happened without your commitment to change and your willingness to make it happen. I know I owe my promotion to the hard work of every person in this plant, but especially to the people who make our product, from design engineer to assembler."

Pete wrapped up his farewell address with a heartfelt thank-you to all of the Hayes employees for their part in the company's success. "I owe my promotion to all of you, and I will never forget that."

As Brian made his way through the crowd and headed for his office, he began to think back over the path he and Hayes had traveled during the last couple of years. All he could think about was the hard work. There had to be an easier way to accomplish this kind of turnaround. He remembered that first daylong seminar that had introduced Joan and him to the ideas that seemed so much a part of his life today. Why hadn't someone told him about them sooner? And where would they be if he and Joan hadn't attended that seminar?

Then he began to think about Georgia and having to travel this path all over again. This time not only would he be trying to implement the shop scheduling and capacity planning processes in a facility twice the size of this one, but also guiding all of the other plants on their journey through Lean Manufacturing to Agile Manufacturing. How could he get the change process to go faster?

Brian knew that one of the keys to making this process work better and faster was to educate all middle management so they would take ownership of the process in much the same way he had. Except in this case, he wouldn't have the time and luxury of discovery. It all had to happen more quickly. The question that kept rattling through his head was how? He needed to find an education process that could aid him in teaching others the concepts he had fought and clawed to understand himself. He clearly remembered the resistance that Dan had put up when Joan first tried to present these new ideas to him and his department. As Brian thought about it, he realized that it wasn't until Dan had to explain it to his own troops that he finally came on board. Why? Because Dan had finally taken ownership. The process now belonged to Dan and his people.

It was obvious to Brian that the involvement of the people made the difference. Each department, supervisor, and operator had to be committed to making things better and be willing to do the work necessary to make it happen. The changes Hayes had to make were not only to the physical processes; they had to change culturally, too.

Suddenly, Brian asked himself whether or not he had ever really shown his appreciation to his people? He knew Ralph had never been one to openly acknowledge his gratitude but that didn't mean Brian shouldn't.

Brian stopped by Roy's office and found him packing a box of books. "I guess this means you're really going to Georgia?" Brian said, as Roy placed a pile of well-read volumes into the box.

"You know, Brian, I asked Pete to have you join us in Georgia. I figured with the work you'd done here, I wouldn't want anyone else helping me start the process all over again."

"That's what worries me, Roy. We worked so hard to get things right here: I'm not so sure I really want to go through all that pain again."

"You won't have to. We're not going to do things the way we did them here." He handed Brian a booklet. It was a checklist of what needed to be done to be a world-class manufacturing company, often referred to as Class A[3]. "That is a guide to help us. It is an accumulation of what hundreds of companies have done and what has consistently worked well. In this plant, we sort of drifted through the implementation process. In Georgia, we're going to take advantage of other people's knowledge. Why reinvent the wheel?

"We'll educate the key managers, because we don't want them be turned off, resentful, or threatened by all the changes that will have to be made to accomplish the good things we've been able to do here. Then, we're going to use the same approach you used in the machine shop, where the boss takes care of the education and training. The behavior changes we saw from that process were incredible."

"That's great, Roy," Brian said, feeling a little better about the prospects, "but it took a lot of work putting that training package together."

Roy sensed Brian's concern. He told him he didn't have to worry so much. Instead of developing all the education training materials themselves, they were going to use some professionally developed education and training material that would supplement and complement the managers' limited knowledge. "We're also going to get some outside help. Not that we have any doubts about your abilities, but we could use some professional guidance to safely accelerate our implementation so we make as few mistakes as possible. That doesn't mean someone else is going to do it for us. It simply means that I'm going to get a qualified expert that has implemented it at a Class A level before, someone who can help us see the forest for the trees, and will be viewed as unbiased and objective."

"You've obviously been doing some thinking about this, Roy. What you say makes sense. In fact, I've got some ideas of my own that may speed things along."

"I was counting on that," Roy said. "This is an exciting opportunity for us, Brian. That's why it's so important that you get down to Georgia as soon as possible. We're a team, partner."

"What about all our work here?" Brian asked. "You don't think as soon as we leave, it's all going to fall apart, do you?"

Roy laughed. "I don't think we have anything to worry about there. Joan will keep Ralph and Lenny on the right track. Besides, as much as Ralph complained about computers, he knows now without them he'd be up the creek. You also have to realize this process has been ingrained in everyone that works here. They all know it's the best way to run the business. If Ralph ever tried to change things back, there would probably be an uproar we could hear all the way in Georgia."

"And we wouldn't be here to bail him out," Brian said. He suddenly realized that he'd already decided to make the move. "Well, I guess I'd better get to work on José. If he's going to be the new machine shop manager, he's going to have to know where all the bodies are buried. Fortunately, he's already got a firm grip on how best to utilize our people's talents."

"More than that," Roy added, "he's got a clear understanding of the importance of planning and not just reacting. He's a good choice.

"I'm also going to work with Joan to set up the ongoing education program using the video tapes we bought," Roy said. "That not only means they'll be enhancing the skills of the current employees, but new employees will have a formal education and training program they'll be put through whether they're just starting with the company or moving to a new job."

"Listen, Roy, I'll let you finish up in here. I've got a Total Quality Management meeting in a minute."

"All right, partner. We'll be in touch as soon as I get to Georgia. I want you in on all the planning so when you show up you can hit the ground running."

"Right," Brian answered. "Pete wants me to start with the scheduling and capacity planning processes in the machine shop just like we did here. You know—the been-there-done-that philosophy. Then I need to start to work on the Agile initiative."

Roy gave him a smile, knowing that as sold as Brian was on the idea, he still wanted to check all the details. "I figure you'll have the Georgia machine shop manager on the right track quickly. Shouldn't be a problem since you can work on it full time. Anyway, all you have to do is get him started because I hear he's a pretty savvy guy. Pete says he's a lot like you."

The two men shook hands. And immediately, in Brian's gut, he knew this was the right move. As he headed off to his meeting, he smiled, remembering Mac's "gut feeling" comment just two short years ago. Finally, with all they'd accomplished at Hayes, and with his future in Georgia presenting an exciting and enticing challenge, he got the "gut feel."

He thought back to what he had always envisioned for Hayes, a company that had what it takes to produce its products on time, without the craziness of constant expediting pressure, of missing parts, of inadequate labor supplies, or a continual tide of unscheduled surprises. Hayes had climbed the mountain of its own inefficiency and come up a winner. It took a lot of education, training, and a willingness to succeed.

Did that mean that all the change was over? Hardly. There was the never-ending job of continuous improvement and the whole new vision of Agile Manufacturing. No matter how much Hayes had accomplished, there was always competition pushing them today to be the leaders tomorrow. Now, however, there was enough information for them to be able to see what was coming their way and plan for what they knew would be happening. They also had the ability to simulate their options, to see with Rough-Cut Capacity Planning how their decisions might impact the plan if it were to change. Because they had the tools to plan with, they could spend their time making the improvements necessary to beat the competition, instead of spending all their time reacting to problems when it was too late for good solutions.

Brian recognized that there was a great difference in the quality of life at Hayes today versus his life when he stepped in as machine shop manager. First, with capacity planning and shop scheduling operating the way they were supposed to, he wasn't working all hours of the day and night. Weekends were now spent doing what he wanted, like taking long, romantic drives with his lovely wife. He hadn't planned on the effect that getting his factory life together would have on his family life. But, most importantly, Brian felt that when he went home at night, he had the satisfaction of a job well done, and now he had the results to prove it, too.

Had it been easy? No. Gaining control of the company by getting years of inadequate processes into shape is never easy. Was it the right thing to do? It was the *only* thing to do. Without the control and knowledge Hayes gained by becoming fully operational with its capacity management and scheduling techniques, the chance of surviving competitively on a national scale, let alone in the global marketplace, were next to none. It took hard work. It took change. It took a willingness and commitment to understand Manufacturing Resource Planning, Lean Manufacturing, Total Quality Control, and the overall concept of total quality management. Now there was the challenge of Agile Manufacturing, which meant taking advantage of the technology that was available and creating an environment that brought out the best in people.

Most of all, it took integrity and guts to stand up and say, "Let's do it right!"

Notes

CHAPTER THREE

1. New York: Harper & Row, 1982.

CHAPTER FIVE

1. Shigeo Shingo, *The Revolution in Manufacturing: The SMED System* (Cambridge, MA: Productivity Press, 1985).

CHAPTER SIX

1. Dr. Eliyahu Goldratt, *The Race* (Croton-on-Hudson, NY: North River Press, 1986).

CHAPTER NINE

1. William A. Sandras, Jr., *Just-in-Time: Making It Happen* (New York: John Wiley & Sons, 1989).

CHAPTER TEN

1. Roger Nagle, Deputy Director, Iacocca Institute, Lehigh University.
2. Roger Nagle (Bethlehem, PA: Harold S. Mohler Laboratory, Lehigh University, 1991).
3. *Oliver Wight ABCD Checklist* (New York: John Wiley & Sons, 1988).

Index